TOWARD PEACE AND SECURITY
IN SOUTHERN AFRICA

TOWARD PEACE AND SECURITY
IN SOUTHERN AFRICA

Edited by
Harvey Glickman
Haverford College

GORDON AND BREACH SCIENCE PUBLISHERS
New York · Philadelphia · London · Paris · Montreux · Tokyo · Melbourne

Gordon and Breach Science Publishers

Post Office Box 786
Cooper Station
New York, New York 10276
United States of America

5301 Tacony Street, Drawer 330
Philadelphia, Pennsylvania 19137
United States of America

Post Office Box 197
London WC2E 9PX
United Kingdom

58, rue Lhomond
75005 Paris
France

Post Office Box 161
1820 Montreux 2
Switzerland

3-14-9, Okubo
Shinjuku-ku, Tokyo 169
Japan

Private Bag 8
Camberwell, Victoria 3124
Australia

Library of Congress Cataloging-in-Publication Data

Toward peace and security in southern Africa / edited by Harvey
    Glickman.
        p.   cm.
    Includes bibliographical references.
    ISBN 2-88124-381-9
    1. Africa, Southern—Politics and government—1975- 2. Africa,
Southern—Relations—South Africa. 3. South Africa—Relations—
Africa, Southern. I. Glickman, Harvey.
DT1157.T68   1990
320.968—dc20   90-2844
                                                                CIP

For my Mother and Father,
Helen and Herman Glickman.
In Memorium

CONTENTS

PREFACE

This volume originates with a conference at Haverford College, April 28-30, 1989. On that weekend an international group of scholars, inside and outside governments, from Africa and elsewhere, assembled to address the theme, "Toward Peace and Security in Southern Africa." The conference was based on a sense of urgency concerning the continuing plight of the region -- reflected in the renewed state of emergency in South Africa and the declining economies in southern Africa -- as well as, paradoxically, a sense of impending opportunity for South Africa and the region, as manifested in the Angola-Namibia accords recently negotiated. It was a ripe moment for exploration of possibilities, pathways and prospects. Conference participants, through prepared presentations, commentaries and orchestrated discussions, exchanged views on how events could be shaped in the near-term future in order to approach a more secure and peaceful region. Our orientation was toward policy and toward how we might contribute to a better future in the region.

A particular attempt was made to capitalize on the advent of the new American Administration by hearing from Herman Cohen, now Assistant Secretary of State for Africa, and by hearing from Howard Wolpe, a leader of recent major U.S. Congressional initiatives on Africa. In order to confront American interests with an African perspective, the Conference heard systematic presentations from African scholars, an African diplomat, and South African journalists. In all, eleven of the thirty-one invited participants were from Africa. The Conference was planned to take place during the college term, making for large and lively audiences of students and faculty from Haverford, Bryn Mawr and Swarthmore Colleges -- audiences which included many students of color, including several from South Africa. This guaranteed a thorough airing of challenges to mainstream, official American policy, also part of the Conference plan. That is reflected in this volume.

It should be clear from the inclusion of commentaries after a number of chapters that an important element in the discussion is the exploration rather than resolution of differing opinions and the expansion of dialogue on major themes, rather than the exhaustive description of major problems. Nevertheless, the editor and the authors of this volume hope to contribute to a clearer understanding of a number of issues that bear on analysis and policy. One such contribution emerges from the dialogue on Afrikanerdom as a "fragment culture" between Peter Ekeh and Harrison Wright. A major question here is whether depriving blacks of citizenship by Afrikaners and other whites in South Africa represents a cultural-historical peculiarity that ultimately leads to the bitter end defense inside the laager. On the other hand, if South African history is singular but comparable to a world-wide phenomena of racially-related hegemonies, then its political barriers can be made permeable in recognizable ways. The implications of such an analysis lead to a second major issue illuminated: the role of violence in increasing the strength of the anti-apartheid extraparliamentary opposition groups, discussed by Henry Isaacs and Joe Thloloe, and the relationship of violence to negotiations and the timing for settlements of disputes, treated by Robert Price, Moeletsi Mbeki and Conor Cruise O'Brien. Price's model for negotiations leading to a political settlement plays down the possibilities for violent revolution and attempts to specify more precisely the nature of mutually hurtful conditions. The question is not whether violence is an alternative to negotiation, but rather at what point violence and political maneuvering lead to mutual exhaustion of alternatives to negotiation. Mbeki expects increasingly effective violent action on the part of the oppressed leading to collapse of the present regime, while O'Brien expects that only international force will bring the same result: both see little hope for negotiations except unconditional surrender. As Kenneth Grundy points out in his chapter, the enormous expansion in police actions and state violence to counter sabotage and rioting creates the potential for long-term militarization as an element in policy, whatever the prospects and terms of political reconciliation.

A third issue joined is that of escaping the reluctant dependence of the states in the southern African region on South Africa, taken up in the exchange between Gilbert Khadiagala and W. Ofuatey-Kodjoe. So vulnerable are the Front Line States that attempts to reduce dependence on South Africa can result in the opposite effect as a consequence of South African retaliation. A policy of seeking Western help to increase regional autonomy versus South Africa could exchange one hegemon for another, or simply wind up as a more devious route for indirect South African influence. Yet advice to South Africa's neighbors from outside supporters to promote a course of action other than negotiations toward the end of violence may be regarded as irresponsible. The question for South Africa's neighbors is not dependence or independence, but the timing and selection of tactics of relative disengagement. This leads to a fourth issue, national self-determination, raised obliquely in the chapters by Joseph Diescho and Harvey Glickman. Both authors survey the possibilities of co-ordinated military and political assistance by the Superpowers and other countries toward intimidating South Africa and its proxies in Namibia and in Mozambique. The global shrinkage in the Soviets' definition of vital interests and involvements has had a stimulating effect on a variety of co-operative activities on the part of European and African countries in the direction of counseling reconciliation of cross-border and internal disputes in this part of the world. An analysis that emphasizes tension reduction narrows the scope for self-determined national interests for victorious nationalist movements, a dilemma apparent to SWAPO in Namibia and to FRELIMO in Mozambique and not lost on the non-parliamentary opposition to the government in South Africa. Finally, there is the issue of the U.S. relationship to South Africa, described as "estranged partners" by Pauline Baker. Authors in this volume all agree that a combination of "carrots and sticks" (specifically focused upon by Walter Barrows) must be applied to South Africa by the U.S. in order to hasten the demise of political-racial exclusion there. Differences exist on the balance between the two, the type preferred and the final objective of policy among authors Baker, Cohen, Wolpe and Gail Gerhart. The limits of U.S. responsibility for internal decision-making in other countries and for the character of international sub-systems must be faced. The concluding chapter comments upon goals and limits of U.S. foreign policy in southern Africa.

All but two of the chapters (8 and 9) in this volume represent papers and commentaries presented at the Conference, thus opinions and information reflect the regional and world situation of spring and early summer 1989. Then, why one more book on South Africa and its neighbors? Special about the approach of this volume is the weight given to international factors in the analysis of the struggle to overturn apartheid and give birth to a more peaceful and secure region. This is clearly reflected in the organization of two of three parts in this volume. But the discussion in Part One, "The South African Cockpit," which addresses internal factors, also regularly draws upon the enormous significance of international pressures. Latent in the thrust of this volume -- with the dramatic exception of the predictions of Conor Cruise O'Brien -- is the recognition of the inevitability of some sort of negotiation process, despite suspicions on the part of the African commentators about Afrikaner intransigence and the danger of premature concessions.

Many people contributed to the enterprise of the Conference and the present volume. Sincere thanks are extended to the Haverford and Bryn Mawr College student rapporteurs: Jonathan McDonald, John M. Cook, Jennifer Neisner, Aruna Chandra, Randy Painter, Rama Mani, Douglas Johnson, Lara Wozniak, Jennifer L. Bills, Ngoc Clark, Blair McGregor Gray, Robyn Gilman (who also served as administrative assistant for the Conference), Susan Robinson, Ben Braslow, Elif Kendirli, Stefan Rosen, Christopher Wilkins, Kristen Thomas, Keino Robinson, and Ted Burnett. In addition to the conferees who contributed chapters and commentaries to this volume, thanks are also extended to the additional invited participants: Robert Allison, Raymond Hopkins, Thomas Karis, Peter Katjavivi, Arthur Klinghofer, Martin Lowenkopf, Blade E. Nzimande, Marc Ross, Barry Schutz, Sonny Venkatraman, and to the three chairmen of panels: Robert Washington, Robert Mortimer, and Thomas Callaghy. Haverford College provided a pleasant and supportive environment for all aspects of the Conference and the production of this volume, reflecting its longstanding interest in peace and international studies. As well as deriving financial support from Haverford College, the Conference and this volume drew on generous grants from the Stinnes Fund to Haverford and Bryn Mawr Colleges and from the MacArthur Foundation to Haverford, Bryn Mawr and Swarthmore Colleges. Wendy Hamilton extended valuable editorial assistance; Sylvia Glickman supplied important technical help; Scott Bomboy compiled the index.

Harvey Glickman
Haverford, PA
July 1989

CONTRIBUTORS

Pauline H. Baker is Senior Associate at the Carnegie Endowment for International Peace, Washington, D.C. She has worked as Research Scientist at the Batelle Memorial Institute and as a Member of Staff of the U.S. Senate Foreign Relations Committee, after more than a decade of teaching and research at the University of Lagos. She has written extensively on Nigerian politics, South African politics and U.S. foreign policy toward Africa. Her most recent book is *The Widening Chasm: The U.S. and South Africa.*

Walter L. Barrows serves as the National Intelligence Officer for Africa on the National Intelligence Council, Washington, D.C. Previously he served as the Defense Intelligence Officer for Africa and as Staff Member in the Office of the Secretary of Defense, International Security Affairs. The author of a book and several articles on African politics and international affairs, he has also taught at the Virginia Polytechnical Institute and in the Overseas Graduate Program of Boston University.

Herman J. Cohen, a Senior Foreign Service Officer in the U.S. Department of State, is Assistant Secretary of State for Africa. He was Senior Director for African Affairs on the National Security Council, 1987-89. His many Africa-related assignments in the USA and in five African countries include positions as Director for Central African Affairs in the Department of State, 1970-74, and as Ambassador to Senegal and Gambia, 1977-80. He has received many Departmental awards for distinguished service.

Joseph Diescho, a published novelist and playwright, is completing research on "Power and Education in South Africa and Namibia" as a Fulbright Scholar at Columbia University in New York, after advanced studies in Germany and at Fort Hare College in South Africa.

Peter P. Ekeh is Professor of Political Science at the University of Ibadan, Nigeria, and Fellow at the Woodrow Wilson International Center, Washington, D.C., 1988-89. Trained as a sociologist, his numerous publications are in several areas and include *Social Exchange Theory*, 1974. His current research is on issues of state and society in the political sociology of Africa.

J. Victor Gbeho is Ambassador and Permanent Representative of Ghana to the United Nations. He is Chairman of the Sub-Committee on the Implementation of Resolutions against Collaboration with South Africa of the U.N. Special Committee against Apartheid and Chairman of the Preparatory Commission of the U.N. Common Fund for Commodities, UNCTAD. He has served as President of the U.N. Security Council and as Chairman of the U.N. Disarmament Commission and other important U.N. Committees. His diplomatic service for Ghana includes many European and Asian postings in the past thirty years.

Gail M. Gerhart has taught political science at the University of Botswana, the University of Nairobi, the American University in Cairo, and (since 1985) at Columbia University in New York. She is the author of *Black Power in South Africa: the Evolution of an Ideology*, and is now working on three new volumes, updating the series *From Protest to Challenge: a Documentary History of African Politics in South Africa 1882-1964*.

Harvey Glickman was Director of the Conference, "Toward Peace and Security in Southern Africa," and is Professor of Political Science at Haverford College. He has been teaching and writing about African politics for many years in the USA and in Africa, including a short period at the University of Cape Town. A former Book Editor of *Africa Report*, he is currently editor of *ISSUE - A Journal of Opinion*, a publication of the African Studies Association of the USA. He edited and contributed to *The Crisis and Challenge of African Development*, 1988.

Kenneth W. Grundy is M.A. Hanna Professor of Political Science at Case Western Reserve University, Cleveland, Ohio. He has taught in Uganda, the Netherlands, Zambia and Ireland. He has published numerous articles and books on ideology, political change, international relations, and violence and politics in Africa. Among his many books are: *Confrontation and Accommodation in Southern Africa*, 1973, and *The Militarization of South African Politics*, 1986, 1988.

Henry E. Isaacs is executive director of African Research and Communications, Inc., a consulting firm in Washington, D.C. A graduate of the University of the Western Cape and a former president of the South African Students Organization (SASO), he has lived and worked in New Zealand, Tanzania and Zimbabwe, held research positions in U.S. universities and written extensively on black politics in South Africa -- most recently, *South Africa: A History of Resistance*.

Gilbert M. Khadiagala is MacArthur Fellow in International Peace and Security in the African Studies Program of the School of Advanced International Studies, Johns Hopkins University, Washington, D.C. where he is completing his work, "The Front Line States in Southern African Politics." He has published articles on Kenya politics and taught in the Department of Government, University of Nairobi.

Moeletsi Mbeki is a research fellow in the Zimbabwean Institute on Southern Africa. He was senior journalist with *The Herald* newspaper in Harare, Zimbabwe, and was a Nieman Fellow at Harvard University, 1988-89. A member of the African National Congress of South Africa, he has worked for the BBC in London, studied at the University of Warwick, England, and has contributed to journals in England, India and USA on politics in South Africa.

Conor Cruise O'Brien, Pro-Chancellor of the University of Dublin, was Distinguished Visiting Professor of History at the University of Pennsylvania in 1989. A practitioner as well as student of politics and diplomacy, in and for the Republic of Ireland, he was Special Representative of the United Nations in the Congo in the early 1960's. A former editor of the London *Observer*, he is a prolific writer, whose books and essays have dealt with intellectual history, literature, culture and political conflict in Europe, the Middle East and Africa. He has also held many teaching and research positions at major universities, including Vice-Chancellor of the University of Ghana. His most recent book is *Passion and Cunning: Essays on Nationalism, Terrorism and Revolution.*

W. Ofuatey-Kodjoe is Professor of Political Science and Director of Research in the African Studies and Research Institute, Queens College, City University of New York, Flushing, NY. He is the author of *Pan-Africanism: New Directions in Strategy, The Principle of Self-Determination in International Law* and articles on Africa and international relations.

Robert M. Price has been a member of the political science faculty at the University of California, Berkeley, since 1970. He teaches courses on South African politics, politics and economic development in Africa, and on the politics of modernization. Among his publications are a monograph on U.S. policy toward Sub-Saharan Africa, a book and numerous articles dealing with South African domestic politics and foreign policy, the Southern African regional conflict and U.S. policy toward Southern Africa. He also closely follows Soviet policy toward Africa and is the co-organizer of an exchange between Soviet and American Africanists that has met bi-annually since 1982.

Joe Thloloe is Deputy Editor of *The Sowetan*, the second largest daily newspaper in South Africa and the largest black daily newspaper. He was a Nieman Fellow at Harvard, 1988-89. Educated at the University of the North and the University of South Africa, he has worked on *The World*, the *Golden City Post, Drum* and the *Rand Daily Mail*. He has been jailed, banned, detained or placed under house arrest on four occasions since 1960 for a period totalling more than five years.

Howard Wolpe is Representative from Michigan in the U.S. House of Representatives (since 1978) and Chairman of the Sub-Committee on Africa of the House Foreign Affairs Committee, where he has been a leader in the development of policies for famine relief, economic assistance and toward a democratic, post-apartheid South Africa. A former professor of political science, he has written two books and a number of articles on African politics and society.

Harrison M. Wright, Professor of History and former Provost at Swarthmore College, has done research in Ghana and South Africa on themes in West African and South African history. His books include *The Burden of the Present: Liberal-Radical Controversy over Southern African History* and *The "New Imperialism" -- Analysis of Late Nineteenth-Century Expansion*.

PART ONE

THE SOUTH AFRICAN COCKPIT

1
A Comparative View of South Africa As Fragment Culture

Peter P. Ekeh

The world history of human civilization has changed dramatically since the sixteenth century through the emergence of a dominant imperial European center that has cast its shadow and substance on the rest of the world. Whether this expansion is seen from the perspective and imagery of an evolving world system or from the point of view of more standard imperial history, it is the case that the sixteenth century is qualitatively different from our twentieth century. Up to the sixteenth century, it could be claimed that mankind was segmented into autonomous enclaves of cultures and peoples, each with its own measure of independence of existence and its native stamp of authority. That innocence and that simplicity of the old world and of old human history have been lost to transformations and expansion that began in the sixteenth century which enthroned European culture and civilization as the new reference point and the new determining centerpiece of modernity in mankind's remolded experience and history.

This remarkable achievement of European culture and civilization was realized through activities directed from within European nations, but also through implantations of European cultural entities outside Europe. Once successfully implanted, the New World European cultures -- in the form of European 'fragment' nations outside the continent of Europe -- have displayed their own independence and have interacted with non-European cultures in ways that could not easily have been predicted from European history and philosophy.

This European cultural and political dominance over the world was established in two waves, leading to two-pronged definitions of European imperialism and colonialism over much of the globe. In the first wave, beginning in the sixteenth century and stretching to the eighteenth, Europeans rendered surplus from massive social changes within Europe, following principally from the upheavals of the Industrial Revolution, sojourned to the Americas and Australia to conquer and settle continents and lands that had been newly 'discovered' by Europeans.[1] This expansion

3

was in the old-style Greek form of colonialism which involved wholesale settlements of colonies of people from Europe on new lands, with their homeland European cultures and political styles preserved in their new settings. Where necessary, indigenous and native peoples of the lands were liquidated to make room for the free flow and transfer of European culture to these new lands. Labor, in the form of slaves and indentured servants, was bought and transferred from other lands to replace weakened native populations.

The second wave of expansion of European culture and power in the nineteenth and twentieth centuries gave a new meaning to colonialism. In this later form, European conquest and colonization were not primarily intended to secure permanent settlement for surplus Europeans on non-European lands; rather, the purpose of European conquest and control of these lands was for the expansion and consolidation of European capitalism and industrialism. Apart from the possible need to export surplus capital there was a neo-mercantilist dimension to this later form of expansion.[2] The need for the provision of raw material and for the guarantee of trade zones and trade routes was an important consideration in the British and European expansion of the late nineteenth century and early twentieth century.[3] Its motives and measure were profits. With respect to the native populations of the conquered lands, the imperatives of this new form of colonialism demanded the exploitation of their labor - - not their liquidation. Their labor and its products in raw materials were needed for working the engines of industry in Europe.[4] Although the British conquest and rule of India clearly belongs here, the prototype of this form of imperialism and colonialism is best revealed in the African encounter and subjugation by European nations in the last decades of the nineteenth century and for the greater part of the twentieth century.

The uniqueness of the South African situation is that it embodies both of these forms of European expansion. While South Africa belonged to early waves of European expansion and settlement of its cultural fragments on new lands in the seventeenth century -- with cavalier disregard for the lives of the native populations of these conquered lands, thus sounding the death knell of their cultures -- South Africa also shares in the demands of the second wave of European imperialism in Africa. Of all the European fragments, South Africa alone is involved in this duality of colonialism. South Africa's history evinces other strands of uniqueness when placed alongside other European fragments in the Americas and Australia. Its racist apartheid doctrine and practice can only be appreciated when discussed in terms relative to the uniqueness of the South Africa 'fragment' of European cultural expansion. That is to say, to understand the South African story, even in its internal dimensions, one needs to have a sense of its kinship to, but also its differences from, the experiences of the other fragments that resulted from the expansion of European culture and power, beginning in the sixteenth century: the

United States of America; British and French Canada; Latin America; and Australia.

THE EUROPEAN WHOLE AND ITS FRAGMENTS

The phenomenal migration of elements of European culture to other lands during the first wave of European expansion to the Americas, Australia, and South Africa represents a congeries of unusual events that are liable to lead to independent laws of existence for the migrants. What happens when there is a wholesale export of European culture to non-European lands along with live full-fledged harbingers of such European cultures? Does it turn into a new Europe or away from it? Is New England a purer or a revised England? Is New York a new-version Yorkshire?

Louis Hartz has painted in bold strokes what has happened to Europe's cultural elements thrust onto other continents.[5] His fragment theory of the development of these cultural outposts of Europe enables us to understand the general character of these peripheries of European culture. It also provides us with a handle for determining the uniqueness and the contributions of each of them to human civilization through the comparative study of these various fragments.

According to Louis Hartz, these European fragments left Europe in different periods and with different pieces of the European cultural whole: Latin America and French Canada, with a feudal piece of the European historical whole; United States of America, British Canada, and (in a more problematic sense) Dutch South Africa, with a liberal bourgeois tradition; and Australia and British South Africa, with a piece of English radical liberalism.[6] Louis Hartz argues that irrespective of what piece of European time-ordered cultural whole any fragment escaped with, they are all subject to the destiny of all European fragment cultures:

There is a problem of traditionalism and change common to the societies -- that...are fragments of the larger whole of Europe struck off in the course of the revolution which brought the West into the modern world. For when a part of a European national is detached from the whole of it, it loses the stimulus toward change that the whole provides. It lapses into a kind of immobility.[7]

Thus, while native Europe progresses from one cultural form to another enhanced civilizational form, there is a mode of fixation which thwarts and stifles cultural progress in Europe's offsprings, in its cultural fragments outside Europe. Europe advances to the point where it experiments with social welfare, to the scare of its American fragment. Europe is able to fondle and toy with communism and socialism, but not Australia with its migrant "radical" liberalism: "Australian radicalism, even after the Labor Party, even after the blood and thunder of the early Commonwealth period, remains morally fixed at the point of its origin."[8]

This intrinsic conservatism and this generic cultural immobility arises from the fact, Hartz argues, that the fragment is freed from the pressures of history and the burden of tradition which in Europe instigate and provoke cultural change. Fundamental change requires a conservative background. The French Revolution would not be possible without the depth of the feudal hierarchies of the *ancien regime*, nor the Bolshevik Revolution without Tsarist traditionalism. The fragment nation is solely able to cherish that piece of European culture it brought in its *Mayflower* and to nourish it tenderly on the new soil because both the past and future are saved from the headstrong and entrenched ideological challenges that torment European nations ingrained with diversities of ideologies. In the bourgeois liberal fragment in America, "Marx dies because there is no sense of class, no spirit of revolution, no yearning for the corporate past."[9]

Thus freed from the travails of ideological confrontations, the fragment is able with depth to nourish its particular element of European culture. To cite Hartz once more, "the fixity of the fragment liberates in the end a rich interior development" to the point of overcompensation. The contrast here works in favor of the fragment: "Europe develops many teleologies but because it intertwines them with one another, because it locks them together in a seething whole, it gives none of them the freedom to evolve"; whereas "[the] fragments provide that freedom -- [and] permit that unfolding of potentialities which the Old World denies."[10]

In so deepening some specialized aspects of the European culture to which the fragments are committed, these European cultural fragments have made special and abiding contributions to human civilization in various ways. Democracy is given special meaning through American emphasis, because the bourgeois liberal fragment in America has entrenched the authority of individual choice. The meaning of democracy is thus sieved through American political and cultural idioms. Canada is able to open its gates to persecuted refugees, because it cherishes the bourgeois liberal tradition of the freedom of the individual to dissent. Latin America has shown humanity that Western civilization can accommodate different races within the ambit of one nation because the spirit of feudal hierarchies that informed its fragment of escape allowed it to "feudalize" race by absorbing it into a composite societal hierarchy. Some worthwhile definition of some contribution could also be found for distant Australia.

The singular exception to this Hartz's law of fragment contribution to deepening Western and human values is South Africa. In South African history we come across a clear case of misadventure with respect to contributions to human values and civilization by way of Europe's expansion. Why is this so? What is there in South Africa's history that makes it so unique?

It would be wrong to claim, of course, that the other fragments have no blemish. They have. Perhaps we should point to areas where they share these ills with South Africa. Even in so doing we will see the uniqueness of the South African fragment.

The Cultural Liabilities of the Fragments

Racism. The lore and scholarship of European history and philosophy before the full range of European expansion outwards had their share of advocacies of ideologies, but they were little prepared for encounter with non-European peoples. The most consistent and substantial encounter with non-Europeans in Christendom was in the format of the Christian crusades, which were resolved in the idiom of conflict between two world religions -- with some respect for the Arabs. On the whole, it may be asserted with a great deal of justice that European philosophy and ideologies were innocent of explicit advocacies of racism. Even the conception of slavery in theology was outside the pale of color differentiation and racism.

It was in the course of the two modes of expansion of European culture to the non-European world that racism in its modern form of distinction between European peoples and non-European peoples attained a clear-cut pattern. This is how the Vatican Pontifical Commission on racism sees it:

Historically, racial prejudice, in the strict sense of the word, that is, awareness of the biologically determined superiority of one's own race or ethnic group with respect to others, developed above all from the practice of colonization and slavery at the dawn of the modern era. In rapidly considering the history of earlier major civilizations in the West as in the East, in the North as in the South, one can already find unjust and discriminatory behaviour, but one cannot in every case speak about racism as such.[11]

Native European ideologies were ambitious because they were inclusive of humanity -- conceived in a catholicism that in its openness embraced mankind. Whatever racism can be attached to them can only be a form of retrospective determinism. In its encounter with the non-European environment in the course of European cultural expansion, the European fragment world burrowed into these ideologies and the Bible for latent intentions of racialism in European thought.[12] It was the fragment world that, in practice as well as in thought, added racism to Western culture.[13] The universalism of the *human condition* in the wholeness of European thought is replaced with the particularism of the *European man* in the fractured perspective of the fragment world.

What was the motivation for racist ideologies in the fragment world? Hannah Arendt sees the origin of racism in "the emergency explanation of

human beings whom no European...could understand and whose humanity
so frightened and humiliated the immigrants that they no longer cared to
belong to the same human species."[14] Such intellectualist conception of
racism probably understates its instrumentality as an avenue for economic
and social differentiation in the new emergent circumstances of the new
World. For in the absence of an aristocracy in the fragment world, race
was readily substituted for class. It is ironic, but fully revealing, that the
fragment that has been most successful in handling race is the one
characterized as feudal in its European time-ordered origins: "Latin-
American treatment of slave and Indian was harsh, but it was far freer
from a sense of property and race, far more involved in distinctions of
status, than was the treatment of the non-Western by the British and the
Dutch."[15]

However, a more dramatic difference can be seen between Dutch South
Africa and the other fragments in the matter of race. The latter -- in
Australia, the United States, Canada, and even Latin America -- have
come to accept discrimination against non-European peoples in their
nations as wrong and have all come to accept racism as an evil that state
and society should work to dismantle. Even as all these other fragments
strive to wipe clean the scourge and taint of racism in their nations,
South Africa has enthroned racism as a moral creed of state and societal
organization. Herein lies the uniqueness of South Africa. And this is
why the Vatican Pontifical Commission on racism has so justifiably
singled out South Africa as the last remaining bastion of overt racism in
the modern world:

The most obvious form of racism, in the strictest sense of the word, to be found today is
institutionalized racism. This type is still sanctioned by the constitution and laws of a
country. It is justified by an ideology of the superiority of persons from European stock
over those of African or Indian origin or "coloured," which is, by some, supported by an
erroneous interpretation of the Bible. This is the regime of *apartheid* or of "separate development." This regime in the Republic of South Africa has long been characterized
by a radical segregation in vast areas of public life, between the black, coloured, Indian
and white peoples, with only the latter, although numerically a minority, holding
political power and considering themselves masters of by far the greatest part of the
territory.[16]

Inter-Fragment Conflicts

With the exception of Australia, the other fragments have been
involved in inter-fragment conflicts in a manner that is not only different
from homeland European national wars and conflicts but that is also
distinctive of these migrant fragment cultures to such conflict.

There are two forms of these conflicts. There is first the conflict
between two different fragment nations, as when the United States went
to war with Mexico over territory. Apart from demonstrating the frontier

mentality of fragment cultures spoiled by excess of territory outside Europe, that boundaries can and should shift, there is not much about these conflicts that has not been recorded in European history.

The second type of conflict has greater significance for the fragment cultures. This is the form of conflict between different fragment cultures in the same fragment nation, or within what Schutz calls "dual-fragment" nation: thus, conflicts between British Canada and French Canada; and between British South Africa and Dutch South Africa.[17] Although in each case the management of power is at issue, the conflict extends beyond power and its control. It also reaches into the soul of the fragment cultures: the preservation of the essential qualities of the European fragment which each side cherishes.

These "dual-fragment" conflicts provide us with examples of how these fragment cultures can resort to reactionary conservatism under pressure and as a design for survival. French Canada's occasional resort to anti-modern forms of behavior illustrates this pattern: thus, typically, "[the] French language of Quebec resembles the Norman of the seventeenth century, but in Paris modern French is spoken."[18] However, this pattern of reactionary conservatism attains its most inglorious height in South Africa where the "dual-fragment" conflict between the British and Afrikaner elements appears to yield to no solution other than avoidance and escape. In Canada there have been solutions that work, through federation arrangements for instance. Indeed, as will be emphasized later, beyond its muddier racist excesses, the South African situation is besmirched by the inter-fragment conflict between the Afrikaners and the English-speaking South Africans.

Citizenship Consequences of the Outward Expansion of European Cultures

There is a distinct area of consideration in which the European expansion has led to political processes to which the fragments have contributed enormously. I emphasize it here because it helps us to understand the crisis in South Africa.

The transition from medieval Europe to modern Europe and its age of outward expansion has been marked by important changes in the relationship between the individual and the state. In the medieval world, the individual was by and large the *subject* of a king of a sovereign nation -- with such subject performing important duties matched by relatively few rights. While the nobility enjoyed enhanced relationships with the king and nation, with due rights and obligations, the ordinary individual's privileges were exiguous. Moreover, the individual's arena for political action was circumscribed, largely limited to counties and boroughs. Unlike the European aristocracy whose international status endowed them with recognition in more than their native countries, the ordinary

individual in pre-modern Europe had less than his country for exercising
his rights, limited as they were.   \

The economic and social developments that ushered modernity into
Europe included the transformation of the status of the individual from
being the *subject* of a king to being the *citizen* of a state.[19] This direct
relationship between the individual and the state, involving the exchange
of the individual's duties to the state for the benefits he gains from the
state, is what T.H. Marshall has characterized as citizenship.[20] The
history of citizenship in England, and indeed in much of Europe, as
narrated by T.H. Marshall, is one of struggle for legal rights in the eighteenth century, political and civil rights in the nineteenth, and social
rights in the twentieth.

The story that has not been as eloquently told is about the impact of
the European expansion in its fragment nations and in colonialism on the
development of citizenship in the modern world. It can be demonstrated
that the expansion of Europe overseas accelerated its pace of development
as well as deepened the scope of citizenship. The proverbial "rights of an
Englishman" which he could obtain and cling to in wide sections of the
globe can only make sense in the context of British expansion overseas.
On the whole, Europeans and European nations benefitted from the
European expansion by enhancing the citizenship possibilities in their
various countries. Moreover, there was considerable transfer of these
citizenship benefits between Europe and its fragment nations as well as
between the fragment nations, as mobility and communications between
the fragments increased enormously. In addition, the fragments have also
directly contributed to the development of the theory and practice of
citizenship. The American rebellion theme of "no taxation without
representation" is a statement of a citizenship principle, denoting the
reciprocity of relationship between the individual and the state, that could
not have received such specification in Europe at that time.

While Europeans, in native Europe and in its New World fragments,
thus benefitted enormously, both the practice and theory of citizenship
suffered severely with respect to those non-European populations with
whom expanding Europe and Europeans interacted. This is particularly
the case with respect to the invidious distinction between *citizens* and
natives. The term *native* came to connote the status of not only being
less than a citizen, but also of being non-European, primitive and being
unworthy of the rights of citizenship. In particular, the distinction carried
with it the empowerment of "citizens" with the privilege of rulership
while the status of "natives" ruled out the possibility of any entitlement
to rulership. The struggle for independence in the European colonies in
Africa and parts of Asia was waged to erase this invidious distinction. It
was also the basis for the fierce struggle for race-equality in the definition
of nationhood in such former settler colonies as Rhodesia.

This seamy consequence of European expansion has been one main source of conflict in various nations in the post-World War II era. It is a tribute to the capability of the modern world to accommodate to new standards that in most nations non-Europeans have acquired citizenship rights and duties and that the distinction between "citizen" and "native" has been erased in most such nations. The singular and obvious exception to this universal expansion in citizenship entitlements is, of course, South Africa which in law and practice has insisted that only Europeans and their descendants are entitled to exercise the power of rulership, even as a minority.

THE UNIQUENESS OF THE SOUTH AFRICAN FRAGMENT

Why is South Africa so different from the other European fragments? What is there in its history that makes South Africa run against the tide of modern humanity? The framework provided in the first section of this chapter should now enable us to elicit the uniqueness of South Africa in comparison with the other European fragment cultures.

Pioneer Migrants and Fragment Culture. Each of the fragment cultures is distinctive because its pioneer migrants were the harbingers of certain mainstream cultural values of Europe at the time of their departure from Europe. Although most of the resulting fragment nations had a motley of migrants--ranging from the inklings of aristocracy to indentured servants or slaves from Europe--their leadership carried with them a strong sense of a European culture profile which it felt compelled to nurture and propagate. Such is the case, for instance, with the conquistador leadership of Latin America or the George Washingtonian bourgeois liberalism of America. In other words, the European culture of the pioneer migrants has left its imprint on each of the various fragment nations.

The South African situation is dramatically different in this respect, largely because there was no preformed design for the Afrikaners to settle permanently in South Africa. South Africa was an accident: servants of the Dutch East Indian Company had been left there in mid-seventeenth century to provision ships of the company in their tedious journeys to and from India. "The [resulting] Afrikaners were poorly educated in comparison with the settlers in Spanish America and in the English colonies in North America."[21] And they rapidly shed European culture: "By 1795 [just 150 years after they had settled in the Cape] the European roots of the white South African community were almost completely severed."[22] It is thus only in a tenuous sense that one can classify even modern South Africa as a Western country.

The Afrikaners and Holland. Holland never really had a South African policy beyond the economic exploitation of the settlement by the Dutch

East Indian Company. Unlike other fragments in which the respective
European mother countries had continuing interests, both political and
cultural, there were only slim relationships between the Afrikaners and
Holland. The Afrikaners did maintain continuing religious ties with
Holland, but their retention and racist application of "primitive
Calvinism" contrasts quite sharply with a fast changing Holland.
Afrikaans, the language of the Afrikaners (a mutation of Dutch with ele-
ments from Portuguese, Malay, and Hottentot), has varied from homeland
Dutch far more than any other fragment language has departed from its
European roots--even including the case of French Canada.

The backwardness of the Afrikaners contrasts in virtually every respect
with the accomplishments of the Dutch in Europe and the world. In this
respect, South Africa is dramatically different from the achievements of
any other fragment relative to developments in its mother European
nation. In some sense the openness of Dutch culture did mean that
Afrikaner culture had lost its European home and alliance. While
Holland, politically and culturally, was becoming an open society, South
Africa and the Afrikaners were pushing with vigor for a closed society.

European colonization and the Afrikaner Fragment. The European
fragments in Latin America, North America, and Australia were largely
shielded from the second wave of European expansion in the colonization
of Asia and Africa. South Africa is uniquely different in this regard.
Apart from being colonized by the British along with other African
territories, South Africa is fenced around by peoples who have experienced
colonial rule by Germans, Portuguese, the Belgians, and the British. Its
attempt at empire building in Namibia appears to weaken its moral hold
on its neighbors and to extend its range of enemies without any indications of admiration and friendship from any neighbors--which can hardly
be said of any other country in the modern world.

In the internal affairs of South Africa, the consequences of
experiencing this double-barrelled European expansion has remained in the
Afrikaner psyche. It has created for the Afrikaner two clusters of enemies
with whom he has to deal: the British and English-speaking South
Africans, on the one hand and, on the other, Africans, both in varying
ways and at different times obstacles to Afrikanerdom. As in Canada, the
British conquest and rule of South Africa implanted an English-speaking
population with a strong allegiance to Great Britain. But because it is
smaller in size than the Afrikaners, it has not been able to dominate the
Afrikaners politically in spite of its economic strength. The inability of
the Afrikaner to control the economic destiny of South Africa has led him
to obsessive preoccupation with the control of political power and to
insist on the near-monopoly of its political kingdom. This separation of
economic power, in the hands of the English-speaking white South
Africans, from political power, monopolized by the Afrikaners, has
created for South Africa a divided ruling elite whose members, although

united in their endorsement of discrimination against non-Europeans, do display different sensitivities in their dealings with the outside world and do respond to internal pressures in different ways.

The Afrikaners and Africans. Although backward compared to other fragments, the Afrikaners were able to liquidate a substantial portion of the native Hottentots in the area of the Cape very early in their history of settlement in South Africa. But their ability to liquidate other Africans was stalled once the Africaners went further inland and came across the stronger Bantu-speaking peoples: "It is important to bear in mind that colonization of America and Australia was accompanied by comparatively short periods of cruel liquidation because of the natives' numerical weakness;"[23] whereas

In understanding the genesis of modern South African society it is of the greatest importance to know that the land beyond the Cape's borders was not the open land which lay before the Australian squatter. It was already an area of settlement, of settlement by a great Bantu population. Much of the energy and determination of the Boers was used more against the natives than against Nature.[24]

The consequences for the Afrikaners has been an unwholesome relationship of hostility against the Africans whom the Afrikaners have struggled to place outside the South African political system.

Problems of South African Uniqueness

Any comparison of South Africa's history with the history of other European fragments in Australia and the Americas can only lead to one clear conclusion: South Africa's experiences are unique. That uniqueness has led the politically dominant Afrikaners into policies and practices that make it the odd distinction in the history of the outward European expansion of its culture and power. These policies and practices have created for South Africa problems that have plagued its history from the Napoleonic War years up to the present time. We may refer to some of these enduring problems as follows:

Apartheid and Fragment Racism. Racism in South Africa was devised as a reactionary creed and doctrine of protection and supremacy in the face of what appeared to the Afrikaners as threats to their isolated cultural existence in Africa. The National Party, the architect of Afrikanerdom, made apartheid its executive policy from its start:

The two pillars on which the party is based remain: apartheid between English and Afrikaans-speaking white South Africans, and apartheid between white and black South Africans...[These] are different sorts of apartheid, admittedly, but the underlying idea is the same. It is that the purity of the Afrikaner race will only be preserved by isolation from other white groups; and that the purity of the white race will only be preserved by isolation from the non-whites.[25]

It is in the irony of the South African situation that the Afrikaners exploited the willing partnership of the English-speaking South Africans (and, at several points in this bizarre history, of the British Imperial Government)[26] to establish the apartheid between white and non-white, while the Afrikaners have employed their majority over the English-speaking whites to ensure that state resources and that the partiality of the Dutch Reformed Church are used to guarantee their ethnic purity and political dominance. In view of the enormity of apartheid between white and non-white South Africans, the significance of the apartheid between Afrikaners and other Europeans in South Africa is liable to be minimized, but it is quite important in assessing the problems of this strange fragment culture. Isolation between the Afrikaners and the English-speaking whites did attain a policy status:

The Dutch Reformed Church has been in the forefront of the Boers' struggle against the influence of Christian missionaries on the Cape. In 1944, they went a step farther and adopted "without a single voice of dissent" a motion opposing the marriage of Boers with English-speaking citizens.[27]

Under the influence of the [Afrikaner secret society] Broederbond, Afrikaners have been encouraged to withdraw everywhere from organizations in which they mixed with the English-speaking, and to establish their own organizations run on their own lines instead.[28]

It is probably the case that outside Europe, among the European cultural fragments, the Afrikaners have maintained the purest ethnic group in South Africa.

From the 1960s onwards, following the Sharpeville Massacre, guarded attempts were made to involve both groups of whites in the destiny and events of South Africa on a common platform. Indeed, P.W. Botha's principal legacy for South African politics is that such accommodation has partially evolved at the level of the corporate world of business in which token Afrikaners have emerged. But the sensitivities remain, particularly in the political realm still heavily dominated by the Afrikaners, especially through membership of their Broederbond (recently bolstered by two reactionary paramilitary organizations: Afrikaner Resistance Movement and Whites' Freedom Movement). As English-speaking white South Africans join the National Party in large numbers, making it less Afrikaner than in its past history, the Conservative Party has emerged as a new expression of Afrikaner political dominance. It has resorted to Dr. Malan's successful tactics of the 1930s, with the insistence that it is "not prepared under any circumstances to negotiate the future of the whites with any other nation of whatever color."[29] That the predominantly Afrikaner Conservative Party could defeat the fatigued National Party in future whites-only elections, on the strength of purity of racist appeals, is one bleak reminder that apartheid remains entrenched in the Afrikaner psyche. Nor has there been any increase in melting-pot inter-marriages between Afrikaners and English-speaking South Africans. Moreover, rural white South Africa with its deep-seated suspicion of Africans and the British is still heavily Afrikaner. In substance, therefore, in spite of changes under Vorster and P.W. Botha, the apartheid between the Afrikaners and the English-speaking white South Africans remains entrenched.[30]

The victims of the two types of apartheid vary enormously, but together they both define the South African crisis and dilemma. While Africans and other non-whites are the victims of one type, Afrikaners themselves are, in the long run, the victims of the enforced isolation between them and other European groups. Be that as it may, these forms of apartheid arbitrarily provide the basis for the laws and the social order that govern economy and society in South Africa.

Citizenship Problems. One major consequence of the outward European expansion in the centuries beginning with the sixteenth has been the enhancement of citizenship opportunities, particularly for Europeans but also for whites in the European fragment nations. Subsequently, non-Europeans in the fragment nations--including African-Americans in the United States--have benefitted from this worldwide explosion in citizenship possibilities. The liberalism in the international arena following the Second World War has also aided in this expansion, leading to full citizenship rights and duties for men and women in the European colonies in Asia, Africa and the Caribbean.

In sharp contrast, the citizenship opportunities for non-whites in South Africa have shriveled since 1948 with the ascendancy to power of the Nationalist Party. The scope of the deprivation suffered by Africans in South Africa in respect of the elements of citizenship is often understated, largely because its degree of exceptionality in terms of world standards in the practice of citizenship is not sufficiently stressed. In such citizenship terms, it needs to be emphasized that Africans in South Africa are the only political entity in the modern world who are forced to live outside the political system by which their nation is run. They are simply *non-citizens*--and share neither in the rights nor in the duties that define the worth of a citizen. They have no political, legal, or social rights as such; they ar treated as "natives" who enjoy whatever the government considers fit for their existence in the system. And they are also not allowed to perform the duties of a citizen--for instance, to develop skills that might compete with those of whites and thus contribute to the economy according to their abilities. South Africa is the only nation known to history where the poor are not allowed to be peasants, for fear that African peasants might compete with the Afrikaner Boer farmers. Clearly, in citizenship terms, South Africa is *qualitatively* different from any other nation on earth.

What is not often realized is that with respect to the tremendous expansion in citizenship opportunities for Europeans, in Europe and in Europe's fragment nations, in modern times, the Afrikaners have also suffered from their own policies. While whites in the European fragments have enjoyed and even exploited the opportunities in this worldwide expansion in citizenship by way of frequent migration and by other special arrangements, the Afrikaners remain relatively isolated inside South Africa. On the other hand, as far back as the 1920s there has been a steady net outflow of English-speaking South Africans who enjoy the coverage of a British worldwide citizenship network. While it is said that Afrikaners who can demonstrate German ancestry may have the opportunity to emigrate to Germany, and while the Jews (the other significant group) have similar opportunity elsewhere, the bulk of the Afrikaners probably do not have such choice. It is doubtful that the Netherlands can, or would be willing to, accord the Afrikaners the openness of citizenship that Britain is now known to have extended to English-speaking South Africans. If, as expected, sanctions bite harder into the South African economy in the face of militant Afrikaner obduracy, most of these other groups are liable to emigrate from South Africa -- leaving the hardcore Afrikaners to battle the consequences.[31]

The Construction of Apartheid Economy. That the South African economy is a subset of its apartheid society is one of the verities of South Africa's history. The implications of this phenomenon are not often appreciated because they have been masked by the relative buoyancy of the South African economy which has been attained through the good fortune of vast mineral resources and through the violence of apartheid economics which expropriates cheap labor from the majority of South Africans by discriminatory laws and wages. At least since 1924, with the "pact" between the National Party and the Labor Party, standard economic principles have been subordinated to policies intended to ensure that white "civilization" with its standard of living is not threatened by allowing economic and social equality between the races:

There was no ideal to which the country was more firmly attached than to the maintenance of a white South Africa. Against this determination even the laws of economics must not prevail. However powerful the opposition of economic arguments, the attempt should be made to raise the poor white population beyond the reach of black intercourse---Reasons of public policy outweigh strictly economic considerations. The solidarity of white society and the integrity of its blood were supreme values [32]

The timelessness of this statement across South Africa's history since about 1924 does not seem to be in any doubt. But buried in this conglomerate white supremacist economics is the hand of Afrikaners' isolationist programs -- after all, the poor whites were virtually all Afrikaners. Chandra Hardy recently noted that "The Government [of

South Africa] employs half the Afrikaner labor force. They have been guaranteed a high standard of living by the state" in so doing.[33]

In the long run, the costs of South Africa's apartheid economics are liable to be enormous. Thus, as Chandra Hardy recently put it, "Apartheid has created structural obstacles to growth in the low purchasing power of the black population and in the acute shortages of skilled labor. Low demand is worsening the problems resulting from the country's weakening currency and rising production costs."[34] Beyond the cataloging of the economic costs of apartheid is its ideological poverty, in not having any coupling means of making its policies and practices even partially acceptable to the majority Africans. In the upshot, apartheid has turned South Africa's majority into an enemy of the Afrikaners. In order to protect itself from reprisals white South Africa has resorted to policies that will prevent Africans from meaningful contributions to the economy, especially in agriculture, with severe and vital costs to its food prospects:

In good years South Africa's well-developed agricultural sector produces enough grain to feed its population and export up to 400,000 tons to neighboring countries. *But in order to reduce the sector's reliance on black labor and the number of blacks living in white areas,* the government encouraged the development of large commercial farms which are very capital and import intensive, and the sector requires huge price supports and budgetary transfers. The domestic costs of agriculture inputs have doubled since 1980 and an increasing number of farmers who are unable to service their debts are being threatened with foreclosures [35]

The cumulative effect of almost a century of such apartheid-controlled economic policies, together with the direct and indirect effects of sanctions, is likely to weaken South Africa's economy further. Indeed, Hardy sees "an economy which used to grow very rapidly, but whose growth rate has now dropped below what is needed either to sustain employment or to provide a basis for adequate profit levels---this sombre perspective suggests that South Africa's economic system will continue to experience great difficulties."[36]

Since the Keynesian Revolution in economic thinking, it has become commonplace to assume that the state would respond to internal and external economic pressures by pursuing fiscal measures that would revitalize its economy by encouraging its growth. However, after virtually a century of being unresponsive to economic laws, South Africa is simply ignoring well-worn laws of economics. Hardy's assessment once more:

Faced with growing fiscal and balance-of-payments problems, the Government needs to pursue deflationary policies and shift incentives to the tradeable goods sector. Instead, the deterioration in the political situation is forcing the Government to pursue expansionary policies--larger subsidies and increased expenditure on security and aggression.[37]

Such are the imperatives of apartheid economics.

South Africa and Its Neighbors. South Africa is the major economic power in Southern Africa, controlling the economic purse strings of the region. In normal circumstances, this should be a major asset to South Africa, especially in view of modern regional groupings of economies in Europe, America, and Asia. But South Africa's politics and its policies of destabilization against its neighbors fly in the face of cooperation within the region and thus of deepening the advantages that South Africa would reap and the common advantages that would accrue to the region. The point is that South Africa needs the region for profitable trade: "A rough calculation suggests that net earnings by South Africa from its trade with [neighboring African states] has been about U.S. $10 billion during this decade. This means that South Africa would, to a large extent, be cutting its own throat if it were to react in a totally hostile way against [these] states. It would not only damage their economies, but it would also severely damage the most profitable part of its external trade in a period of acute foreign exchange scarcity."[38] And yet such is the lack of rationality in apartheid economics that South Africa's adventurism in Southern African international politics may well ruin its own prospects of benefitting economically from the region.

THE WAY FORWARD: INTEGRATING SOUTH AFRICA INTO WORLD ETHICS

When compared to the other European fragments formed outside Europe since the seventeenth century, the clear conclusion is that South Africa represents a case of misadventure. All the other fragments have sought to resolve problems arising from their settlement into new non-European environments, and in the process, have contributed enormously to human civilization. But South Africa stays apart. Thompson's assessment of the poverty of the South African situation is still fully valid twenty-five years after he made it:

The history of the Afrikaner is a striking illustration of the conservatism which may encrust a fragment of European society after its transplantation to a new environment. Although the Afrikaner has now mastered modern educational, industrial, and military techniques, the basic ideas of the majority, including their political leaders, remains those which crystallized in the seventeenth and eighteenth centuries. Bred in isolation from the main stream of Western thought, they have rejected three of its dynamic modern impulses--liberalism, socialism, and democracy. A fourth--nationalism--they accepted; but they have perverted it because, unlike other nations, they do not form a majority of the inhabitants of their country. Today their position vis-a-vis a hostile outside world and a restless internal proletariat is based upon sheer physical power. But they themselves are the victims of their past. So tyrannical is tradition over them that they are left with no room for effective manoeuvre, no means of genuine reconciliation. The last and most dangerous of the tribes of Africa, they are an anachronism in the second half of the twentieth century.[39]

It seems to be the judgment of the international community and the direct victims of apartheid that solution will partially come from the outside world. Assistance from the outside world would have to include efforts that will: (a) reorder the citizenship opportunities for the Africans and Afrikaners in terms of possibilities inside South Africa and in the outside world; (b) introduce free market economics and policies in place of apartheid economics and logic; and (c) help and enforce the normalization of relations between South Africa and its African neighbors.

Citizenship Prospects. What the world is asking South Africa to do is to extend citizenship rights to all its citizens as well as grant them the privilege of performing requisite duties, including contributing to the economy and serving in the armed forces. It is also important that the Afrikaners be helped to end their self-imposed isolation in a world in which vast citizenship opportunities abound. It is important that the Afrikaners be specifically helped out of this isolation. This means that the assumption that all South African whites are the same should be abandoned. In the end, the propensity of the Afrikaner to incline toward illiberal doctrines and practices is in direct proportion to his degree of isolation within South Africa. Citizenship opportunities, especially in the other fragment nations, will help to induce the Afrikaner to see the world as more than South Africa
and to open up greater choices for him than the limited ones he is now able to exercise.

Free Market Economics vis-a-vis Apartheid. South Africa will have to be persuaded that its own fate is not immune to the adversities that have been visited upon the economies of nations with protected economies. It is fair for outsiders and international organizations to insist that the restructuring of South African economy away from apartheid logic--away from the infamy of discriminatory "civilized" wages for Afrikaners--is natural and ultimately in South Africa's own best interest.

Since the 1970s, especially since President Jimmy Carter included South Africa in his human rights campaigns, Western nations and the Western world generally have been less reluctant to criticize South Africa for its unjust racial policies. As anti-communism disappears, with the Cold War, as a bargaining weapon for South Africa and as a reason in the West for overlooking South Africa's evil system, the decade to come will severely test the sincerity and the degree of commitment of Western champions and professors of humanitarian and democratic ideals as the civilized beacons of modernity that must be nourished and protected in all parts of the world, in the East as much as in the West, in Latin America as much as in Black Africa. It is going to sound thoroughly insincere for any Western nations to insist, as the British Government has done with respect to Poland for instance, that investments and participation by the West in Eastern European economies will be conditional on political and economic reforms without applying the same or similar measures to the far more inhumane circumstances of South Africa. For Great Britain and West Germany, in particular, South Africa will represent an acid test of their valuation of humanity: whether the rights of Englishmen or of Germans are all that count; and whether the gold and lucre that accrue from their investments in apartheid South Africa weigh more than the freedom of the Africans whose toil produces their profits in the apartheid regime.[40]

South Africa and Its Neighbors. The momentous events of our age include the growth of regional marketing and economic organizations, largely patterned on the European Economic Community. In sub-Saharan Africa, there exist two major attempts to form such regional organizations: (i) the Economic Organization of West African States (ECOWAS); and (ii) Southern African Development Coordination Conference (SADCC). SADCC was formed in 1980 to promote cooperation among the nine member nations and balanced growth in the region. Its fortunes have, however, been besmirched by South Africa's destabilization policies against this organization: "The SADCC Secretariat has estimated the cost of actions taken by South Africa to destroy their economies at over $10 billion between 1980 and 1984."[41] South Africa will have to be persuaded or else forced to abide by international rules of behavior as well as recognize that the future growth of its own economy depends on the growth of the economies of the SADCC countries.

The reasons for emphasizing South Africa's relations with its neighbors are not limited to the mutual economic benefits that both sides will derive from stable international relationships in the South African region. Any final settlements of the problems created by apartheid in South Africa will ultimately involve participation by South Africa's responsible neighbors in Southern Africa. At critical points in any future negotiations, African neighboring nations may be the right parties to put pressure on South African Blacks for requisite compromises. The Afrikaners may indeed need the good will of Africans outside South Africa for their continued stay and for their full citizenship rights in South Africa--in much the same way that Ian Smith and other Englishmen (and Scotsmen) are staying in former Rhodesia with full rights. It would, therefore, be counter-productive for the Afrikaners to extend their reign of terror beyond South Africa's borders--even if one were to assume that such policy would not lead to greater militarization in the region, including foreign military alliances, such as Angola was able to secure with Cuba to South Africa's fright.

*   *   *

The bitter irony of the South African situation is that in the end, when the madness of apartheid will have been dissolved into history, the two groups that will have to share South Africa are the Africans and the

Afrikaners. The earlier both groups are persuaded to recognize this possibility, the less contentious that end will be. The Afrikaners are, in spite of appearances of strength, the victims of their own machination. Centuries of virtual isolation from the current of humanism that has changed so much of the modern world have led the Afrikaners to stick to uncivilized policies that deeply injure and humiliate non-whites in South Africa. But the Afrikaners are in fact emerging as victims of their own outmoded notion of dominance. Perhaps the season of reawakening in international cooperation occasioned by the acclaimed principles of *perestroika* and *glasnost* may be able to blow some fresh breeze of modernity to this archaic land of apartheid and sweep away this piece of atavism into history.

Notes

This chapter was prepared while the author was a fellow at the Woodrow Wilson International Center for Scholars, Washington, D.C., and on leave from the University of Ibadan, Nigeria. The author thanks the Senate of the University of Ibadan, for granting leave, and the Woodrow Wilson Center for its generous research facilities. Neither of these institutions is responsible for the views expressed herein.

1. It is an indication of the Eurocentric dimensions of the new composite world that 'discovery' took on a European meaning. The world was henceforth to be seen and measured from the convenience and the point of view of Europe.

2. J.A. Hobson, *Imperialism: A Study* (London, 1902).

3. C.C. Wrigley, "Neo-Mercantile Policies and the New Imperialism," in Clive Dewey and A.G. Hopkins, eds, *The Imperial Impact: Studies in the Economic History of Africa and India* (London: The Athlone Press, 1978), 20-34.

4. Eric Williams, *Capitalism and Slavery* (London: Andre Deutsch, 1964).

5. Louis Hartz (with contributions by Kenneth D. McTae, Richard M. Morse, Richard N. Rosecrance, Leonard M. Thompson), *The Founding of New Societies: Studies in the History of the United States, Latin America, South Africa, Canada, and Australia* (New York: Harourt, Brace and World, Inc., 1964).

6. See Barry M. Schutz, "The Concept of Fragment in Comparative Political Analysis," in *Comparative Politics*, 1(1) (1968), 111-125 for a rich and extensive review of Louis Hartz's thesis, which also extends the categories of the fragment cultures.

7. Hartz, *op. cit.*, 1

8. *Ibid.*, 8

9. *Ibid.*, 7

10. *Ibid.*, 6,9.

11. Pontifical Commission, "Iustitia et Pax," in *The Church and Racism: Towards A More Fraternal Society* (Vatican City, 1988), 9. Race-thinking and racism appeared in Europe as a backlash from its imperialist and colonialist expansion. The view that race-thinking and racism were "a German invention" to the contrary, "the historical truth of the matter is that race-thinking, with its roots deep in the eighteenth century, emerged simultaneously in all Western [European] countries during the nineteenth century. Racism has been the powerful ideology of imperialistic policies since the turn of our century. It certainly has absorbed and revived all the old patterns of race opinions which, however, by themselves would hardly have been able to create or, for that matter, to degenerate into racism as a *Weltanschauung* or an ideology. In the

middle of the last century, race opinions were still judged by the yardstick of political reason: Tocqueville wrote to Gobineau about the latter's [Gobineau (1853-55)] doctrines, 'They are probably wrong and certainly pernicious.' Not until the end of the century were dignity and importance accorded race-thinking as though it has been one major spiritual contribution of the Western world." Quoted in Hannah Arendt, *The Origins of Totalitarianism* (New York: Harcourt, Brace and Company, 158).

12.   "For example, the interpretation that some fundamentalists gave to the curse made by Noah on his son Shem, condemned, in his grandson Canaan, to be his brothers' slave is well-known (cf. Genesis, 9:24-27). They [sic] misunderstood the meaning and scope of the sacred text which referred to a certain historical situation: the difficult relations between the Canaanites and the people of Israel. They wanted to see in Shem or Canaan the ancestor of the African peoples whom they subjugated and, consequently, they considered them marked by God with an indelible inferiority which destined them to serve whites forever." Although the Vatican paper did not name the "fundamentalists" who promote such outrageous views, the totality of its documentation points critically to South Africa where the Dutch Reformed Church historically provided theological justification for apartheid. In its 1985 synod, the Dutch Reformed Church decided to repudiate apartheid and to open its membership to all races--leading to the break-away formation of a new all-white church in 1987, with all the supremacist interpretation of the Bible as the bedrock of apartheid theology. See Pontifical Commission, *op. cit.*, 13n.

13.   "Two new devices for political organization and rule over foreign peoples were discovered during the first decades of imperialism [during the second wave of European expansion]. One was race as a principle of the body politic, and the other bureaucracy as a principle of foreign domination." See Arendt, *op. cit.*, 185.

14.   Arendt, *op. cit.*, 185.

15.   Hartz, *op. cit.*, 18.

16.   Pontifical Commission, *op. cit.*, 17.

17.   Schutz, *op. cit.*

18.   Hartz, *op. cit.*, 12.

19.   Walter Ullman, *The Individual and Society in the Middle Ages* (Baltimore: The Johns Hopkins Press, 1966.

20.   T.H. Marshall, *Citizenship, Social Class and Social Development* (New York: Doubleday & Co., 1985).

21.   Leonard M. Thompson, *The South African Dilemma* in Louis Hartz. *The Founding of New Societies* (New York: Harcourt, Brace and World, Inc., 1964), 189.

22.   *Ibid.*, 187.

23.   Arendt, *op. cit.*, 187n.

24.   C.W. de Kiewiet, *A History of South Africa: Social and Economic* (London: Oxford University Press, 1941), 59.

25.   Brian Bunting, *The Rise of the South African Reich* (Harmondsworth, England: Penguin Books Ltd), 21.

26.   The complicity of the British Government, both in its imperial era and in modern times, in the evolution of Afrikaner apartheid discrimination against South African Blacks easily represents the ugliest blemish in what many justifiably regard as the most illustrious history of colonialism and imperialism in Europe's expansion overseas. Following the defeat of the Afrikaners by the British in the Boer Wars (1899-1902), the British Government negotiated away the rights of the "native" Africans by allowing the Afrikaners to do what they

pleased with them. This extraordinary concession to the Afrikaners was apparently made to appease the Afrikaners because Europeans were generally unhappy that the British had extended their strong hand of imperial conquest to those seen in Europe in romantic terms as innocent and harmless farmers in the wilds of Africa. Similarly, South Africa acquired South West Africa (formerly ruled by the Germans) at the end of World War I with the cooperation of the British Government. While both of these deals with South Africa were by Liberal Governments, it is significant that Margaret Thatcher's Conservative Government is seen by many as the greatest supporter of apartheid South Africa in modern times. While this modern-day British *de-facto* support for apartheid South Africa may have a lot to do with sizable British investments in South Africa, it has been said that it has a great deal more to do with the fear that sanctions will cause many English-speaking white South Africans to flood Britain by escaping South Africa in the wake of a deteriorating economy.

27. Arendt, *op. cit.*, 195n.
28. Bunting, *op. cit.*, 54.
29. Pauline H. Baker, "South Africa: The Afrikaner Angst" *Foreign Policy*, 69 (Winter, 1987), 70.
30. The sentimental value of Afrikaans, the language of the Afrikaners, is a major factor in defining the political power of the Afrikaners. While most Afrikaners are now bilingual, speaking English and Afrikaans, the South African Government imposed Afrikaans as the official language in Namibia. It is also their design that the "coloureds" use Afrikaans as their official language, although Blacks use English, rather than Afrikaans. It is one source of fear among the Afrikaner ruling elite that with Namibian independence and the possibility of majority rule in South Africa, Afrikaans may be wholly replaced by English as the language of government and commerce in Southern Africa.
31. The history of migration into and from South Africa has been one major indicator of the differences between Afrikaners and the English-speaking white South Africans. The non-Afrikaner whites in South Africa today came with the gold rush in the last decades of the nineteenth century. The flow of migration for all the other groups, except the Afrikaners, has followed the economic fortunes of South Africa. In times of economic boom, migration into South Africa picks up; in periods of down-turn in the economy, net emigration registers strongly. Thus, Arendt, *op. cit.*, 187-88, noted, "Although today [in the 1950s, that is] South Africa belongs to the Commonwealth, it was always different from the other dominions; fertility and sparseness of population, the main prerequisites for definite settlement, were lacking, and a single effort to settle 5,000 unemployed Englishmen at the beginning of the nineteenth century proved a failure. Not only did the streams of emigrants from the British Isles avoid South Africa throughout the nineteenth century, but South Africa is the only dominion from which a steady stream of emigrants has gone back to England in recent years." Also see Baker, *op. cit.*, 72: "Nearly one-third of the electorate did not vote [in the 1987 South African general elections won by the National Party, with major gains by the pro-apartheid Conservative Party], including many who have dual citizenship and retain the option of leaving. For the first time since 1977, more people--mainly English-speaking professionals--are leaving the country than settling in. Net emigration of whites in 1986 was about 6,000; by comparison, South Africa experienced net annual immigration of more than 20,000 in [the relatively good years of] 1983 and 1984."
32. Kiewiet, *op. cit.*, 222.
33. Hardy, *op. cit.*, 55

34. *Ibid.*, 35

35. *Ibid*, 36; emphasis added.

36. *Ibid.*, 37.

37. *Ibid.*, 55.

38. *Ibid.*, 38.

39. Thompson, *op. cit.*, 215-216.

40. It is entirely possible that developments in independent Namibia may have something to do with future changes in the political attitudes of the British and German governments toward South Africa. Although Britain would be pleased to see Namibia opt for membership of the British Commonwealth of Nations, the weakened influence of that body after a decade of neglect under Prime Minister Margaret Thatcher makes such choice unattractive for a new independent African nation. If Namibians were to be tempted not to exercise such choice of membership, then there would exist the clear possibility on their side of seeking for a European anchor in their old, pre-World War I, ties with Germany. In such eventuality, West Germany would have to consider its position in Southern Africa in more than economic terms.

41. Hardy, *op. cit.*, 46.

A "South African 'Fragment' Culture"?
A Comment

Harrison M. Wright

In order to address the problem of apartheid we must try to determine what the origins and nature of the problem are. Utilizing the enormously stimulating and suggestive ideas of Louis Hartz's *The Founding of New Societies* (1964), Peter Ekeh argues that the essence of the South African problem may be found in the particular "fragment" of Dutch society that emigrated to South Africa in the seventeenth century. He maintains that this original Dutch "fragment," developing and combining with other historical influences over time, made South Africa uniquely backward and counterproductive in its race relations.

"Fragment" theory, despite its stimulating and suggestive character, has never been without problems when applied to individual cases. In this brief and necessarily oversimplified discussion I will first consider a few, mostly recent, historical approaches that tend to undermine a fragment interpretation of South Africa. I will then consider some of the implications and problems that both fragment theory and these historical approaches raise with respect to thinkng about policy toward South Africa today.

Interpretations critical of a fragment approach to South African history are difficult to categorize or group. There are overlappings between and differences within them. It will be simplest -- if somewhat arbitrary -- to divide the interpretations into three groups of approaches that run contrary, respectively, to a fragment interpretation's emphasis on the continuity, the uniqueness, and the importance of Afrikaner history.

Some recent studies accept the uniqueness and importance of the Afrikaners in shaping present-day South Africa but question an emphasis on historical continuity. In particular they question the idea that the ideology behind today's apartheid can be traced to certain seventeenth-century developments. The proponents of this approach -- André du Toit, Irving Hexham, T. Dunbar Moodie, and others -- argue that there is no evidence to support the presumption that the early European settlers at the Cape were unusually religious, let alone that they adhered to some "primitive

25

Calvinism" that gradually intensified through frontier isolation and fear of change and led directly to the makers of apartheid.[1] These scholars suggest, on the contrary, that for over two centuries after 1652 Afrikaners were, while undoubtedly racist, relatively indifferent to religious ideology; that during that time Afrikaner society was characterised by extreme political and social disunity; and that present-day Afrikaner religious and political ideologies are, therefore, not seventeenth-century in origin.

Du Toit, Hexham, and Moodie argue that the seeds of present-day Afrikanerism and the Afrikaner state were sown only in the late nineteenth century. The various and severe Anglo-Boer crises of the time resulted in movements aimed toward increased unity and nationalism, and some Afrikaner leaders began to be influenced by the neo-Calvinist ideas of the conservative nineteenth-century Dutch theologian and statesman, Abraham Kuyper. (Among Kuyper's ideas was the concept of separate social spheres each responsible only to God, a concept that could later provide a theological justification for apartheid.) Du Toit, Hexham, and Moodie disagree as to the nature and importance of the early Afrikaner movements -- as to the particular ideological influence of Kuyper, or the personal influence of the nationalist S.J. du Toit or of the Dopper Paul Kruger, or the influence of the broader political and social changes of the nineteenth century. But they agree that Afrikaner nationalism, broadly-speaking, began in this period with the desire of Afrikaner nationalists to unify the Afrikaners in their struggles against the power of the English and against the economic threat of the Africans -- to make the Afrikaners appear unique and powerful by providing them with a special language, with special grievances, with special strengths and character, and with a heroic and consistent history. And they agree that modern Afrikaner Calvinist ideology itself -- specifically Christian Nationalism -- is, basically, a deliberately constructed (and in its extreme views by no means widespread) phenomenon of the period after 1910 that did not reach maturity until the 1930's and 1940's.

Du Toit and his colleagues, in short, while accepting the importance of modern Afrikaner political and religious ideology, argue that there was no continuous "Calvinist paradigm" and that modern Afrikaner ideology is recent and non-"fragmental" in origin. If their view is correct, then the fragment interpretation of South Africa, which has relied on the South African liberal historians' idea of a continuous development of Afrikaner character since the seventeenth century, is not only incorrect but has reinforced the recent Afrikaner nationalist historical myth -- even though it has substituted a critical and negative judgment for the glorifying one of the Afrikaner nationalists.[2]

The second group of approaches that tends to undermine a fragment interpretation of South African history questions an emphasis on the uniqueness of South Africa. This approach is not so much a school of thought as it is an analytical frame of mind. It embraces those social scientists who, examining social issues broadly, look on South Africa as simply one example of more general phenomena.

The Afrikaners can best be understood, these social scientists argue, as a subset of broader groups and broader generalizations. Taking, for example, roughly the areas covered by Hartz's theory, Pierre van den Berghe, in *Race and Racism*, used racism in Brazil, Mexico, the United States, and South Africa not to show the uniqueness of the areas but to illustrate his typology of the causes and nature of racism generally.[3] Even as he borrowed heavily from liberal history (the dominant interpretation at the time he wrote), he resisted its tendency to find the Afrikaners unique. Although he acknowledged significant differences among the four societies, he found the differences not as important as the similarities -- similarities that could help him understand broad, general problems of group conflict, social integration, power, social stratification, culture change, and assimilation.

Of course van den Berghe used as cases only four ex-colonial states. We may also study South Africa as one of a broader range of societies -- western or even non-western -- with racial or ethnic problems. Instead of considering the Afrikaners a unique consequence of a particular fragment development, we may find it useful to consider them as exhibiting, in general terms, characteristics common to the dominant social groups in India, Sri Lanka, Burundi, North Ireland, or other societies where one social group imposes inequality on other groups on the basis of race, religion, or ethnicity. Or we may, going in another direction, consider Afrikaners in the general context of nationalism -- perhaps late nineteenth-century European nationalism, or even anti-colonial nationalism in Africa.

In their book, *Ethnic Power Mobilized*, Heribert Adam and Hermann Giliomee have a long chapter that investigates general approaches and theoretical concepts -- Marxist and non-Marxist -- that social scientists have applied to South Africa.[4] They divide the perspectives into six major categories: those that focus on Calvinism and religiously induced prejudice; fascist analogies and police state methods; racism as a social phenonmenon; the concept of plural societies; class formation; and colonial analogies, especially those pertaining to internal colonialism. Generalizing approaches such as these are based on the assumption that we can gain understanding if we will reduce our fixation on what makes South Africa different from everywhere else and will, instead, consider South Africa's problems in their broader context.

The third group of approaches that tends to undermine a fragment interpretation of South African history questions not only the continuity and the uniqueness, but also the importance, of the Afrikaners and Afrikaner ideology. This group is the "radical" or "neo-Marxist" school that has so influenced South African historical writing over the past twenty years.[5] By emphasizing the crucial impact on South African history of late-nineteenth century international capitalism, radical historians question continuity. By their emphasis on general theory, they question uniqueness. And by minimizing the ultimate role of Afrikaner ideology in the shaping of apartheid, they question importance.

Many varieties of radical history have developed since the early 1970's: for example, traditional Marxism, underdevelopment theory, structuralism, and history-from-below. But these approaches all have Marxist antecedents in one way or another, and they all assume the crucial influence of capitalist power. Despite their many disagreements and differences in theory and subject matter, therefore, they are all agreed in their objection to interpretations that depend on what they would consider to be ultimately non-materialist forces or independently derived ideologies.

Radical historians, as is well known, consider capitalism rather than racism as the driving force in modern South African history. To radicals the shaping of twentieth-century South Africa stemmed not from the ultimate rise to power of anachronistically racist Afrikaners but from the arrival of modern international capitalism after the discovery of diamonds and gold. It was this new force, with its capitalist need to exploit the available labor supply and its inevitable internal competitions within an increasingly differentiated class structure, that led to modern segregationist ideologies, to apartheid and, more generally, to the South Africa of today. What is important to understand about the Afrikaners gaining control over the government in 1948 is, therefore, not how racial and social anachronism triumphed, but how the Afrikaners took advantage of the class structure for their own empowerment. Consider the Afrikaner Broederbund, for example: Traditional liberals see the Broederbund as the triumph of reactionary Afrikanerdom. Dunbar Moodie and other revisionists see it as a carefully contrived effort of modern nationalist ideologues to bring unity and power to a politically apathetic and divided Afrikaner population. The radical scholar Dan O'Meara, on the other hand, sees the Broederbund as the vehicle of an Afrikaner petty bourgeoisie struggling to achieve full bourgeois status.[6]

To demonstrate their conviction that the apartheid of the Afrikaners in no way flies in the face of capitalist self-interest, the radicals point to ongoing labor exploitation and other racist policies among the capitalist English in South Africa and to the extraordinary economic growth that South Africa experienced in the decades after 1948. They argue that the development of the Afrikaners before the late nineteenth century is, in short, while interesting in some respects, in the final analysis not very significant.

The radical approach is a powerful one. It brings a remarkable amount of analytical sophistication to bear on class relations -- an aspect of South African development relatively neglected in traditional liberal interpretations. And, like the other two approaches, it tends to undermine fragment interpretations.

Set out in brief comparison, the differing historical interpretations described above may not seem important when considered against the urgent and serious problems of South Africa today. But because to a considerable degree they correlate with differing approaches to present-day policy toward South Africa, they have in fact contemporary and functional implications of the utmost significance.

If present-day apartheid is, as the traditional liberal and fragment interpretions have it, the result of a unique Afrikaner character and ideology developed over the past three centuries -- anachronistic, ingrained, and running contrary to economic good sense -- then the problem of apartheid is largely the problem of uprooting the Afrikaners. The solution presumably lies in a political assault on entrenched Afrikaner power while at the same time expanding the economy so that the natural laws of economic growth will help break down the atavistic shackles of the outmoded ideology. The liberal approach is naturally attractive to non-Afrikaners, and it has been especially attractive to English-speaking South Africans. Its supporters tend to point to the AWB and the Conservative Party as the essence of present-day Afrikanerdom and as evidence of the correctness of their view.

If, on the other hand, as du Toit and others argue, Afrikaner ideology is primarily a deliberate nationalist construct of the relatively recent past, then there is hope that Afrikaner ideology can be in fact reformed. The solution then presumably lies in appealing to the pragmatic self-interest of Afrikaner leadership, in persuading it that a significant change of ideology is now in its best interests in order to meet changing circumstances. This solution has clear overtones of C. Vann Woodward's approach to reform in the American South in the 1950's, as exemplified in *The Strange Career of Jim Crow*.[7] It is particularly attractive to reform-minded Afrikaners and to political pragmatists generally -- to individuals such as du Toit, Hermann Giliomee, Heribert Adam, and Kogila Moodley.[8] Its supporters can point to the verligte wing of the National Party and to many liberal Afrikaners in opposition to the government as evidence of the correctness of its view.

If the Afrikaners are not really important in themselves, but should be considered primarily as just one of many groups who have imposed social inequality on others throughout history, then the solution should lie in some approach that might be appropriate for not only the South African problem but for other, similar problems as well. This general approach, with its many different interpretations and policy implications, while perhaps attractive in theory, does not in itself suggest any particular course of action. But it does tend to promote skepticism toward policies based too heavily on the supposed uniqueness of South Africa.

If, finally, apartheid is based on class exploitation, then a purely political solution is simply inadequate. Even universal suffrage is not sufficient to overthrow capitalist oppression. For a proper solution there must be a socialist revolution -- whether or not it is in one or two stages, whether or not it is complete or results in a mixed economy. This approach is naturally attractive to Marxists. To support their view Marxists can point to the striking coincidence in South Africa today of those who are poor and those who are black and to the increasing urban proletariat.

After even a quick perusal of the different historical and contemporary approaches to South Africa we must be sobered by the complexity of the problems they present. Each interpretation offers evidence that supports its point of view, that challenges the other interpretations, and that suggests the wide variety of influences that have gone into shaping South African history and society. Each interpretation also clearly contains not only historical analysis but some elements of historical rationalization for its approach to the problem of South Africa. In this dilemma let us return to Peter Ekeh's chapter to see if it can help us find our way.

I must say to begin with that there are certain suggestions in Ekeh's chapter I have to question directly: that there was no European racism before the European "fragments" went overseas; that resorting to "reactionary conservatism under pressure and as a design for survival" is especially characteristic of "fragments"; and that "South Africa is simply ignoring well-worn laws of economics" because of its unique "fragment" background.[9] At the same time these statements are -- except perhaps for the last one -- more important to fragment theory itself than they are to an understanding of South Africa. And fragment theory, I think, is clearly more a stimulating heuristic device than a literal rendering of the past.

The model of a specific fragment of European culture working out its own ideological destiny in isolation and over a long period of time is dramatic and compelling. But even Hartz -- even as he tried to concentrate on the pure unfolding of the individual fragments -- kept bringing in external influences from Europe and kept making concessions to the differing geographical and human environments in which the different fragments found themselves. All Hartz's followers made similar concessions to reality. (One of the real problems with fragment theory when applied to South Africa, for example, is that in focussing so intently on the European "fragment" it tends to overlook the enormous influence the black population -- especially the African population -- has had in shaping the South Africa of today and, by implication, the enormous influence it will inevitably have in shaping the South Africa of tomorrow.) In short we should not apply fragment theory narrowly, I believe, although we may well find Hartz's ideas highly suggestive when we investigate Europe's settlement colonies overseas.

Ekeh writes largely in this vein. Although he uses the rhetoric, or idiom, of fragment theory, he also keeps referring realistically to outside influences that have helped to shape South Africa: the late nineteenth-century wave of economically motivated European imperialism that needed to exploit indigenous labor for its profits, for example; or the large and vigorous indigenous populations that the Afrikaners have faced both within and without their borders.[10] And yet is not Ekeh's basic premise, consistent with fragment theory, correct -- that the South African situation is unique in an important way? Despite characteristics undeniably shared with other similar societies, is it not a specific South African situation that we are trying to resolve? Do we gain as much by trying to explain South Africa through a general theory of social relations as we do by testing general theories against the specific situation in South Africa? Do we not do better, as Adam and Giliomee argue, to attempt "to utilize insights from various perspectives without elevating a particular approach to the sole truth"?[11]

Beyond this point I do not wish to assert a particular interpretation but to raise various issues as to the nature of the current crisis. To what extent are class and material conditions at the heart of the South African problem, so that a radical solution may become appropriate? (Here comparing the radical historical interpretations with those that see racial and ethnic issues as central may help us find an answer.) Can Afrikaner society change or is it irredeemably locked into a seventeenth-century social mentality? (Here the du Toit et. al. theory of ideological discontinuity -- of the intentional change that lies behind modern Afrikaner attitudes and practices -- may help provide an answer.) Is white society already changing under the influence of inexorably evolving economic and political realities? (Here some of the traditional liberal views -- which also assume the ultimate power of economic change to alter political and social policy -- may, along with the radical interpretations, help provide an answer.) These are all questions with significant historical ramifications that we will have to address as we consider what is to be done with respect to South Africa today.

The basic dilemma -- both for us and for South Africans -- is that the South African problem is at the same time extremely urgent and extremely complex. Urgency and complexity are difficult challenges to respond to simultaneously. Should there be bold and forceful actions because of the urgency of the problem -- actions that may risk making matters worse? Or should there be careful and cautious actions because of the problem's complexity -- actions that may risk achieving little, or nothing at all?

Notes

1. For the clearest expression of these views see André du Toit, "Ideological change, Afrikaner Nationalism and Pragmatic Racial Domination in South Africa," in Leonard Thompson and Jeffrey Butler, eds., *Change in Contemporary South Africa* (Berkeley: University of California Press, 1975), 19-50. Also see André du Toit, "No chosen people: The Myth of the Calvinist Origins of Afrikaner Nationalism and Racial Ideology," *American Historical Review*, 88:4 (October 1983), 920-52; and André du Toit, "Puritans in Africa? Afrikaner 'Calvinism' and

Kuyperian Neo-Calvinism in Late Nineteenth-Century South Africa,"
Comparative Studies in Society and History, 27:2 (April 1985), 209-40. See also
Irving Hexham, "Dutch Calvinism and the Development of Afrikaner
Nationalism," *African Affairs*, 79:315 (April 1980), 195-208; and Irving
Hexham, *The Irony of Apartheid* (New York: Edwin Mellen Press, 1981); Gerrit J.
Schutte, "The Netherlands, Cradle of Apartheid?," *Ethnic and Racial Studies*, 10:4
(October 1987), 392-414; and Hermann Giliomee, "Constructing Afrikaner
Nationalism," *Journal of Asian and African Studies*, 18:1-2 (1983), 83-98; and T.
Dunbar Moodie, *The Rise of Afrikanerdom: Power, Apartheid, and the Afrikaner
Civil Religion* (Berkeley: University of California Press, 1975). While not as
extreme as some of the later work, Moodie's piece was most influential in the
development of this point of view.

2. Probably the best-known and most influential liberal history may be found in the
works of W. M. Macmillan, C.W. de Kiewiet, Eric A. Walker, and Leonard M.
Thompson. See Leonard M. Thompson, *The Political Mythology of Apartheid*
(New Haven: Yale University Press, 1985).

3. Pierre L. van den Berghe, *Race and Racism: A Comparative Perspective* (New
York: John Wiley & Sons, 1967), 37, 141 especially.

4. Heribert Adam and Hermann Giliomee, *Ethnic Power Mobilized: Can South Africa
Change?* (New Haven: Yale University Press, 1979), pp. 16-60. For a Marxist
discussion of different general approaches, see Stanley B. Greenberg, *Race and
State in Capitalist Development: Comparative Perspectives* (New Haven: Yale
University Press, 1980), 7-25.

5. The most important theorists of radical history have probably been Harold Wolpe
and Martin Legassick. For a recent, not-unsympathetic review of radical history
(and of South African historiographical trends generally) see Ken Smith, *The
Changing Past: Trends in South African Historical Writing* (Johannesburg:
Southern Book Publishers, 1988). See also Christopher Saunders, *The Making of
the South African Past: Major Historians on Race and Class* (Totowa, NJ: Barnes
& Noble Books, 1988). (Barry M. Schutz, "The Concept of Fragment in
Comparative Political Analysis," *Comparative Politics*, 1:1 [October 1968],
116-7, specifically points out incompatibilities between "fragment" and class
analysis.)

6. See Dan O'Meara, "The Afrikaner Broederbond 1927-1948: Class Vanguard of
Afrikaner Nationalism," *Journal of Southern African Studies*, 3:2 (April 1977),
156-86; or Dan O'Meara, *Volkskapitalisme: Class, Capital and Ideology in the
Development of Afrikaner Nationalism, 1934-1948* (Johannesburg: Ravan
Press, 1983), 59-95 especially.

7. C. Vann Woodward, *The Strange Career of Jim Crow* (New York: Oxford
University Press, [1955], 3rd ed. revised, 1974).

8. See, notably, Heribert Adam and Kogila Moodley, *South Africa Without
Apartheid: Dismantling Racial Domination* (Berkeley: University of California
Press, 1986).

9. See the preceding chapter by Peter P. Ekeh, "A Comparative View of South Africa
as Fragment Culture," pp. 5-7, 13-14, 16 These statements largely reflect liberal
positions that were dominant when Hartz wrote.

10. *Ibid.*, 2, 9-10.

11. Adam and Giliomee, *Ethnic Power Mobilized*, 16.

2
The Dynamics of Conflict in South Africa: Routes to Peace?

Henry E. Isaacs

INTRODUCTION

Soweto, June 16, 1976, marked the beginning of a decade of black protest that steadily sapped and hemorrhaged the white power structure from below. Reaching new heights during 1984-86, the final showdown appeared imminent: Blacks* were more organized, militant and united than ever before, while Whites were weaker, divided and on the retreat.

The reality was more complex. Probably the most militarily powerful Third World regime was facing a popular rebellion of largely unarmed masses. By 1986 this conflict had reached stalemate: the state was militarily strong but politically weak, while the popular movement and its leading representative, the African National Congress (ANC), was politically strong but militarily weak. Neither side had the combined military and political capacity to decisively seize the strategic initiative. Refusing to accept the inevitability of majority rule, the regime declared a State of Emergency in June 1986. This gave the state a defensive shield for launching a new "national security" strategy aimed at "countering the revolutionary onslaught."

"Revolutions," a senior military officer said, "are made by revolutionaries [who] exploit the grievances of the poor for their own purposes."[1] For a solution the generals modified the "low intensity warfare" strategies pursued by some Latin American regimes. This involved using extensive repression to "eliminate the revolutionaries" and massive "socio-economic upgrading" programs to deal with some black grievances. By combining repression and "reform," the regime hopes to dissipate the revolution.

*The term "Blacks" refers collectively to persons classified as Africans, Coloureds and Indians in South Africa. Where precision is required, the racial categories will be used but this in no way indicates acceptance by the author of the racial classifications imposed by the Pretoria regime.

To manage this ambitious repressive reform program, a complex hierarchy of 400 security committees called Joint Management Centers (JMCs) has been activated at national, regional and local level. The committees, whose activities are kept secret, are chaired by military of police officials. So-called "hard war" sub-committees decide who is to be detained or killed, and "soft war" sub-committees deal with welfare, economic and constitutional matters. Each township has a JMC that aims to achieve the right balance between "hard" and "soft" responses.

The overall strategic objective is to forcibly rip the Black communities apart, extract and incarcerate the leadership kernel that helped organize them, and then to put the pieces together again on terms that leave white domination intact. The regime believes it can outflank the liberation movement by re-molding the communities in its own image. By removing their base, the regime hopes to remove the need to negotiate with legitimate Black leaders.

Black political organizations do not deny how damaging the state's ferocious retaliation has been. However, given that blacks remain politically disenfranchised, it is unlikely that the state's current strategy will achieve more than temporary compliance. Black co-operation, not simply compliance, is the regime's deepest desire. But this will elude its grasp as long as the white minority refuses to accept the inevitability of majority rule.

In the interregnum, the white right-wing has become increasingly prominent. This is not because more Whites are voting for the right. Before 1987 the governing National Party (NP) faced a liberal official opposition in parliament. The crudely racist Conservative Party (CP) became the official opposition following its gains in the white general election of May 1987.

Conservative Party policies in 1987 were identical to NP policies during the 1981 general election. As the NP moved fractionally leftward in line with reform policies which conceded that Black exclusion from the 1983 constitution was a mistake, it split in two in 1982, leaving behind the CP and its loyalty to orthodox racism. One in two Whites voted NP in 1981, while one in four voted for the same policies in 1987, but this time espoused by the CP. It is not the electorate that moved right, but the political parties that moved (slightly) leftward as they responded to Black protest.

The root problems in South Africa will not be resolved until the government agrees to negotiate a settlement with the African National Congress and other legitimate leaders. By rejecting the Commonwealth Eminent Persons Group's proposals for such negotiations in 1986, the regime told the world it still has other options. The fundamental question in future till be how a militarized white state uses co-optive strategies to achieve a critical mass of moderate Black support. Can the white autocracy create a multi-racial veneer to sell to the world? The survival of radical Black opposition, despite massive repression, suggests the state's strategy will fail in the long run. In the end, genuine all-party negotiations will have to take place. Meanwhile violence, breakdown and degeneration will persist as the old order refuses to die and the new order struggles to be born.

The chapter paper examines the dynamics of conflict in South Africa in the period following the 1976 Soweto uprising. It analyses the qualitative growth in Black political consciousness and resistance, particularly the armed struggle for liberation and working class resistance. We also examine the Whites' response and capacity to respond. Finally, we answer the question whether, in the face of massive repression such as the State of Emergency, detention and torture of political activists, incarceration of leaders, political assassinations and proscription of organizations, Black resistance will survive. This will assist in determining whether peaceful solutions are possible or whether future trends are towards increasing conflict.

SOWETO STUDENTS' REVOLT

June 16, 1976 saw the beginning of national uprisings precipitated by African students in South Western Townships (known by their acronym Soweto), outside Johannesburg, protesting against a government decree forcing instruction through the medium of Afrikaans. In eighteen months, anti-apartheid protest spread to almost 200 communities throughout South Africa; about 1,000 people were killed; an estimated 4,000 youths fled the country to join the exiled national liberation movements, the African National Congress (ANC) and Pan-Africanist congress (PAC); finally, in October, 1977, the South African government banned eighteen organizations, most of them black Consciousness-oriented groups, and two Black-run newspapers, *The World* and *Weekend World*. It detained prominent Black leaders and journalists and banned several of its liberal white critics, including Donald Woods, editor of the East London *Daily Despatch*, and Dr. Beyers Naude, director of the ecumenical Christian institute.[2]

The crackdown, effected by Prime Minister B.J. Vorster after consultations with his National Party caucus and the white business community, was aimed at silencing right-wing Afrikaner critics who charged that Vorster was "too soft," and at convincing the international businessmen and financiers that the country was still a safe haven for investment. In the whites-only general election that followed the crackdown, the National Party increased its parliamentary majority, which indicated that the white electorate preferred authoritarian rule over any negotiations that might result in a loss of white power and privilege.

The crackdown induced a temporary calm, but did not create permanent stability. The Soweto rebellion convinced elements within the ruling National Party and big business that changes were necessary to stave off Black revolution. But this would not be effected while Vorster and the government intelligence agency dominated. Vorster, the architect of the modern police state that emerged in the post-Sharpeville period, was elevated to the ceremonial position of State President and P.J. Botha, a veteran National Party organizer who was then Defense Minister, succeeded him as Prime Minister.

Soon after the National Party's election victory and the change in leadership, however, the party was rocked by a scandal that sparked a fierce power struggle. A government-appointed Commission of Inquiry, led by a Supreme Court judge, discovered that public funds were laundered to finance various secret projects aimed at winning friends for Pretoria and favorably influencing international public opinion. The Information Department scandal led to the resignation in disgrace of Vorster, Dr. Connie Mulder who was Information Minister when the secret projects were launched, and the former head of the Bureau of State Security, General Hendrik van den Berghe.[3]

NATIONAL SECURITY DOCTRINE AND TOTAL STRATEGY

Botha's leadership was accompanied by the ascension of the military within the white power structure. Faced with the successes of national liberation movements against colonial regimes in the former Portugese territories and Southern Rhodesia, as well as Black resistance domestically in the wake of the 1976 Soweto uprising, the military leadership in South Africa was preoccupied with the need for the regime to regain the initiative and go on the offensive.[4] The National Security Doctrine, elaborated for the first time in 1977 at a symposium on "National Security" at Pretoria University's Institute of Strategic Studies, was an attempt by the politico-military ideologues to adapt to their own situation doctrines which have evolved in other parts of the world, particularly in regimes which have been involved in "counterinsurgency" and in attempts to crush popular resistance led by national liberation movement. They closely studied the imperialist wars of expansion, including those of nineteenth century Prussia and Nazi Germany, and the lessons of the French in Algeria, the British in Malaysia, the United States in Indo-China and Israel in the Middle East.

"Total strategy," a politico-military philosophy, has its origins in the National Security Doctrine. The military claimed that South Africa faced a "total onslaught" that was political, diplomatic, economic, military and psychological. A "total strategy" was necessary, if this "total onslaught" were to be successfully countered. One of the first explanations of "total strategy" was proved in 1977 by General Magnus Malan (himself a graduate of West Point) while still Chief of the Defense Forces:

In a mature state the fundamental concepts of conflict entail far more than war. It means the formulation of national objectives in which all the community's resources are mustered and managed on a co-ordinated level to ensure survival. Every activity of the state must be seen and understood as a function of a total war.[5]

Two key elements necessary for the survival of white minority rule in South Africa were, according to the military, (i) the maintenance of a strong defense force and (ii) commitment to domestic reform.

Strong Defense Force

The period after the Soweto uprising saw a significant increase in military expenditure. In September 1981 the Whites-only central parliament approved a record budget of R2.6 billion. During the discussion of the budget, the Defense Minister justified the increased expenditure on two grounds. First, he claimed that South Africa faced a threat from the Soviet Union and Cuba which were committed to the overthrow of the regime so as to capture the country's wealth. The overthrow of the white minority regime, he argued, would enable the Soviet Union to deny the West access to the Cape sea route. Secondly, he foresaw an expanding role for the defense forces in "safeguarding internal strategic pieces" and ensuring the "maintenance of law and order." To support his contention that the "internal threat" was likely to increase, he cited the fact that there had been a two hundred percent increase in the number of incidents of sabotage during the first six months of 1981 compared with the last six months of 1980.

Domestic Reform

The military leadership was aware, however, that while the South African Defense Forces might be able to resist any external threat, they could not simultaneously deal with internal unrest. For this reason, the military supported a program of limited domestic reforms in the hope of winning over sections of the Black community. During his tenure as Chief of the Defense Forces, General Malan expressed the view that fighting a guerilla war was primarily a matter of winning "hearts and minds." The solution to the problems in South Africa, he said, was only twenty percent military and eighty percent political.

With the emergence of P.W. Botha as Prime Minister after the fall from grace of Vorster, van den Berghe and the BOSS/DONS (Bureau of State Security/Department of National Security), the military leadership consolidated its control within the white power structure so as to implement "total strategy" effectively. By reviving the State Security Council which, since its inception in 1972, had been dormant even though its ostensible purpose was to advise the Cabinet, Botha was able to by-pass even his own party caucus. The State Security Council became the regime's main think tank, taking over a function that belonged to the Broederbond. By virtue of the decisions it made it became an alternative Cabinet.

Botha implemented a rationalization of the administration: The number of government departments was reduced and a new Cabinet structure set up, reducing the number of Cabinet committees from forty to five. These cabinet committees assumed responsibility for the important decisions regarding the economy, security, the constitution, and social affairs. Describing the influence exerted by the military, a journalist wrote:

Military advisers sit on the fifteen departmental committees coercing all the main aspects of government whose recommendations are coordinated through the State Security Council. Senior officers can be found on many of the public commissions set up by the Botha administration...The military's influence even extends to grassroots level through joint planning centers which have been set up in the country's nine "commando areas." These act as information-gathering centers about potential threats to the country, and their information is fed back to the State Security Council.[6]

Even Afrikaner academics expressed concern about the emergence of a "military dictatorship" in South Africa, but saw it as a necessary evil if there was to be a gradual evolution to "peaceful change."

THE CONSTELLATION OF SOUTHERN AFRICAN STATES

Pretoria's military strategists also formulated the concept of a "Constellation of Southern African States," as an integral part of their counterinsurgency strategy. According to their plans, Pretoria would use its political, economic and military might to establish a grouping of moderate "anti-Marxist" states in the African subcontinent. The idea was further propounded by P.W. Botha in Parliament in April 1979 and subsequently clarified by various National Party spokespersons, academics and analysts. Pretoria hoped that the formation of a regional bloc, in which it would play a dominant role, would enable it to achieve several objectives.

First, in return for certain economic benefits, the independent African states which could be enticed into the alliance would cease criticism of Pretoria's *apartheid* policies. Botha envisaged the establishment of friendly relations with neighboring states on the basis of non-interference in each other's internal affairs. The corollary of this would be that member states of the alliance would also deny support to the ANC and PAC, the national liberation movements fighting for the overthrow of white minority rule in South Africa.

Secondly, Pretoria hoped that if the independent African states could be persuaded to join the alliance, international criticism of *apartheid* would similarly be blunted. In response to international criticisms and campaigns for economic sanctions, Pretoria would be able to point to the co-operation with sovereign and independent African states.

Thirdly, the creation of a regional bloc would have military benefits for Pretoria. In the wake of the independence of Mozambique and Angola, the exodus of thousands of young Blacks after the Soweto uprising of 1976 and the successes of freedom fighters in Zimbabwe, there were expressions of concern within the South African military establishment about the security implications.

Having lost the protection of the buffer states, the Pretoria regime hoped that the Bantustans, together with the independent African states prepared to join the Constellation, would provide a new *cordon sanitaire*. Guerillas of the national liberation movements, if they succeeded in infiltrating from "hostile" countries, would be contained on the periphery of "white South Africa" which would assist its partners in the alliance in dealing with threats to their security. Dr. Piet Koornhof, then Minister of Cooperation and Development, explained in March 1980 that the members of the Constellation "would not threaten each other and would present a united front to any external threat."[7] In other words, a non-aggression pact was envisaged for the Constellation.

The desirability of a regional bloc was emphasized by government, as well as opposition spokespersons, who noted the benefits for South Africa's security and economic development. The idea was enthusiastically supported also by businessmen and industrialists who pointed out that the Southern African region is South Africa's natural hinterland and market for its manufactured goods. The idea of a "constellation of Southern African states" was presented by Botha to a conference of the country's leading businessmen and industrialists with much fanfare in November 1979.

Pretoria's hopes were dashed by the convincing victory won by Robert Mugabe in the first elections held following the Lancaster House Agreement concluded at the All-Party Conference on Rhodesia convened by Britain. Robert Mugabe, who became Prime Minister of independent Zimbabwe in April 1980, joined the leaders of Angola, Botswana, Lesotho, Malawi, Mozambique, Swaziland, Tanzania, and Zambia to form the Southern African Development Coordination Conference (SADCC). The stated objectives of SADCC are to decrease economic dependence on South Africa and to promote regional economic cooperation. Even though Botswana, Lesotho and Swaziland are members of the South African Customs Union, and other SADCC member states continue to

trade with South Africa, none of the independent African countries in the
region joined the proposed "Constellation of Southern African States."

Regional Destabilisation

Having failed to secure the cooperation of the independent African nations in the suppression of the exiled national liberation movements, particularly the ANC, which increased its presence in South Africa and the
region after 1976, Pretoria embarked upon a policy of regional destabilisation to make difficult the tasks of national reconstruction in those countries that accede to independence after years of armed struggle. In this
way, the conflict in South Africa was transposed in the region. The policy of destabilisation had four prongs:

(1) Direct military incursions and commando raids: Mozambique
(1981 and 1983); Lesotho (1982 and 1985); Angola (1977 and every year
through 1987); Botswana (1985, 1986 and 1987); Zambia (1986);
Zimbabwe (1983 and 1986).

(2) Training and supporting dissident groups in the African Front Line
States: These included Jonas Savimbi's UNITA in Angola, RENAMO in
Mozambique, the Lesotho Liberation Army in Lesotho and Zimbabwean
dissidents in the troubled southern province of Matabeleland. Evidence in
the trial of four White Zimbabweans charged with murder, following a
series of bombings in Bulawayo in January, 1987, indicated that South
Africa recruited die-hard racists in Zimbabwe to spy on ANC personnel
and to carry out acts of sabotage in that country. They worked under the
supervision of former Rhodesian security and intelligence officers who
migrated to South Africa in independence.

(3) Economic pressures, including the withdrawal of locomotives on
loan to Zimbabwe and insistence that the Preferential Trade Agreement between the two countries be renegotiated at ministerial level despite
Zimbabwe's policy of prohibiting such high level contacts; and the 1986
economic blockade against Lesotho which precipitated the military coup
that toppled the government of Prime Minister Leabua Jonathan.

(4) Kidnapping and assassination of ANC personnel and other South
African refugees and exiles. These include ANC representative Joe Gqabi
in Harare, Zimbabwe (August, 1981); Ruth First in Maputo,
Mozambique (August, 1982) and dozens of others in the countries neighboring South Africa.

The extent of the devastation caused by South Africa's regionalisation
of the conflict was described in stark terms by Joseph Hanlon, a political
analyst who spent many years in Mozambique:

Since 1980, 700,000 people have died in neighboring states due to South African destabilisation. More than four million have been made refugees. The cost to the nine

states, which are members of SADCC, is at least $25 billion. This is nearly triple the total foreign assistance received by the SADCC states in that same period.[8]

Initially South African military strategists denied involvement in the escalating regional conflict. As evidence mounted of their deploying surrogate forces in Angola and Mozambique, they indicated that they would cease support for such groups when the African countries deny support to the ANC. By 1983, however, Pretoria's spokespersons repeatedly stated that the objective was to effect the evacuation of the ANC from the Southern African region, a goal which would be achieved through a combination of military and diplomatic pressures. Swaziland, which secretly signed a non-aggression pact with Pretoria in 1982, was offered a portion of land bordering on Northern Natal and Zululand in return for the expulsion of the ANC from its territory. Mozambique, its economy devastated by RENAMO's campaign of terrorism and sabotage, and natural disasters (particularly the floods of 1981 and the three successive years of drought from 1982) ultimately signed the Nkomati Accord with Pretoria in March 1984. Mozambique agreed to expel all but four ANC representatives in return for a promise from Pretoria to cease support for RENAMO -- an agreement that was observed more in the breach by Pretoria.

There was a realization, however, that progress in the achievement of Pretoria's regional economic and security objectives would be enhanced by changed in internal policy. For this reason, P.W. Botha's succession to the National Party leadership was accompanied by much rhetoric about "reform" and "change." The "reforms" envisaged by the white establishment aimed at creating for Blacks an illusion of change, through such measures as desegregation of certain public amenities and sports facilities, as well as limited access to economic and educational opportunities, while retaining political and economic power firmly in white hands. A knowledgeable journalist who returned to South Africa after an absence of almost five years to cover the Whites-only general election in April 1981, summed it up:

While there is great ferment in intellectual circles and a continuing debate about the need to introduce genuine change -- to "adapt of die," in the dramatic phrase of the Prime Minister -- there is neither blueprint nor strategy, nor even some sense of subterranean common purpose on the part of the government to alter the underpinnings of South African society. Nor is there, as far as I have been able to discover, an "explicit commitment" by that government to domestic change in anything other than the vaguest rhetorical terms.[9]

Even the mere rhetoric about the need for change has not been without cost to the ruling National Party and to Afrikaner unity. In the April 1981 Whites-only general election the extreme right-wing Herstigte Nasionale Party (HNP), which remains implacably opposed to any liberalization of *apartheid,* increased its share of the popular vote from two percent in 1979 to thirteen percent, although it did not win any parliamentary seats. Subsequently sixteen National Party members led by Dr. Andries Treurnicht, former leader of the powerful Transvaal region, were expelled because of their opposition to Botha's acceptance of the idea of limited "power-sharing" with Coloureds and Indians. Treurnicht and the other expelled members later merged with Dr. Connie Mulder's Conservative Party. Although superficially the splits and divisions within Afrikanerdom may appear to the casual onlooker as a struggle between "reformers" and "reactionaries," they also manifest shifting class alliances within the White establishment. What emerged in the post-Soweto period as the dominant force was a military-industrial alliance with strong interests in domestic reform and an expanded regional role for Pretoria with the objective of preventing Black revolution.

The dilemma was how to effect change without radically altering capitalist economic relations and white power and privilege on which they were based. In an attempt to modernize *apartheid* the recommendations of several government-appointed commissions were accepted. The Riekert Commission, appointed to examine the status of urban Africans, recommended both the retention of Bantustans and recognition of the permanence of urban Africans, whose political and material connection with the Bantustans had been undermined by urbanization. The Commission pointed out that the urban Africans were also the basis for an expanded market and labor aristocracy. While abandoning the fiction that urban Africans were "temporary sojourners," the Riekert Commission's recommendation meant in fact that "urban insiders" had to be separated from rural poverty, which in turn necessitated more rigid enforcement of influx control. The Orderly Movement and Settlement of Black Persons' Bill (1982), which was designed to intensify influx control in order to keep out "rural outsiders," generated such intense opposition that it was never promulgated into law. But the government's acceptance of the Riekert Commission's recommendation facilitated implementation of various other reforms: the right to form trade unions, see labor "on the free market" and without a contract, the right to leasehold, and the right to trade.

Legalization of trade unions for Africans was effected in 1979, following the report of the Wiehahn Commission. The regime initially attempted to fit the Labour Relations Amendment Act within the framework of the Riekert Commission by excluding migrant workers from the provisions of the new law. The trade union movement opposed the exclusion of "rural outsiders" from the new dispensation, thus jeopardizing the regime's labor reforms.

Black responses to the 1982 Black Local Authorities Act and the 1983 South African Constitution Act similarly rendered the reforms meaningless or undermined their intended purpose. The Black Local Authorities Act created fully autonomous municipal entities for urban Africans. They were empowered to allocate housing and trading licenses. The regime also hoped that because they were presented as Black self-government they would defuse grievances. Since the Black Local Authorities lacked a revenue base, they could only derive capital for the costs of upgrading programs by raising the rents, which in turn proved to be their undoing. Moreover, since the Black Local Authorities were connected politically with the Bantustans, the Africans were still disenfranchised, further fueling Black anger. For the same reason, the extension of limited political rights to Coloureds and Indians under the 1983 South African Constitution Act, which created the tricameral parliament, instead triggered massive Black protest. In other words, measures that the Whites regarded as major reforms precipitated Black anger and protest. To understand this phenomenon it is necessary to examine the developments in internal opposition to apartheid in the post-Soweto period.

INCREASING DOMESTIC OPPOSITION TO APARTHEID

The 1977 crackdown did not result in a long period of political quiet, as followed the bannings of the ANC and PAC in 1960, the imprisonment of their leadership and, by 1963, the destruction of their military organs, Umkhonto we Sizwe and POQO, respectively. Six months after the bannings of the eighteen organizations, Black Consciousness activists formed the Azanian People's Organization (AZAPO) and even though the first leaders of this new organization were detained and subsequently restricted without trial, by September 1978 it was operational. Many activists from the banned organizations also joined existing, or formed new community, youth, student and women's organizations. Others joined the labor movement.

The independent labor movement that emerged following the 1972-73 Black workers' strikes also grew in strength and organization, to the alarm of both capital and the state. The two umbrella labor organizations, the Federation of South African Trade Unions (FOSATU) and the Council of Unions of South Africa (CUSA), formed in the late 1970's, devoted considerable time and energy to the development of organizational infrastructure and working class leadership to enable the fledgeling labour movement withstand attacks by the state.

Pretoria's legalization of African trade unions in 1979, was an attempt to bring the independent labor movement under control. In its report, the Wiehahn Commission pointed out that the new unions formed in the wake of the 1972-73 strikes operated outside the existing framework of industrial relations yet enjoyed widespread support and legitimacy among Black workers in contrast with the discredited, officially-sanctioned workers' committees. When the independent labor movement resisted the controls the regime proposed in the 1979 Labour Relations Amendment Act, the regime relented. In an amendment in 1981 it expunged all references to race in the law, thus permitting the registration of nonracial unions.

The organization and pervasive mood of resistance was evident during the 1980 revolt which began as a protest against *apartheid* education but developed into a generalized campaign against the *system of apartheid*. Coloured students in the Western Cape demonstrated against the inferior system of education, but rather than take to the streets in large numbers as in 1976, used the physical facilities for meetings and political education. In addition, they sought community support for their protest: community meetings were held throughout the Western Cape, to explain to parents their grievances. In this way, the inter-generational conflict of the 1976 student revolt was obviated. Another qualitative difference between the 1976 and 1980 student revolts was the involvement of Black workers. Students supported a strike by workers at Fatti's and Moni's company and, when management refused to reinstate dismissed workers, assisted the workers in organizing a successful community boycott of red meat. An added feature of the 1980 student revolt was the sharper analysis in the students' pamphlets of the nature of the struggle, which was increasingly defined as anti-capitalist. This enabled students to define their own struggle against the inferior system of education more clearly and to demonstrate to workers their understanding of the inter-relatedness of the inferior educational system and the exploitation of workers.[10]

The 1980 revolt was not restricted to Coloured students and workers, or confined to the Western Cape. It involved African and Indian students throughout the country.[11] The students elected representatives to a body called the "Committee of 81" which coordinated their activities. During that time, there also emerged a shadowy organization called the "Black Eye Movement," which coerced Black school principals and teachers who were not fully supportive of the school boycott. In Natal, Inkatha, the tribal political-cultural movement formed by Bantustan leader Chief Gatsha Buthelezi, violently suppressed the anti-apartheid demonstrations -- an action that permanently alienated Inkatha from the emerging broad-based anti-apartheid movement.

Student protests and workers' strikes took place against a background of increasing sabotage by ANC freedom-fighters. In June 1980 the anti-apartheid movement was given a tremendous boost of morale when ANC freedom-fighters successfully sabotaged South Africa's oil-from-coal plant at SASOL. The SASOL attack demonstrated Pretoria's vulnerability to guerilla attack, while the sophistication of the operation further enhanced the image and political fortunes of the ANC in South Africa and internationally.

ECONOMIC FAILURE

Political strife was exacerbated by economic failure in the decade of the 1980s. Despite the severity of the economic recession in the period following the 1973 oil crisis, South Africa's military intervention in Angola in 1975 and the costs of supporting the beleaguered Smith regime in Rhodesia (about half-a-million Rhodesian dollars a day by mid-1976), and the Soweto uprisings, the South African economy experienced a boom between 1979 and 1981. The economic boom was brought about by the spiralling gold price. Unpegged from the dollar in 1971, gold was pushed to $200 an ounce in 1974 by pressure on the dollar. The price rose steeply again from 1978 to 1980, reaching an all-time high in late 1980 of nearly $800 an ounce.

The flood of foreign exchange into South Africa that resulted from the bonanza was accompanied by increased spending. Between 1975 and 1980, the value of imports more than doubled. A "natural" balance-of-payments deficit was transformed by gold sales into surplus. But, by the end of 1981, the gold price plummeted almost fifty percent. With it, the economy as a whole skittered on a sharp down-curve. Gross Domestic Product, which in 1980 grew by eight percent, was static in 1982.

The immediate consequence was a balance-of-payments crisis. In November 1982, South Africa turned to the International Monetary Fund (IMF) for a loan of 1.25 billion rands. The economic downturn pressed particularly heavily upon Blacks. Official inflation figures of around fifteen percent bore little relation to the impact on household budgets in the townships as basic foodstuffs and rents rocketed. Estimates of African unemployment levels ranged in 1982 from one and one-half million to three million, or roughly from fifteen to thirty percent of the workforce. Workers' strikes, community protests against rent and bus fare hikes increased during this period and spawned hundreds of community organizations to address local issues.

In the last quarter of 1983 and the first quarter of 1984, the economy experienced another brief upward turn. The mini-boom of 1984 coincided with diplomatic and military developments that occasioned a huge (but, as it turned out, premature) collective sigh of relief in government and business circles. In March 1984, Pretoria signed the Nkomati Accords with Mozambique. The Mozambican government agreed to restrict ANC operations in that country. The effect was that the ANC was deprived of a major launchpad in its strategy of sabotage and guerilla war. ANC military attacks decreased from 146 in 1983 to 56 in 1984.

Pretoria hoped that the Nkomati Accords, together with the proposed new tricameral parliament with separate chambers for Coloured and Indian representatives, and the other reforms, would effect long-term stability on which continued foreign investment, so crucial to the South African economy, was dependent. P.W. Botha undertook an eight-nation

European tour in May and June 1984 that was widely publicized in the
South African media and interpreted as a reacceptance of the country in the
world community But this was not to be. South Africa's political and
economic crisis deepened. With it, the conflict worsened.

ECONOMIC RECESSION, "REFORM" AND POPULAR RESISTANCE

At the beginning of July 1984, the Governor of the Reserve Bank cau-
tioned South Africans "not to panic," as the price of gold dropped below
the "psychological support level" of $364 per ounce and the rand -- in
1980 worth $1.25 -- shrank to 68 U.S. cents. In the same week as this
jittery bid to dispel anxiety, the general sales tax was increased from seven
to ten percent and overdrafts hit twenty-five percent. Then, at the beginning of August 1984, the Finance Minister announced a classic monetary
deflationary package. Interest rates were increased further. Imports and
consumer spending were to be cut. The money supply was to be decreased. These indications of economic distress (and the acute effects of
inflation on Black consumers) could hardly have happened at a less auspi-
cious time. On August 22 and 28, 1984, elections were held for Coloured
and Indian representatives to the new tricameral parliament. The elections
provided anti-apartheid groups across the country with a potent focus for
hostility to a constitution which entrenches racial distinctions and ex-
cludes Africans who constitute seventy-one percent of the population from
its electoral provisions. Political, religious, labor and community leaders
urged people not to vote. AZAPO and the United Democratic Front
(UDF), an umbrella organization comprising some 600 affiliates, formed
in 1983, campaigned to reject the new constitution and boycott the elections. Media campaigns, pamphlet campaigns, door-to-door campaigns,
mass rallies and demonstrations were organized throughout the country to
protest the tricameral parliament.

On the eve of the Coloured election, leading members of the UDF and
AZAPO were detained -- later to face charges of treason, before the state
withdrew its case in late 1985. Against this backdrop of state repression
and violence, an estimated eighteen percent of eligible Coloured and sixteen percent Indian voters went to the polls, a turnout the regime declared
"acceptable."

On September 3, 1984, "reforms," economic pressures and popular resistance intersected and fused. The new Constitution creating the tricameral parliament and executive presidency came into effect. A one-day stay-
away by students and workers in the Transvaal took on an insurrectionary
air. The town council of Leakoa, responsible for several densely popu-
lated African townships (including Sharpeville and Sebokeng), south of
Johannesburg, announced rent increases of almost six rand per month.

Township residents demanded the resignation of the Black councillors, denounced as "stooges." During the stay-away, clashes between police and residents left more than sixty people dead.

In November 1984 an even bigger stay-away in the Vaal triangle was organized by students and workers to protest state repression and the increased cost of living. Between 300,000 and 500,000 workers downed tools for two days, and 400,000 Black students boycotted schools. The November stay-away marked the beginning of a new phase in the history of protest.

A similar fusion of issues operated over most of South Africa through 1985. The balance of emphasis differed from one town or rural area to another. Unemployment, high prices, increases in rents and the costs of transport, attacks on Black policemen, informers or councillors, the deaths in police custody of local activists and community leaders in different communities became precipitants for new levels of organization and militancy. The gulf between the maximal reform proposals touted by the regime, and the minimal demands of the Black opposition widened perceptibly. Those Black politicians who accepted office under the new Constitution or in the Bantustans are now implicated beyond any forgiveness in state repression. Constitutional or welfare provisions which only a few years ago might have won a measure of Black acceptance, are now ringingly repudiated as irrelevant.

The heightened political consciousness and organization among Black South Africans was evident in the successful consumer boycotts in the Eastern Cape coastal city of Port Elizabeth. In the Black townships of Port Elizabeth, an average of ten Blacks per month were killed by the South African security forces in 1984 and 1985. In May 1985, three community leaders -- Sipho Hashe, Qaaqwuli Godolizi and Champion Galela -- disappeared en route to Port Elizabeth airport for a meeting with the British ambassador. Led by Mkhuseli Jack, a twenty-eight year-old building supply salesperson, Blacks in July 1985 organized a consumer boycott. Their slogan was "One South Africa, One Person, One Vote." Mkhuseli Jack and sixteen other Black leaders were detained by the South African authorities in an effort to break the back of the boycott, but to no avail. Blacks continued the boycott which seriously affected White businesses because the Blacks' purchasing power exceeds that of Whites. White businessmen, brought to their knees by the consumer boycott, sided with the Blacks. The Port Elizabeth Chamber of Commerce mediated between White businessmen and Black consumers, and made representations to the government for the release of the detained Black leaders. The government released Mkhuseli Jack and the sixteen other Black leaders and also agreed to withdraw the troops from the townships for a while. The Blacks called off the consumer boycott.

In March 1986, after lifting the state of emergency that was imposed in July 1985, the South African government banned Mkhuseli Jack and

Henry Fazzi, a former ANC member who spent twenty years on Robben Island. Jack successfully challenged his banning order in the Supreme Court. After South African security forces murdered eleven Black people in March 1986, however, the boycott resumed.

Similar successful consumer boycotts were organized in Port Alfred and Cradock in the Eastern Cape, resulting in the collapse of the government-created Black Local Authorities and in negotiations between the community leaders and local White councils and the central government. In Cradock, for example, the Cradock Residents Association (CRADORA), a UDF affiliate, negotiated with the deputy Minister of Education.[12]

By the beginning of 1986 it was evident that the South African police had lost control of the Black townships where, in contrast to earlier uncontrolled Black anger and frustration, rudimentary revolutionary government structures emerged in the form of "area committees," "street committees," and "people's courts." In Alexandra outside Johannesburg, where twenty-seven people were killed by police in a rent protest in February, the "area committees" and "street committees" collected rents and provided patrols to prevent crime, while "people's courts" heard complaints and meted out punishment. People providing essential services could only enter the townships under heavy guard. Formerly, the government proscribed organizations and detained leaders, but by 1986 organization was so widespread that such repressive measures were ineffective.

The nationwide state of emergency declared in June 1986 was aimed at the destruction of the "alternative structures" which emerged in the townships where they enjoyed a great deal of legitimacy and popular support. The state of emergency also marked the abandonment by the regime of its "reform strategy" and the implementation of its "counter-revolutionary" strategy. This combines severe repression with socio-economic upgrading in key areas, termed "oilspots," thirty-four of which have been identified. While hundreds of political activists have been detained and thousands of others incapacitated by restrictions and court trials, thirty-four organizations banned and community newspapers shut down, the regime has begun to implement its program in such townships as Alexandra, Bonteheuwel, Walmer, and Mamelodi outside Johannesburg, Cape Town, Port Elizabeth and Pretoria respectively. The dimensions of the state's counter-revolutionary strategy were clarified by Major General Charles Lloyd, secretary of the State Security Council:

Firstly,...the specific areas of dissatisfaction identified by the ANC need to be addressed - education, housing, health care and freedom of movement.... Secondly...the security forces must protect government, must protect the masses against intimidation, and must "eliminate revolutionaries...." Thirdly...to win the support of the masses by communicating and demonstrating a "realistic new future" to them.[13]

In the light of this strategy, the question that has to be considered is whether Black resistance will survive.

WILL BLACK RESISTANCE SURVIVE?

Six critical factors can be considered in determining whether or not Black resistance will survive.

National Movement

There has emerged in South Africa a social movement that has completely transformed that society. It is a movement that is national, and cuts across race, class and gender.

Deeply Rooted in the Black Community

The movement is deeply rooted in the Black community. The state has lost credibility and legitimacy among the broad mass of the disenfranchised: it governs not by consent but by coercion.

Church Support

The churches (with the exception of the Dutch Reformed Church), under Black leadership, support the struggle. Recent developments within the Dutch Reformed Church (DRC) have also served to undermine the theological underpinnings: The DRC has stated that there is no theological basis for apartheid and recently also confessed to, and sought forgiveness from, the Black "daughter churches" for previously supporting apartheid. In addition, the moderator of the DRC has rejected the regime's precondition for negotiations with the ANC that the latter should "renounce violence."

Trade Unions Organized

The trade unions are nationally organized and despite the restrictions imposed on COSATU, the largest labor federation, in February 1988, they will continue to play an important role. This was seen in June 1988 when, without a formal call by the labor unions, more than two million workers stayed away in observance of June 16 (Soweto Day). The recent labor summit conference, in March 1989, also augurs well for the future of the labor movement and its involvement in the struggle for a nonracial democratic society.

Internal and External Movement Linked

The internally-based UDF is ideologically linked to the ANC but does not support the ANC's strategy of armed struggle. They share the vision of a nonracial, democratic society and despite the regime's efforts to prevent contact with the exiled organization, dozens of delegations of South Africans have traveled to Lusaka and Harare for discussions with the ANC leaders. The links with the ANC, which currently enjoys a high profile and international support, facilitate access to diplomatic and other forms of support for the internally-based movement. Although it is not as well organized or internationally supported, the PAC has also had discussions with a small number of internally-based organizations, including the National Congress of Trade Unions (NACTU).

Support Services

One of the notable features of the popular resistance in the part decade is the wealth of support services in the form of information, skills training, policy analysis and research provided by a range of organizations. This has enabled the resistance to explore alternative models of development, challenge theses put forward by the regime, effectively counter the regime's propaganda and, where negotiations have been held, as between management and labor, to negotiate skillfully.

We have attempted to show that resistance to apartheid has grown qualitatively and quantitatively since the 1976 Soweto uprising. In 1976 protests were sparked by educational issues; in 1984 the legitimacy of the state was at issue. In 1976 the regime was in control; in 1984 it appeared indecisive and vulnerable. In 1976 collaborators were socially ostracized; in 1984 they were executed. Black police fled their homes in the townships and had to be protected in makeshift encampments. The 1976 rebellion was almost entirely a student struggle; the 1984 revolt was broad-based. It has survived a state of emergency in effect since June 1986; bannings of organizations; detentions and torture of leaders; political assassinations and "disappearances;" trial and convictions of various layers of leadership on charges of treason, sedition, public violence aimed at criminalizing political opposition; and, crippling restrictions on individuals.

Between September 1984 and December 1988, more than 4,000 people were killed in political violence in South Africa.[14] More than 2,000 of the fatalities occurred after the state of emergency was imposed in June 1986 -- a draconian measure the government justified on the grounds of having to put an end to violence. The state of emergency has been successful in curbing anti-apartheid activity, but it has not reduced the overall levels of conflict in the society. As the ruling class attempts to maintain and reproduce itself, it reproduces the conflict. Only a thorough restructuring of the economy, political system, ideology and culture will resolve the conflict.

There is no evidence that the South African regime is prepared to negotiate with authentic Black leaders, a new political dispensation that would resolve the conflict. The extra-parliamentary opposition has stated four minimum demands for a negotiated settlement:

(1) The legalization of the ANC, PAC and other political organizations;

(2) The release of Nelson Mandela and all other political prisoners;

(3) The return of all political exiles and their free participation in the political process; and

(4) A national convention to draw up a new Constitution.

The history of Southern Africa indicates that colonial and white minority regimes have been persuaded to negotiate when faced with a credible military challenge by the oppressed and their national liberation movements. At present the military balance between the regime and its principal challenger, the ANC, is far too heavily weighted in favor of the regime. It believes that it can defeat the ANC militarily and contain a radical challenge domestically through severe repression. In the face of Pretoria's intransigence the future seems to be fraught with strife.

Notes

1. Major-General Charles Lloyd in a confidential briefing for South African businessmen, quoted in Philip Frankel, "Reform and Counter-Revolution: South African State Strategy during the 1980's," mss, presented at Defense Intelligence College, Washington, D.C., February, 1988.

2. John Kane-Berman, *South Africa: The Method in the Madness* (London: Pluto Press, 1979); Batuck Hirson, *Soweto: Seeds of a Revolution? Year of Fire, Year of Ash!* (London: Zed Books, 1979); Tom Lodge, *Black Politics in South Africa Since 1945* (Johannesburg: Ravan Press, 1983).

3. Survey of Race Relations in South Africa 1978 and 1979 (Johannesburg: South African Institute of Race Relations, 1979 and 1980).

4. "The National Security Doctrine: the Origins of 'Total Strategy,' " *Resister*, (London: Committee on South African War Resisters, December 1981-January 1982).

5. *Ibid.*

6. N. Ashford, "South Africa's Generals in the Corridors of Power," *The Times* (London, September 1, 1980).

7. Survey of Race Relations in South Africa 1979, (Johannesburg: SAIRR, 1980), 643.

8. Joseph Hanlon, "Regional Destabilisation in Southern Africa," *CUSO Journal* (Ottawa: CUSO, Summer 1987), 18. See David Martin and Phyllis Johnson, eds., *Destructive Engagement*, (Harare: Zimbabwe Publishing House, 1986) for a detailed account of South Africa's destabilisation.

9. *Muslim News*, (May 9, 1980); *Cape Times*, (May 27, 1980); *New Statesman*, (June 6, 1980).

10. J. Hyslop, "School Student Movements and State Education Policy," in William Cobbet and Robin Cohen, eds., *Popular Struggles in South Africa* (New Jersey:

Africa World Press, 1988), 188. See also F. Molteno, "Reflection on Resistance -- Aspects of the 1980 Schools Boycott," in M. Lawrence, ed., Kenton-at-the Stadt 1983 Conference *Proceedings* (Mafikeng: University of Bophuthatswana, 1984); R. Levin, "Black Education, Class Struggle and the Dynamics of Change in South Africa," *Africa Perspective*, 17 (Spring, 1980).

11.   *Sunday Express*, (June 1, 1980).
12.   "Resistance in the Eastern Cape: Caradock," *Work In Progress*, 38 (Braamfontein: Southern Africa Research Service, August, 1985), 4-8.
13.   Quoted by Kate Phillip, "State Strategy and Popular Response," *Work in Progress* 56/57 (Braamfontein: Southern Africa Research Service, August, 1985), 23. See also William Cobbett and Robin Cohen, eds., *Popular Struggles in South Africa*, (New Jersey: African World Press, 1988) for excellent essays detailing the mass struggles and state responses.
14.   *New York Times*, (March 5, 1989).

The Intensifying Armed Struggle:
A Comment

Joe Thloloe

I suggest that in order to get a better perspective you probably need to stand back and get a wider view of the struggle that has been taking place in South Africa. Immediately after that I will try to zoom in on a specific area to try to get at events inside the country. If you do not get this wider view, you can easily get trapped into a position of believing that the final show-down is imminent. That is a problem we had around 1986. Again, if you don't get too close and look very intimately at the developments you miss some of the feedback that is necessary in understanding the country.

If you stand back and look at South African history in the last thirty years, you will see a series of ridges and plateaus. That very first ridge would be 1960 to 1963; the second ridge would be from 1976 to 1977 and the third ridge would be 1984 to 1986. Between those ridges you have plateaus. The interesting thing is that each plateau is higher than the one that went before and each ridge is higher than the one that went before. If you look at the plateau between 1964 and 1976, it is twelve years, and the one between 1977 and 1984 is only seven years. Henry Isaacs has given us some indications of what happens at these ridges. Between 1984 and 1986 more than two thousand people were killed and in the ridge between 1976 and 1977 about a thousand people were killed. These are the figures that are quoted.

What is happening in the country now that we have dropped to a plateau? This plateau is very important in the sense that there was too much blood-letting during 1984-86 period. So the black community has withdrawn into itself to lick its wounds. But the anger is still there, the resentment is still there and it is still being expressed. Last June 6th, 7th and 8th we had the biggest-ever strike in the country called by NACTU and COSATU. The anger is being expressed by way of rent boycotts. Today local government structures are collapsing because communities are refusing to pay rents. The anger is expressed by the way people are refusing to participate in phony elections like they did October 26 last year.

So the anger is still there, we might have dropped to a plateau, but it is still a very important plateau.

Here is a quick picture that I am trying to draw. The first graph would indicate spontaneous unorganized resistance to apartheid. But we need to look at another graph. This time it would indicate a steady upward movement. This graph would show organized armed resistance to apartheid, organized by the African National Congress and the Pan-Africanist Congress. Last September, the South African Minister of Law and Order, Adrian Vlok, gave statistics of guerrilla attacks. He said between 1976 and 1984 eighty-three people were killed in these attacks, and between 1984 and the time he was talking in 1988, one hundred forty-four people were killed. So we see a steady climb. I don't have comparative statistics here, but last year twenty-eight guerrillas of the pan-Africanist Congress and one hundred eleven of the African National Congress were killed by the so-called security forces.

Another interesting development last year was just before the October 26th election. There was an intriguing coincidence between reports of unorganized, spontaneous acts and the organized armed struggle. In September, there were more than thirty bomb explosions in various places in the country and in October there were more than thirty. It came to an average of more than one explosion per day. I would say it was the first time there was this coincidence of the unorganized spontaneous resistance, and the organized armed struggle. Some people have tried to dismiss armed struggle, but I think we should accept that it is still in the nascent stage, just starting. We can trace its history from 1976. I know there was an earlier period 1961 to 1963-64, but at the end of the period the government reacted very viciously. A number of guerrillas were executed in 1963-64 and a number of people were sentenced to life imprisonments. So the vicious attack brought a halt to the armed struggle at that point. What the liberation movements were doing between 1964 and 1976 was laying down an infrastructure. So there are still possibilities in armed struggle.

Earlier I spoke about the ridges. The interesting thing is what happens at the ridges. The South African government has done two things every time. It has gone for reform and then increased repression. Talk about a "total strategy" is not new; it is just that we have given it a label at this point. During the 1960-63 ridge, the South African government finalized its Bantustan concept; that was by way of reform at the particular period; at the same time they started detention without trial. That is when you had 90 day detention coming in, that is when you had the Terrorism Act coming in, so that repression was increasing. The reaction of the international community was also particularly interesting. After the Sharpeville shootings in 1960, the international community pulled its capital out of South Africa and there was an economic crisis, along with the internal crisis. But immediately after South Africa tightened its repression and gave us this pseudo-reform, capital flowed back and everything went back to normal. That has been the pattern throughout. The international community is encouraging South Africa's reluctance to look at a long term solution to our problems. The South African government is not looking at any long term solutions. It is just fire-fighting and crisis management. That is what Total Strategy is all about, and the international community is encouraging that type of response.

Isaacs passed very quickly over the reforms in labor legislation that were introduced in 1979, but a closer examination of these will give us an insight into the nature of the conflict and change in South Africa.

The Wiehahn Commission was appointed because there was a shortage of skilled, *i.e.* white, labor. Following the 1976 revolt by blacks, whites in Europe and other parts of the world refused to immigrate into the country. The international community was expressing its disgust against the June 16 shootings and the apartheid system generally.

At that time too the labor movement was growing and had been growing since 1973, indifferent to the government's attitude to it. The black unions were not illegal, but they were not recognized by the government and the bosses.

It was thus a combination of black revolt and action by the international community that brought about the changes to the country's labor laws.

Faced with this shortage, the Wiehahn Commission opened the way for blacks to move up to jobs from which they had been excluded by legislation. But the interesting thing was that the vertical line of apartheid was shifted up: whites moved to even better jobs and blacks came in below them. Up to now there has been no significant breakdown of the line that separates white workers from black.

All that the Wiehahn Commission accomplished was to clear the decks for the real struggle against apartheid at the workplace to start. The black trade unions that were legalized by the legislation that followed the report of the commission are now fighting that battle at the factory floor. This explains why much of the recent struggle has been waged by the trade unions.

3

Some Thoughts on the Demilitarization of South and Southern Africa

Kenneth W. Grundy

All modern polities depend, to one degree or another, upon coercion or the threat of it to maintain order and control. In many countries, if not most, the armed forces are coercive organizations that serve political purposes. Regardless of the size, professionalism, loyalty or reliability of the arms of state, they are crucial to the exercise of political power.

Occasionally the armed forces seek to shape state policy unencumbered by civilian authority. Frequently our attention is drawn to the direct seizure of power by the armed forces. The military *coup d'etat* is the most dramatic form of military involvement in politics. It is, however, by no means the most common. The coup is an identifiable act. It is usually accompanied by a public declaration of achievement, of a manifest transfer of power. Seldom, however, does someone openly announce that the armed forces have persuaded a public official to act as they prefer or that they have influenced a decision of state, or that the officers have gotten their way in budgetary negotiations, or that they have threatened to undermine a head of government unless that official pursues a certain policy line.

In the last dozen years or so, we have witnessed the increased involvement of the coercive arms of the South African state in politics in that country and in the surrounding region. Moreover, the South African Defense Force (SADF) has spawned and protected a variety of proxy formations comprised of elements hostile to established and legitimate governments in the region and prepared to destabilize those governments and their societies. Because of these diverse open and clandestine activities, we have come to refer, almost axiomatically, to the militarization of South African politics.[1]

But militarization is not just the exercise of force and coercion. It can be discerned in the pervasive role of the security establishment in policy making and in various aspects of life -- in education, the media, the economy. In the rise of the State Security Council and the all-pervasive National Security Management System there exists a dyarchy or alternative government ready to assume control should the elected (albeit limited) agencies of government prove incapable of maintaining control in a crisis. And these offices are headed by military and in some cases police.

It is not a new phenomenon, just an intensified one. To one degree or another, it affects virtually all sectors of public policy, all racial segments of the population, all regions, all age levels. Violence, coercion, repression are today as they always have been in South Africa, instruments of the racist order. For generations of white settler rule, a pervasive and elaborate superstructure of social control has been put in place to thwart African resistance.

Nevertheless, one can discern in recent years, clearly since Soweto in 1976 and especially since P.W. Botha became head of government in 1978, a further systematic militarization of the South African polity and, because of Pretoria's centrality in regional affairs, throughout southern Africa.

Some have speculated that F.W. de Klerk, the new head of the National Party and the most likely successor to P.W. Botha as State President, has fewer links to the security establishment and is less dependent upon them. While this may be accurate in the narrow partisan sense, these relationships are fluid, as situations change and as perceptions of threat and personal ties are altered. At base, the South African regime rests upon power relationships that are founded upon the exercise of force.

Militarization is not an end product. Militarization is the process of trying to imbue selected individuals and hence institutions and groups with a belief that their lives and fortunes are dependent upon the exercise of coercive power. Militarization is the process by which a people and their institutions prepare for the use of force. Insofar as it is perceived to be successful in achieving expectations and aims, militarization has the further effect of legitimizing the exercise of force and coercion. And as those institutions specifically charged with the tasks of mobilizing force grow in stature, they tend to be relied upon and looked to by policy makers in shaping state policy. In other words, the militarization of a society leads to a militarization of the polity. And the process is interactive -- militarization of the polity can contribute to the militarization of a people.[2]

As a result of this process reaching deep into a society, a sort of Gresham's law of militarization emerges, by which the cooperative, negotiable and compromisable are driven out by the violent and assertive. It is not automatic and it is by no means unidirectional. It can be reversed, from sheer exhaustion and pain. But too frequently, in high-stakes situations of tension, distrust, when the struggle appears to be a zero-sum game, the violent mode takes precedence. We can observe it in the white population in the rise of the Afrikaner Weerstandsbeweging and other, even more pugnacious and inflexible racist elements and in government's responses thereto. Even when the armed forces appear to favor reform and to advocate negotiation, they do so in a firmly confined and limited setting, one in which the parties to negotiation are co-opted and the true proponents of revolution are excluded.

In the black community, divisions exist that are played upon, encouraged, and even provoked by government and its security agents, in order to precipitate destructive and self-defeating internecine civil strife, as in, for example, Pietermaritzburg and Crossroads.

If what is sought is a demilitarization of southern Africa, it becomes necessary to remove the conditions that contribute to the rise of militarization -- in short, to provide for the well-being or at least the promise of well-being and greater freedom and self-expression for a wide segment of the people, to provide for alternative avenues for the just and peaceful settlement of disputes, and to establish greater security for the populace, all segments of it, without the exclusive or nearly exclusive reliance on fear, coercion, and the unequal distribution of power and wealth. In a setting of appalling inequality and scarcity, that may be more than a tall order -- it may be a pipe dream. Nevertheless, it is worth an attempt to see how such a transformation might be brought to pass.

THE CURRENT SITUATION IN SOUTHERN AFRICA

It would be easy to dedicate this entire paper to describing and analyzing the current state of militarization in the region. Fortunately, that subject has been relatively well studied and documented. Instead, I intend to highlight key events and situations, to look for trends and patterns, to cite the relevant literature, and to set a framework for the underlying purpose of this paper, which is to examine the prospects for reversing the militarization and for reducing its attending violence in the area.

It appears that, for the time being at least, South Africa's militaristic policies in southern Africa have been forced into remission.[3] The December 1988 agreement regarding elections in Namibia, and mandating South African force withdrawal from Angola and Namibia and Cuban troop withdrawal from Angola contains within it an opportunity for a major settlement in that part of the sub-continent.[4]

What is more, it appears that the war-making or violent revolutionary capacity of the African National Congress (ANC) will be deeply affected as these arrangements come into force.[5] The ANC is expected to vacate its bases in Angola. It is unlikely that an independent Namibia will risk (at first at least) hosting ANC bases. This agreement, therefore, means that the ANC will not have a military presence nearer than Tanzania.

It is true that the ANC withdrawal from Angola will not mean an end to ANC infiltration and guerrilla strikes inside South Africa. Insurgents are being trained within the Country and this trend will probably grow. But without external support and sanctuary near at hand, operations will be more difficult and probably more random. And hence, ANC strikes will likely prove to be less or an immediate and concerted military threat to Pretoria.[6]

But the ANC is far more than a military organization. Its leadership has always insisted that the political struggle is paramount. Depending on how that organization chooses to pursue its goals and who prevails within the organization, the chances are that the ANC will have to strengthen its links with the non-violent anti-apartheid forces within South Africa. And the ANC could be forced to step up its diplomatic activities (as it has of late) to increase foreign pressure on Pretoria. The ANC cannot be expected to abandon its armed struggle, but it might get even more politically engaged -- domestically among a wider swath of anti-apartheid groups and internationally to raise and enhance its profile and effectiveness.

On the other hand, the failure to include either UNITA or SWAPO directly in the negotiations and the continued support for UNITA from the United States and South Africa and, presumably elsewhere, could contribute to a re-escalation of warfare and to the re-deployment of South African and Cuban forces. In one respect, the fighting that marked the first weeks after April 1, 1989 in Namibia can be traced to SWAPO's official absence from the negotiating table. Given the vulnerability of the Angolan government, the dissatisfaction of UNITA with the terms of the settlement, South Africa's record for procrastination, duplicity and intransigence, and the volatile politcal situation in Namibia and within South Africa itself, the outbreak of large-scale fighting in Angola and Namibia is not entirely out of the question.[7] Simply because Foreign Minister Pik Botha stated publicly that continued aid to UNITA would be a "clearcut violation" of the agreement and that such aid would cease does not mean that Pretoria (and especially the SADF) is going to abandon a fighting force so painstakingly built up over the years. The South African dossier on RENAMO should be consulted on an analogous although different situation. And there is little evidence that the United States intends to close down UNITA or to end its military assistance to UNITA. In fact, there are repeated rumors that UNITA may move its base closer to Zaire, where U.S. assistance can be expedited even as the South African link is loosened.[8] On its own, UNITA still has the capacity to devastate large segments of southern and central Angola and to immobilize the economy in those areas where it operates. In secretive concert with the SADF, it would be a formidable force for destruction.

In addition to the proxy role of UNITA, one can expect the more notorious South African fighting units in Namibia -- 32 Battalion and Koevoet -- not to be demobilized, but to be restructured and relocated either across the border into Angola, or back into South Africa, to serve the SADF's perception of its immediate needs.[9] There are already claims that

South Africa is forming a proxy force of dissident Namibians to unsettle a future SWAPO government in Windhoek. Moreover, there is no absolute assurance that all the black ethnic groups in Namibia will accept a SWAPO victory.   In January 1989, for example, Kaptein "Hans" Diergaart, leader of the Basters of the Rehobeth region, told the South Africa authorities: "Abolish the Rehoboth authority and Resolution 435 will become Revolution 435." Some regard the 65,000-strong Basters as an irritant, at most. Yet coupled with other disenchanted minorities, they could add to the overall level of violence and require greater military mobilization of a new Namibian central government.[10]

This agreement on Angola and Namibia and the generally reduced levels of violence are by no means a product of South African benevolence and choice. The South African military defeat at Cuito Cuanavale, other military failures, the swift deployment of a large Cuban force near the Namibian border in southwest Angola, thereby outflanking the South African formations and posing an immediate threat to Namibian security, and the long-term costs of the Angolan war and occupation of Namibia have forced Pretoria to be more serious about negotiations.[11] The days of South African domination of the air over Angola and their "recce" group's casual free run on the ground in southern Angola are over. Pretoria has been forced to recognize its limitations.[12] Bear in mind, however, that although the exposure of South Africa's military vulnerabilities may have compelled Pretoria to reassess its overt military aggression in the region, it has not abandoned its strategy of covert destabilization or the selective use of terror and dirty tricks.

Also of promise is the fact that hostile military activities in Botswana and Zimbabwe have been curtailed. The Matabeleland-based armed dissidence and banditry that plagued the Harare government after independence seems to have been ended after the 1988 unification of the ruling PF-Zanu and the opposition Zapu-PF. In April and May 1988 an amnesty was in force and many rebel dissidents responded to the offer. Army units, in turn, were withdrawn from Matabeleland. The most critical current military threat to Zimbabwean stability are cross-border raids into eastern Zimbabwe by RENAMO (Mozambique National Resistance) fighters. They seek to end Zimbabwe's military assistance to the Frelimo government in Maputo.   The extent of South African involvement in RENAMO activities will be touched upon later. South Africa itself has been accused of a series of attacks and assassination attempts on alleged ANC officials and facilities in Zimbabwe and elsewhere, although observers agree that their frequency has been reduced. Special operatives from South Africa have even sought to "lift" from a Zimbabwean prison people accused of murder, espionage and sabotage.

In both Zimbabwe and Botswana, South African raids and assassination attempts have become more secretive, selective and focussed and have also been less successful than in past years Occasionally, Pretoria's agents are captured and put on trial. In general, Pretoria has been forced to re-assess its regional strategy. Repeated military rescues of UNITA fores have taken their toll, in South African treasure, materiel and lives, and in weakening diplomatic relations with South Africa's Western colleagues.

Perhaps the one country in southern Africa where there appears to be little if any let up in the magnitude of violence is Mozambique. There, RENAMO continues its banditry and wholesale brutality and destabilization. South Africa's policy toward RENAMO is clouded. Officially it insists that it abides by the terms of the Nkomati accord and that it seeks to improve relations with the Maputo government. Policies regarding private investment, transport links and even military assistance to the Mozambican forces give the appearance of cooperation but not cordiality. Yet reports of South African assistance to and supervision of RENAMO fighters continue to surface.[13] The SADF and diverse other components of the security establishment, including military and civilian intelligence, have been able to mount schemes that either subvert or complement the Department of Foreign Affairs, the State President's Office, and various state economic, infrastructural and private commercial entities.

Elsewhere in the region, the prospect of violence and the use of force grow. The military government in Lesotho is none too stable and re-quires support from the SADF. Malawi faces an impending struggle for succession. President Banda is around eighty-three years old, and he is re-luctant to designate a successor. Zambia drifts closer to economic chaos. Rumors of conspiracies and coup attempts and of corruption are widespread. Government austerity programs, in an effort to rein in state subsidies and a bloated bureaucracy, have led to clashes in the streets, strikes, and greater evidence of government ineptitude and dislocation. In short, opportunities abound throughout the region for flash fires of unrest, leading to military responses. Barring long-term plans and prospects for rectifying the underlying social inequities and institutional inadequacies, coercion would appear to be the short-term state response. And thus the cycle of frustration and dissatisfaction continues.

When one addresses the issue of the demilitarization of southern Africa, it is necessary to appreciate that governments can be complex or-ganizations, capable of dual or even more complicated strategies and tac-tics, or even of contradictory strategies, pursued by diverse offices, com-peting rather than coordinating with one another. The question: "who makes regional policy for Pretoria?" may not admit of simple answers.[14]

In the short run there appears to be a great deal of vacillation in Pretoria's strategies and tactics. What is emerging is what might be called a double dual strategy. Domestically, government pursues simultane-ously a strategy of calling for negotiation and reform from the top and an all-pervasive and brutal suppression of serious opponents of the regime. Likewise, in foreign policy, we get the deployment of force and an ongoing diplomatic minuet. In foreign affairs, the swings of the pendulum tend to be more marked. Domestically, the pattern is more patently synchronal. Still, there is considerable debate among analysts as to what Pretoria is trying to accomplish and how it arrives at this double dual emphasis.

Some feel that this is a coldly calculated oscillation in order to confuse opponents -- a Pavlovian effort to force Pretoria's enemies themselves to salivate on signal and then to be immobilized in confusion or indecision. Opponents are forced to debate which policy signals are more important and whether they should do nothing and await a more conciliatory gesture from Pretoria.

Others see less guile and more confusion in Pretoria's policy circles. Government is indecisive because government doesn't know how best to achieve its ends, or worse, isn't sure what it wants. In such a policy vacuum there is room for considerable "free lancing" (especially by groups within the security forces). By their initiatives they can, in effect, commit government without prior approval at the top. The government waffles and those who think they have the answers seize the moment.

Still others subscribe to a "struggle at the top" thesis. This competitive model of decision making is one characteristic of a part pluralistic and part conspiratorial system. The RENAMO documents seized by Frelimo at Gorongoza attest to this view.[15] South Africa's foreign policy zigs and zags, its spasmodic hostile strikes coupled with a willingness to talk is thereby a product of institutional and personal competition at the center of power. that all this can be linked to domestic white politics, electoral and communal, is evident.

Levels of violence vary over time. The high point of South Africa's overt incursions into neighboring territories (in terms of numbers of operations and forces deployed) was probably 1980 to 1984; and domestic South African bloodshed peaked from 1984 to 1986. The present lull does not represent either a reduced desire on the part of apartheid's enemies to undermine the regime. Nor does it reflect a willingness to the National Party and other apartheid supporters to compromise or surrender power. In some respects, regionally the lull may represent a diminished ability of Pretoria to project power beyond its borders and a heightened capability of neighboring states to protect themselves. Domestically, by diverse means (mostly coercive) the regime has been able to deflect and damp down resistance. Overall, however, the current decline in fighting presents opportunities to diverse actors with complex tactical and strategic motives to slow down further the cycle of violence.

Although the SADF may be the single most powerful military force in the region, it is not the only armed force that contributes to the patterns of militarization. Other states that confront the SADF and its proxy forces do not merely react in response to Pretoria's stimuli. Their own governments may be able to take advantage of opportunities to develop

and employ their own arms of state.[16] Similarly, domestic opponents of
Pretoria and apartheid resist South African Police and SADF and other official formations, but they also have their own intra- and well as inter-
communal agenda. They, too, are in positions to initiate and thereby
shape policy. Too frequently we become accustomed to thinking that
Pretoria alone sets the tone from all conflicts. South Africa's oppressed
peoples, and other southern African governments and parties are not pas-
sive actors.

THE DEMILITARIZATION OF THE REGION

Is it possible to demilitarize southern Africa, that is, to reverse the
process by which the use of coercion and military power have become the
customary, if not the preferred, methods for dealing with public policy
among population groups and states? The principal reason to maintain a
ready armed force is to defend a regime that is threatened from abroad. But
it is also self-evident that coercive forces are indispensable to maintain in
power a minority regime when that regime has lost its legitimacy among
important segments of the population. Pretoria tries to sustain the fiction
that the opposition to it is largely external. But what Pretoria seeks to
label an external threat is in reality a domestic challenge, forced into exile
or underground because of the closure of legal domestic political outlets
and the suppression of majoritarian opposition.[17] In most cases coercion
is a surrogate for a lack of legitimacy and political credibility. No longer
able to maintain the rationale that the white minority rules because it is
civilized, superior, efficient or chosen by the deity, South Africa's government must now rest its case on something apparent to most observers
and what, in fact, had enabled the white minority to gain power in the
first place -- it rules because it is militarily stronger.

It follows that to reduce the role of coercion in politics, it is necessary
to reduce the threats to the regime -- both domestic and external. And to
reduce threats to the regime, the regime must be replaced by one that is
legitimate for all, or for most all South Africans. There is little doubt
that South Africa's domestic racist regime is the single most important
factor that shapes South Africa's foreign policy. To demilitarize South
Africa, in short, power must be transferred from a privileged racial minority to a government with a more widespread popular base. This is a necessary step, but not always a conclusive one. Well-organized minorities
can pose a concentrated threat to even a well-ordered state. Without such a
transformation of the regime, however, demilitarization in the long run is
impossible.

But this may be a simplistic, even naive proposition, for several reasons. In a divided society, there are degrees of commitment to and rejection of the status quo. The regime may be able to buy off some segments

of society with non-political rewards or politically hollow payoffs, mollify others, and isolate still others, or some combinations of rewards, punishments, promises and threats. In situations of scarcity, maintaining anti-regime solidarity is not easy-- small rewards and threats by those in power go a long way.

South Africa is a regime that is militarily strong in the region. Yet it lacks political legitimacy -- militarily rich, politically bankrupt. Yet those military riches are not unlimited.[18] Military riches are a non-convertible currency -- military power cannot buy political legitimacy. It may purchase order and control, but at inflated prices. As Shlomo Avineri says in another context: "An army can beat an army; an army cannot beat a people."[19] Even among its supporters, most white South Africans are prepared to accept enlarged military demands, but not indefinitely. And many have not endorsed the bellicosity associated with those demands.

The South African elite's successful use of violent conflict (domestic and foreign) in the past led to the emergence of polity in which the armed forces (including the police) reinforce the elite political culture that is inclined to employ coercion when inevitable disputes arise.[20] More recently, however, the cross-border raids and large-scale incursions have had less favorable outcomes. Eventually, a calculating elite, faced with the likelihood of defeat or expensive stalemate, will come to explore nonmilitary strategies for the future. South Africa may be entering such an era, one in which demilitarization becomes possible because militarism has become counter-productive or to a lesser extent thwarted. The optimist in me hopes that this is so; the realist thinks it is premature.

Throughout South African history, recurring deadly conflicts have been accompanied by the establishment and expansion of state power. As a result, the disposition of the rulers is to use that power. Not that force is the exclusive mode of governance in South Africa. But it is and always has been the *ultima ratio regnum*. Because of this, the specialized organizations charged with exercising and enforcing state power have gained a respected place in the state's decision making machinery, especially over the past fifteen years. The dominant political culture in South Africa has come to accept if not acclaim the inspirational utility as well as the reality of "patriotic gore." There is, however, considerable resistance to this bellicosity.[21] But with such institutions highly professionalized and central to state operations, and with such a political culture entrenched in the white political elite, it will be difficult to displace such a mentality without a series of unfavorable outcomes stemming from militaristic state policies. In other words, rational policy makers will have to lose more battles or pay more dearly for "victories" before they begin to realize that there are serious costs attending the calculated and often unconstrained employment of force and coercion in state policy. Just such a result in Angola has had this impact.

Strictly speaking, South Africa today is more of a police state than a militarized state. A police state focusses chiefly on the domestic threat. It maintains a large internal security establishment and is ruled by an elite that relies frequently on coercion to control domestic resistance and to implement policy *vis a vis* the majority community. It is a police state defended when necessary by military means. To a lesser degree is South Africa militarized. Compared to other similarly situated unpopular regimes, its military establishment and budget is not especially large. The rate of growth, however, has been remarkable -- officially increases of 19.9 percent in 1986, 30 percent in 1987, 22 percent in 1988, and 17.3 percent in 1989. there are massive "hidden" items of military expenditure sprinkled throughout the budget so that where the official defense budget in 1988 is R9.1 billion, the total "security" budget could be as high as R15 billion.[22]

The key concern, however, is what the military machine is used for, not how large it is. There is little evidence that the SADF seeks to "capture" the polity or that it seeks to intervene in favor of one faction or another within the ruling party. If anything, the armed forces have been politicized, that is, "captured" by the ruling party, and there have been incidences when the partisan employment of the SADF has been challenged by the Progressive Federal Party and by the Conservative Party.

In South Africa, the military performs a police function in a military fashion. Even the police can mount military operations when so deployed. Indeed, military force is as likely to be used to put down domestic resistance as it is to be assigned to so-called defensive functions, that is, defending the borders. As a result, it can be expected that as the challenge to the regime widens, the military institutions and the police institutions will blend and expand. This is, of course, as much a function of the actual threat on South Africa's international borders as it is a matter of policy choice. The fact is, however, that South Africa's regional policy is designed to defend the internal racist system of super- and subordination. Moreover, as the international environment makes it increasingly dangerous for South Africa to project its power abroad too blatantly, Pretoria risks forcing the hands of Western governments that would more comfortably stand on the sidelines rather than invoke sanctions or do even more in support of revolutionary change.

Should the regime fail to suppress the revolutionary challengers, what is the likely outcome? The expected result of a failure to defeat revolutionary challengers is a full-scale war and eventually a defeat for the regime or an effort at securing a compromise outcome.[23] Typically, new revolutionary governments would be committed to strengthening their grasp on the state. They usually are preoccupied with securing their power against counter-revolutionaries and would-be separatists. Knowing what we know of South Africa's social structure, and especially what we know of white (largely Afrikaner) para-military tendencies, to say nothing of the possibility of dissident units within the arms of state taking to the field against a new regime, one cannot expect the new regime to have inhibitions about using force against violent opponents.

Repression of the black majority has been the model for a long while in South Africa. It is part of the political culture of apartheid. It is hard to imagine that apartheid's opponents, tempered in that environment, can avoid reflecting their political culture. As Ronald Weitzer paraphrases the argument as it applies to Zimbabwe: "...it might be too much to expect the 'culture of repression' to be transcended overnight, however archaic and inappropriate these survivals may be."[24]

A post-revolutionary South African state, especially if its regime gains power in a particularly violent and prolonged struggle, is likely to build up its own apparatus of internal security, even as it tries to dismantle the institutions of the ancien regime. This is understandable until the regime is securely in power and the threat of counterrevolution is ended. Such institutions can be expected to be no less political than their predecessors. Moreover, one cannot imagine an end to the states of emergency and even, in places, martial law.

Historically, such new regimes tend to take on the characteristics of states with little tolerance of dissent, as they seek to stabilize and institutionalize their power in the face of disparate threats and claims. The white minority community is heavily armed. In opposition, it or portions of it can be expected to engage in sporadic armed resistance against even a most reasonable and open majority government or to try to foment dissent among black elements. For that reason, a post-revolutionary South African government would, of necessity, be forced to be prepared to employ force to defend itself and its constituents.

In addition it will require a long and successful record of conflict management, concession, compromise and good government in order to displace and outflank proponents of confrontation and revenge. Given South Africa's history and complex social composition this will not be easy. But it is, I think, the only way in which the norms and institutions of democratic rule can be established and defended.

Much of what can be said turns on the nature of the transition to majority rule. As a general proposition, the more violent and protracted the struggle for revolution, the more difficult it is to reduce the role of the armed forces in political life afterwards.

The structure and composition of the SADF, especially the presence of distinct black units and ethnic-cum-proto-bantustan forces, make it less likely that the SADF will behave as a single force in a chaotic or disintegrative struggle for power. So far, intramilitary rivalries have been minimal. But tensions and successful challenges have a way of driving wedges into outwardly unified institutions. The outlines of such future divisions are discernable, especially as policy responses are debated. Carried to an extreme, the prospect of diverse, well-armed and well-trained fighting units, akin to private armies, marauding the countryside is chilling. South Africa could well become Lebanon writ large.

There is, of course, the possibility as developed in Mao's concept of the protracted war and Regis Debray's corollaries thereto, that the ancien regime, by its ruthless defense of the status quo, may inadvertently unify the enemies of the regime and thereby actually facilitate the post-revolutionary demilitarization process. In a fashion, this is happening among South Africa's resistance groups. But this does not address the presence of "bittereinders" and white supremacists totally opposed to any compromise, least of all a transfer of power. Certainly many of these will flee the new order. But not all. Moreover, the Pretoria regime has entrenched malleable black political interests, particularly in the bantustans, who are disinclined to surrender their marginalized power to a majority central government determined to end the territorial fragmentation of the state. The ANC, for example, has never defined the geographic boundaries of South Africa. Presumably, its unitary state will include the so-called "independent" states of Transkei, Bophuthatswana, Ciskei and Venda. Bringing these territories into the fold will entail confrontation. And this says nothing of how the ANC will address the equally large challenge of KwaZulu and Inkatha.[25]

As a second general proposition, the more that the productive physical mechanisms of the economy are left unscathed in the transitional process, the easier it is to bring off a peaceful transition to civilian majority rule. This does not rule out (indeed, there needs to be) some structural alterations in the economy, especially regarding ownership and management and the distribution patterns of the ultimate product. A regime with rewards to hold out to those who cooperate has an additional non-coercive tool to employ. Otherwise, compulsion is its chief means to secure compliance with policies that demand sacrifice or surrender.

As selected groups within the polity seek to assert their claims to secede or to be heard or to be rewarded or to be protected in terms of political and civil rights, outside forces that are determined to influence the outcome of the political struggle within South Africa may seek to take advantage of internal dissent by encouraging and assisting regime opponents. Thus the new regime needs political acumen to balance the tendencies of dissenters to exploit their political rights in order to destabilize the regime with the need to extend those rights and defend them in order to preempt and dissipate dissent. It is a difficult situation demanding sensitivity and political maturity and skill, qualities not easily acquired in the current militarized setting in which serious resistance is regarded as treasonous and hostile.

The Zimbabwean example may be encouraging.[26] What has been accomplished there, in the decade since independence, is nothing short of miraculous. The old regime has been dismantled, despite a recognizable element of continuity. Parts of the economy have been reformed and others left largely intact. The most racist elements have been encouraged to leave. Two, and in some respects three, large armed forces have been integrated and then reduced in size. We have seen how the issue of control of the security forces was the sticking point in the numerous failed negotiations for transition in Zimbabwe and Namibia. There is little reason to suspect that South Africa can be as easy. In Zimbabwe regionally-based center of opposition has been pacified by a combination of (at times vigorous) coercion and conciliation. It has not been a perfect arrangement, but given the challenges at independence, an admirable transition.

But South Africa is different and far more difficult. The racial proportions, the explicit and self-conscious divide and rule policies going back centuries, the territorial/cultural fragmentation of the state and its peoples, the absence of a facile escape hatch (as Rhodesians had in South Africa), and the long history of white presence on and identity with the land serve to complicate the South African future. The first condition for serious and general negotiations to be launched is a stalemate. Both sides must realize that they cannot achieve their optimum aspirations by escalating their efforts. South Africa is in a state of stalemate. But is is not as yet a "mutually hurting stalemate."[27] Instead it appears that both sides are readying themselves for a protracted struggle. The majority, counting on the inevitable wave of history, expects to negotiate the surrender of the minority. The government feels that it can, through its superior security apparatus, dole out constitutional "dispensations" from above, or co-opt pliable black voices and divide genuine black spokespersons. In short, South Africa is not ripe for resolution. And until it is, significant demilitarization and democratic rule have little hope of becoming realities.

Notes

1.   A more complete discussion of the process appears in Kenneth W. Grundy, *The Militarization of South African Politics* (Bloomington: Indiana University Press, 1986) and an updated version (Oxford: Oxford University Press, 1988). A rejection of the militarization thesis appears in Annette Seegers, "The Military in South Africa: A Comparison and Critque," *South Africa International* 16(4) (April, 1986), 192-200.

2.   For specific discussion of the security establishment, its diverse public and private institutions and agencies see Grundy, *op. cit.*, chap. 3; Gavin Cawthra, *Brutal Force: The Apartheid War Machine* (London: International Defence and Aid Fund for Southern Africa, 1986); and, Philip H. Frankel, *Pretoria's Praetorians: Civil-Military Relations in South Africa* (Cambridge: Cambridge University Press, 1984).

3.   Cf. With the period discussed in Joseph Hanlon, *Beggar Your Neighbours: Apartheid Power in Southern Africa* (London: James Currey, 1986); Richard Leonard, *South Africa at War: White Power and the Crisis in Southern Africa* (Westport, CT: Lawrence Hill & Co., 1983); Robert S. Jaster, ed., *Southern Africa: Regional Security Problems and Prospects* (Aldershot: Gower, 1985); Robert S. Jaster, *South Africa and Its Neighbours: The Dynamics of Regional Conflict*, Adelphi Paper 209 (London: International Institute for Strategic

Studies, Summer, 1986); and Robert M. Price, "Creating New Political Realities: Pretoria's Drive for Regional Hegemony," in Gerald J. Bender *et. al.*, eds., *African Crisis Areas and U.S. Foreign Policy* (Berkely: University of California Press, 1985).

4. See "Agreements for Peace in Southwestern Africa," *Selected Documents No. 32* (Washington, D.C.: United States Department of State, Bureau of Public Affairs, December 1988).

5. This argument is developed more fully in *Weekly Mail* 5(1) (Johannesburg, January 13-19, 1989), 12. See also *New York Times* (January 10, 1989).

6. For historical comparison, see the discussion of the impact of the Nkomati accord on the ANC in Tom Lodge, "The ANC after Nkomati," *SAIRR Topical Opinion* (Johannesburg), PD 8/85. ANC future strategy is discussed in *New York Times* (May 7, 1989), 8.

7. John Seiler, "South African Security Forces in Namibia: Unwitting Agents of Social Revolution," in Simon Baynham, ed., *The South African Security Establishment* (London: Croom Helm, forthcoming).

8. For example see *The Star* (Johannesburg), July 3, 1988, 14.

9. *Weekly Mail* 5(2) (January 20-16, 1989), 11; and *New York Times* (January 15, 1989).

10. *Weekly Mail* 5(9) (March 10-16, 1989), 11.

11. *Weekly Mail* 5(5) (February 10-16, 1989), 15.

12. See *Weekly Mail* 5(8) (March 3-9, 1989), 13, for an account of the changing balance of military power in the region.

13. Among the numerous reports, see *Facts and Reports* 19(A) (Amsterdam, January 6, 1989), items A100 and A101; *Africa Confidential* (London, September 9, 1988); and *Africa News* 29(8) (Durham, NC, April 18, 1988), 6-8.

14. See Grundy, *op. cit.*, postcript to 1988 edition; Robert Scott Jaster, *The Defence of White Power: South African Foreign Policy Under Pressure* (London: Macmillan, 1988), chap. 3; and Deon Geldenhuys, *The Diplomacy of Isolation: South Africa's Foreign Policy Making* (Johannesburg: Macmillan South Africa, 1984).

15. See "Counting on Colonel Charlie," *Africa News* 15(9) (November 4, 1985), 8-12, in which sections of the diaries are translated and reprinted.

16. See Ronald Weitzer, "Responding to South African Hegemony: The Case of Zimbabwe," (unpublished paper), 111-12.

17. This argument is presented in a purportedly reasonable and enlightened defense of South Africa's foreign policy by the Chief Director of Communications and Planning in the Department of Foreign Affairs. See Gerrit Olivier, "Recent Development in South African Foreign Policy," *Optima* 36(4) (Johannesburg, December, 1988), 196-203.

18. See Christopher Coker, "South Africa's Security Dilemmas" *The Washington Papers*, no. 126 (New York: Praeger, 1987); M.F. Blatchford, "The Last Drop of Blood," *Work in Progress*, no. 55 (August/September, 1988), 42-44; and Steven Friedman, *Weekly Mail* 4(10) (March 18-24, 1988), 14.

19. Quoted in Hermann Giliomee, "The Elusive Search for Peace," *Optima* 36(3) (September, 1988), 14.

20. Many of the ideas developed in the following pages emerged from a close reading of Ted Robert Gurr, "War, Revolution, and the Growth of the Coercive State," *Comparative Political Studies*, 21(1) (April, 1988), 45-65.

21. Blatchford, *op. cit.*; and Mary Crewe, "Black and White in Khaki: Education and Militarization in the South Africa," presented at the conference on Militarization in the Third World, Queen's University, Kingston, Canada, January 15-17, 1987.

22. See *Weekly Mail* 5(9) (March 10-16, 1989), 14; *Weekly Mail* 5(10) (March 17-22, 1989), 16; and *Jane's Weekly* (April 1, 1989). A discussion of military budgets appears in Grundy, *op. cit.* (1988 ed.), 19-21.

23. The negotiation process, and especially the ideas of a "mutually hurting stalemate" and the "ripe moment" are discussed in I. William Zartman, *Ripe for Resolution: Conflict and Intervention in Africa* (New York: Oxford University Press, 1985); and Zartman and Maureen Berman, *The Practical Negotiator* (New Haven: Yale University Press, 1982).

24. Ronald Weitzer, "Continuities in the Politics of State Security in Zimbabwe," in Michael G. Schatzberg, ed., *The Political Economy of Zimbabwe* (New York: Praeger, 1984), 83.

25. See Oscar Dhlomo, "Piecing Together a New South Africa," *Weekly Mail* 4(39) (October 7-13, 1988), 7.

26. A good discussion of "relevant pasts" appears in I. William Zartman, "Negotiations in South Africa," *The Washington Quarterly* (Autumn, 1988), esp. 149-152.

27. Zartman, *Ripe for Resolution.*

Carrots as Well as Sticks in Demilitarizing Southern Africa: A Comment

Walter L. Barrows

My comments will focus on an issue touched on in this chapter: What are the lessons learned from the recent Angola/Namibia agreements, and what are the implications of the Quadripartite talks that led up to them for reducing violence and promoting peaceful political accommodation in South Africa and the region?

I am carving out only a portion of what Ken Grundy has attempted to do, primarily because my time horizon is much less ambitious than his -- on the assumption that the white regime in Pretoria will remain in power for a long time to come, and that discussion of its replacement puts us far into the cloudy future. I would prefer to stick to the here and now and discuss how recent developments might affect immediate prospects for reducing the role of violence in southern Africa.

The accords signed in December are potentially the most significant settlement in modern southern African history, even more important than the Lancaster House agreement on independence for Zimbabwe -- primarily because in this case South Africa, the regional hegemon, has been a direct participant. Why did Pretoria choose diplomacy over continued coercion? Grundy's answer is incomplete. He stresses the military and other pressures that "forced" Pretoria into negotiations. Without question, these factors were vital, but there were other factors as well.

(As an aside in discussing the military pressures on South Africa last year, I suggest deemphasizing the much-ballyhooed "battle of Cuito Cuanavale" and paying more attention instead to the deployment of a powerful Cuban force near the Namibian border in southwestern Angola, far from Cuito Cuanavale. The former was as much a propaganda event

---

The opinions expressed in this comment are the author's and do not necessarily reflect the views of the U.S. Government or Intelligence Community.

as a battle; the latter was a brilliant maneuver that indeed "forced" South Africa to make strategic recalculations.)

First among the attractions to Pretoria of a settlement was a changing Soviet approach to South Africa and the region. As part of its "new thinking" in foreign policy, Moscow now stresses the need for accommodation and negotiations. In contrast to its earlier hostile attitude toward U.S.-sponsored peace negotiations, the Soviets played a helpful behind-the-scenes role in the Quadripartite talks. Pretoria has been receptive to this emerging Soviet approach, encouraging contacts and exploring possibilities for a less confrontational relationship than in the past.

Second, Cuba pursued a two-sided policy, using the lure of a negotiated settlement as well as the threat of force. Castro's strategy effectively combined diplomacy and "militarization," to use Grundy's term. Specifically, he held out the possibility of removing his troops from Angola in return for South African departure from Angola and Namibia.

Finally, South Africa could entertain talks because there was something already on the table to talk about. UNSCR 435 and associated understandings about Namibian independence had already been negotiated, and South Africa had something concrete on which to hang its ongoing assessment of the costs and benefits of remaining in Namibia. The government, in fact, had probably already decided to cut its losses by leaving the territory but was in a quandary over how to do it. UNSCR 435 helped Pretoria define its self interest and provided an internationally acceptable way of serving it. Moreover, the U.S. had in place the firm outlines of a comprehensive settlement that included the key issue of Cuban forces in Angola. The U.S. role in bringing and keeping the parties together was considerable.

I have no doubt that had these positive factors been absent, the white regime and its formidable military arm would have chosen to meet force with force -- and the consequences would have been deleterious if not disastrous for the region well beyond the immediate battlefield.

My point is simple: carrots as well as sticks are necessary for inducing a power such as South Africa into adopting a less combative posture. Assuming that the Angola/Namibia settlement stays on track, the demonstration effect of negotiations in which all sides gain may well have an impact elsewhere in the regions.

Especially as outside military factors diminish, prospects for a political settlement in *Angola* will improve. The spirit of "no losers" that underlay the Quadripartite talks has extended to efforts promoting reconciliation between the Angolan government and the UNITA rebels. The U.S., Soviet Union, and Cuba mutually recognize the need for a political solution, and Angola's neighbors (including Front Line States) are anxious to maintain the momentum created by the December accords.

Key African and external actors sense that Angola has reached an historic moment. Angolan war weariness combined with an externally applied set of incentives (for talking) and disincentives (against continuing the fight) stands a much better chance of convincing the Dos Santos government to sit down with UNITA now than before the December accords.

As long as South Africa demonstrates continued commitment to Namibian independence, and therefore builds trust (or at least reduces distrust), the incentives for talking rather than fighting in *Mozambique* will improve. South African Foreign Minister Botha, waxing enthusiastic in the wake of the December accords, suggested that the U.S. and U.S.S.R. launch an effort to reconcile the Maputo government with its RENAMO opponents in the bush. South Africa itself, of course, would have to play a constructive role in any such undertaking; President Chissano will keep a close watch on his powerful neighbor for signs of renewed interference in Mozambican affairs. The trust that would make a serious effort at reconciliation easier to contemplate will depend primarily on South African actions toward Mozambique, such as the recent delivery of non-lethal materiel to government forces. But it will also be affected by wider regional developments, particularly Pretoria's ability or inability to demonstrate the genuineness of its recently resurrected "good neighbor" policy.

The regional settlement could have a beneficial spin-off within *South Africa itself*. Pretoria will look to the international community for rewards for its good behavior towards Namibia. For their part, South African blacks will carefully note Pretoria's treatment of Namibia. If the government concludes that genuine accommodation pays off, and blacks conclude that the government might be trusted enough to sit down for at least exploratory talks, South Africa will take a step towards becoming less polarized and less "militarized." Certainly the obverse is true: Breakdown of the Namibia settlement or instability after independence that leads to racial antagonisms would have adverse repercussions in the Republic itself and set back whatever tentative gains had been made toward constructive dialogue.

The fate of Namibia and Cuban troops in Angola will set the tone for nascent reconciliation efforts in southern Africa. This is not to say that the demonstration effect of successfully implementing the Angola/Namibia accords will necessarily produce positive results elsewhere in the region. On the contrary, the obstacles to reconciliation in Angola, Mozambique and South Africa are daunting. Bitterness and distrust run deep in all three cases, and the main internal actors are not particularly susceptible to external pressure. But the kind of careful mix of carrots and sticks that underlay the December accords has a better chance of promoting peace in southern Africa than sticks alone.

4
Majority Rule in South Africa:
The Role of Global Pressure

Robert M. Price

This essay is concerned with the role played by the international community in the fundamental political transformation of South Africa. How does South Africa's external environment enter the dynamics of internal political change and how does it influence the prospects for majority rule? I will first deal with these questions in the abstract, attempting to think systematically and speculatively about the change process. I will then relate these ruminations to a discussion of observable trends in the South African situation. This will then provide the basis for extrapolation and prognosis in regard to the near-term future.

PROCESS OF POLITICAL TRANSFORMATION: THE INTERNAL VERSUS THE EXTERNAL

In discussions of the future of South Africa both the governing group and its "left" opposition agree on the essential irrelevance of international factors. The South African government has frequently declared the international environment and the varied pressures emanating from it to be inconsequential in respect to either determining its policies or influencing the direction of change within the Republic. The "theory" of the 'laager mentality' is meant to explain this outcome. Supposedly, when Afrikanerdom comes under external pressure, Afrikaner culture produces a response that entails enhanced ingroup solidarity and greater recalcitrance in the face of external influences. The notion of the laager mentality is a convenient creation for a South African government seeking to avoid and deflect external pressure. If accepted by external actors it would convince them that the exertion of pressure is counter-productive. But the actual behavior of the South African government under National Party rule belies the notion of an insular governing elite acting without regard to developments in its external environment. Pretoria has used both foreign

and domestic policy in an effort to prevent developments in its international environment from undermining white rule within the Republic.

   A major preoccupation of the governing elite, during the very
first decade of National Party rule, was the fundamental change in the international state system occasioned by the process of post-war decolonization. To Pretoria, that process, along with the Cold War context of East-
West rivalry within which it was occurring, contained significant potential threats to white rule in South Africa. The governing group realized
that in a world in which many newly formed "non-white" states were being competitively wooed by East and West, the denial of political rights
to the black majority in South Africa would constitute a liability. They
feared that under these circumstances South Africa's important diplomatic,
military, and economic relations with the Western industrialized countries
would be jeopardized, with dire consequences for the survival of white rule
in South Africa. Hendrik Verwoerd described the situation created by decolonization in Africa this way:

In this auction between the Western nations and the East or Communism, the spirit is
cultivated in Africa of standing...by one who offers most...always to ask for more and
to make bigger demands.... In this struggle between East and West, the Western nations
are evidently prepared to abandon all the White people in Africa....[1]

It appears that a world psychosis has arisen of thinking only of the rights and privileges of freedoms of the non-Whites....I would like Britain, the U.S.A. and the other
Western nations seriously to ponder that they will lose the only staunch friends they
have -- the Whites in Africa -- if the white man in Africa is swamped by the Black
masses....[2]

In the face of this perceived threat from an altered global situation,
Verwoerd did not recommend withdrawal into the laager; on the contrary,
he argued for adaptation to changed international circumstances. "[We]
cannot govern without taking into account the tendencies in the world and
in Africa." "We must have regard to them."[3] To Verwoerd these tendencies required eliminating the international stigma of black disenfranchise-
ment within South Africa. His solution was the policy of Separate
Development -- the metamorphosis of native reserves into ten independent
and sovereign states within which all South Africans of African descent
would henceforth be citizens. When, through legal and administrative
means, tens of millions of black South Africans had been transformed
into citizens of Transkei, Bophuthatswana, Ciskei, and so on, South
Africa would no longer contain a black majority; white minority rule
would thus be eliminated. "We can only take [the global changes] into
account and safeguard the White man's control over our country,"
Verwoerd told Parliament in 1959, "if we move in the direction of separation ... in the political sphere."[4] This is something he would have liked
to avoid, Verwoerd told his followers some time later. But, he argued --

In the light of the pressure being exerted on South Africa, there is however no doubt that eventually this will have to be done, thereby buying for the White Man his freedom and the right to retain his domination in what is his country.[5]

Some twenty years later, P.W. Botha warned his followers that they must "adapt or die," and ushered in an era of adaptation intended, like Verwoerd's earlier efforts, to "buy for the White Man...the right to retain his domination." The late 1970s like the late 1950s were a period of both rising black opposition domestically and increasing international pressure from abroad. Pretoria recognized a linkage between the two and the need to alter course in order to avoid the threats inherent in the domestic-international connection. Thus, the Wiehahn Commission, inquiring into the industrial relations system and seeking to defuse a situation of increasing organization and militancy among black workers, took frequent note of the global aspects of the domestic labor situation. At one point it observed:

The strikes and labour unrest of 1973 brought the position of the Black worker and his organisation under the focus of international attention, giving rise to a preoccupation among pressure groups and various institutions, including trade union organisations, with Black trade unionism and the conditions of employment of Black workers. [This constituted] a development of historical significance.[6]

Thus, in the 1980s reform became simultaneously a means to defuse and divide the internal opposition and a means to deflect mounting pressures for change from abroad. Because of the unique position that racial rule establishes for South Africa within the global state system, Pretoria's domestic policy is also the essence of its foreign policy. Internal changes are meant to reduce the effectiveness of organized opposition **and at the same time** to present South Africa to the world as a "normal" country. As the Chief Director of Communication and Planning in the South Africa Department of Foreign Affairs explained in 1988, in arguing for further internal change: "Our greatest foreign-policy challenge right now is to regain moral legitimacy in world politics...This is the only way in which we can get back into the mainstream of international interaction."[7]

Academics and activists who identify with the liberation struggle exhibit an ironic parallelism with Pretoria on the question of the significance of international factors in the change process. Like the government, they act one way and talk another. While seeking comprehensive international economic and other global sanctions against South Africa, "left" intellectuals usually assert, as an article of faith, that it is internal factors that are both the dynamic and decisive element in producing liberation. In so doing they marginalize the role of the international environment in their analysis.

A comparative perspective on modern revolutions suggests that such a dichotomous view of internal and external factors is misplaced and thus misleading. It is generally recognized, for example, that the involvement of Russia and China in the First and Second World Wars, respectively, contributed significantly to their revolutionary transformation by undermining the power of the state. Such a recognition in no way precludes the simultaneous understanding that the organizational and political capacities of the Bolshevik and Chinese Communist parties, as well as the internal socio-economic systems of the two countries, were essential ingredients in the Russian and Chinese revolutions. Trotsky, in the concluding paragraph of his treatise on the 1905 insurrection recognized the interrelationship of international and domestic factors in revolutionary transformations -- "The tempo at which the revolutionary process will unfold...depends on many factors, military, political, national, and international. These factors may speed up the development or slow it down, ensure the revolution's victory or lead to another defeat."[8]

The way in which a particular state is situated politically, militarily, and economically within the international system has a powerful effect on the resources available to the state to both avoid revolutionary social situations and to resist efforts by domestic opponents to alter the political status-quo. At the same time, domestic socio-political upheavals can affect the situation of a state within the global inter-state system as well as the consequences of that situation for the flow of resources to the state. The process is an interactive one; the development of a situation conducive to fundamental political transformation can not be adequately understood unless both aspects -- domestic and transnational -- are appreciated and their inter-relationship fully grasped. Theda Skocpol, in her seminal work on social revolution, *States & Social Revolutions*, puts the matter aptly --

If our aim is to understand the breakdown and building-up of state organizations in revolutions....we must...focus upon the points of intersection between international conditions and pressures, on the one hand, and class-structured economies and politically organized interests, on the other hand. State executives and their followers will be found maneuvering to extract resources and build administrative and coercive organizations precisely at this intersection. Here, consequently, is the place to look for the political contradictions that help launch social revolutions.[9]

As we will see presently, the South African case provides an excellent illustration of the wisdom of Skocpol's view.

MODES OF POLITICAL TRANSFORMATION

An analysis of the role of international factors in South African political transformation needs to be situated in a conceptualization, however rudimentary, of the South African change process. Unless we have some general conception of how fundamental political changes take place, and a more specific notion of the dynamics of change in the South African situation, we are unlikely to be able to understand the way the international factor fits into the picture. Because observers of change in South Africa rarely make explicit their understanding of the dynamics or ultimate direction of change they often end up at odds on the most basic of phenomenon. Do economic sanctions and armed resistance retard change or make a fundamental change in the South African situation more likely? We are unlikely to be able to answer this type of question unless we are first clear about the nature of the change process itself, and that is not an easy task.

Two often discussed scenarios for how political transformation will occur in South Africa can be relatively easily dismissed. One holds that comprehensive international economic sanctions will produce a rapid collapse of the South African economy, leading to the capitulation of Pretoria and the introduction of majority rule. Both the complex international linkages of the South African economy and the unwillingness on the part of the many relevant actors abroad to exercise the level of coercion and coordination that would make such an outcome possible, make this scenario highly implausible. As we will see, this does not mean that international economic pressure is irrelevant to the change process, but rather that its impact is neither immediate, nor direct. It is because the proponents of sanctions have justified them in terms of the above scenario, linking economic pressure directly and rapidly to political transformation, that the critics of sanctions have been able to convince many that the existing international economic sanctions have been a failure. Proponents have defined an inappropriate measure, and critics have been only to happy to use it.

A second scenario relies on external military rather than economic power to force the end of white supremacy in South Africa. Here, the military forces of one or more industrialized countries, or more often, some joint African military operation, is seen to produce Pretoria's capitulation. This idea seems even less plausible than the first. There is not the slightest evidence that industrial countries would engage the South African Defence Force in an effort to transform South Africa domestically. And, the imbalance between the militaries of African countries and the SADF, as well as the inability of the former to cooperate sufficiently, seriously weakens this scenario. It is true that the development and modernization of the militaries of Angola and Zimbabwe in the 1980s do show that military balances are not fixed. The events of 1988 in southern Angola indicate that Pretoria may have lost its unchallenged military hegemony in its region. But challenging Pretoria's regional hegemony is a very different matter than invading South Africa and forcing its unconditional surrender. This remains an extremely implausible occurrence for the foreseeable future.

Yet another transformation scenario involves armed resistance by an externally based but domestically active liberation movement. Umkonto we Sizwe, in the most common version of this conception, will confront and neutralize the South African security forces in a war of national liberation. Much as the collapse of the Kuomintang in China in 1949, in the face of the Peoples' Liberation Army, led to a takeover by the Chinese Communist Party, the African National Congress will replace the existing regime of white supremacy. In recent years the significance of revolutionary armed force in producing a transition to majority rule has been viewed with increasing skepticism. And this skepticism has come from surprising quarters. Soviet experts on South Africa have joined liberal academics in the West not only in their skepticism about the real and potential military capability of the ANC, but also in suggesting that continued pursuit of armed resistance may be counterproductive. In both the Soviet and Western liberal view a negotiated settlement is viewed as a "political" alternative to armed force, and the continued pursuit of the latter is seen as making the former less likely.

We can, I think, accept the liberal and Soviet assessment that the ANC is unlikely to be able to mount a successful war of national liberation against Pretoria.* The scenario of political transition through military victory can be grouped together with the scenarios of collapse *via* either economic sanctions or external invasion and filed under "wishful thinking." However, the idea that armed resistance has **no** significant role to play in producing a transition to majority rule, or that it is indeed counterproductive to that end, is a different matter, and requires further consideration.

NEGOTIATIONS AND POLITICAL TRANSFORMATION

The dichotomizing of force and negotiations, suggesting that the latter is a peaceful and **political** alternative to the violence of the former, is analytically misleading because it suggests the two are unrelated except as complete alternatives. But, in fact, armed force is often a pre-requisite for meaningful negotiations. Few wars actually end by total surrender or the utter collapse of one side. Most wars end by negotiations. The negoti-

---

It should be noted the ANC does not now, and to the best of the author's knowledge, has never considered armed resistance the sole or even primary means to accomplishing the overthrow of the regime of white supremacy. Its position differs from that of the critics of armed force, however, in that it sees a role for it along with other means of undermining Pretoria.

ated phase of conflict resolution is often simply the end of a path paved by violence. Armed conflict, by imposing costs on the combatants alters their political positions until these converge enough to allow for agreement by negotiation. This is the essential meaning of Clauswitz's seminal observation that "war is politics by other means." Figure I presents a formalized version of this notion. Two adversaries, Combatant 1 (Co_1) and Combatant 2 (Co_2) adopt positions c and w along a continuum of positions on some important political matter. The difference between their positions at T1 (c-w) is so great as to provide no basis for agreement. Armed conflict imposes costs on both combatants so that at T2 they are willing to accept outcomes (i and j) as a way of ending the war which at the earlier period, T1, they would not seriously have contemplated. Their positions converge, so that now the distance between them is represented by segment i-j. Within this narrow range, what we might call a "zone of agreement," they can find a basis for negotiating a settlement of their differences. The amount of pain imposed by the conflict will determine the extent of movement or convergence for each combatant. If costs are unevenly distributed amongst them, as is usually the case, one combatant will move (converge) further than the other, as is the case in our diagram. Although we have been discussing armed conflict as the mechanism for imposing costs, these can of course be imposed by other means as well.

This formal statement of what might seem quite obvious, can nevertheless help us think systematically about the change process in South Africa. Let us reconsider our "continuum of conflict" but this time thinking in terms of the South African situation (see Figure II). The continuum a-z represents the range of possible positions on the issue of majority access to political power. The ANC/UDF's current stand -- majority rule based upon a non-racial mass franchise in a unitary state -- is represented at point d. The shaded segment d-f represents the ANC/UDF's "zone of agreement." Within it fall various arrangements of majority rule -- guarantees for the white minority, for example -- that the liberation movement might accept in negotiations. The outer limit of this zone, point f, might be some form of federalism with a strong center and with constituent units defined in non-racial-non-ethnic terms.

Pretoria's position, in contrast, is an explicit rejection of majority rule. According to the National Party's Schlebusch Commission of Inquiry into the South African Constitution: "The so-called one man, one vote system would probably lead to minorities dominating majorities and [therefore]...did not offer a solution for the constitutional problems of the Republic."[10] The Constitutional Committee of the President's Council reiterated this view. "There is near unanimity," it reported, "on the unworkability of a system of undifferentiated majoritarianism ... or what is conventionally described as 'one man, one vote, in a single political system.' "[11] Pretoria's alternative to majority rule is what it terms "power

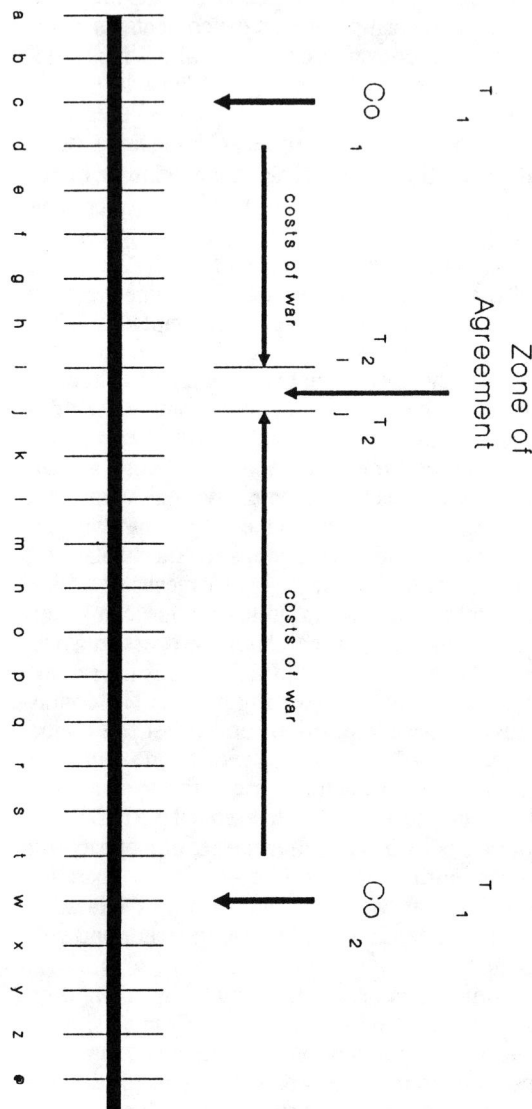

Figure I

CONTINUUM OF CONFLICT

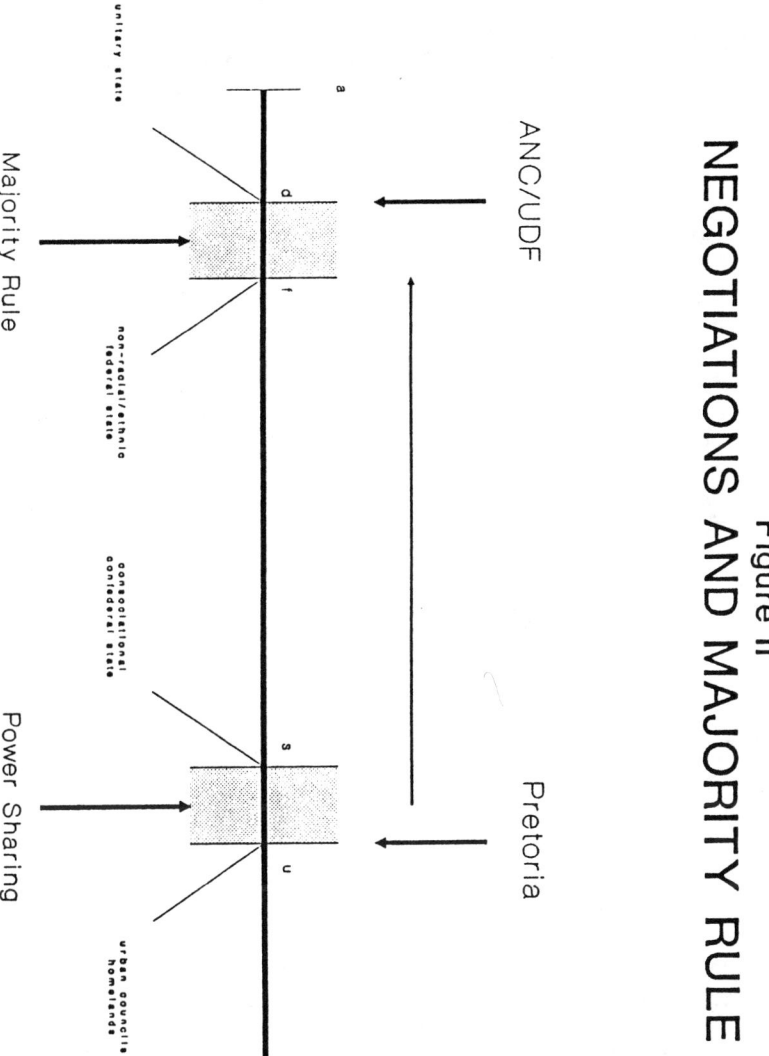

Figure II
NEGOTIATIONS AND MAJORITY RULE

sharing." "We are prepared ... to share power," proclaimed State President
P.W. Botha, "but not to relinquish it...."[12]

The meaning of the National Party elite's use of the term power sharing is illuminated in interviews conducted with NP leaders by sociologist
Lawrence Schlemmer.[13] A white determining voice in the major affairs
of state is viewed, Schlemmer reports, as essential for protecting what the
political elite terms "white culture." As one Nationalist Member of
Parliament explained, whites have a political interest in maintaining their
"lifestyle" -- a combination of material well-being, psychological
health, and cultural standards -- and, consequently they require
"sufficient control over the allocation of resources and the maintenance of
security to ensure the continuation of these benefits." The outer-limit of
what the governing group considers acceptable in respect to the sharing of
power was laid out by Willem de Klerk, then editor of *Rapport*, in a 1985
interview with the *Economist*. It should be noted that Mr. deKlerk is
considered a leader of the *verligte* wing of Afrikanerdom, and thus his
views can be considered indicative of the most "progressive" position
within the ruling group's 'zone of agreement.' De Klerk listed what he
consider the "non-grantables" in any negotiations. These are: one-man-
one-vote in a unitary state; the surrender of "the white power-base;" the
same laws and institutions for all South Africans, in contrast to separate
ones for different ethnic groups; and a fourth chamber for Africans in
Parliament.[14]

In short, the governing group's current position is that they can accept
changes which involve access to some power resources for the black majority but which do not at the same time threaten white control of the political system. The sharing of power without the loss of control; that is
the essence of the South African government's position on political
change. It is represented in Figure 2 by the shaded segment s-u. At present Pretoria adheres to the idea that political participation for those of
African descent can take place *via* town councils and homeland government structures (point u). At the same time, some sort of consocia-
tional/confederal arrangement, within which urban black townships and
homelands would be incorporated while whites maintained control at the
center, is being contemplated among the National Party intelligentsia.
Such a consociational constitution within a loose confederation might
well be considered the outer limit of the government's current "zone of
agreement" (point s).

As Figure 2 illustrates, the zones of agreement of the liberation movement and the South African government are far apart; and, as a simple
logical matter, until the zones of agreement of two adversaries overlap
there is no basis for a negotiated agreement. One way for that overlap to
occur is for the ANC/UDF, as a consequence of exhaustion, weakness, or
collapse, to give up the goal of majority rule and shift toward the gov-

ernment's zone of agreement. Negotiations might well take place, but there is little reason to expect that they would lead to majority rule. Only when Pretoria shifts from its current position at point u to converge on the ANC/UDF's zone of agreement at point f can a negotiated transition to majority rule be considered feasible. The basic challenge for the black opposition is to accomplish such a shift so that negotiations could be the prelude to a fundamental transformation in South Africa's political order. One of the most vexing tasks for the analyst of South Africa is comprehending exactly how such a shift might be accomplished.

RISKS, PERCEPTIONS AND MAJORITY RULE

An actor's "zone of agreement" will shift, as in the above example, when he alters his assessment of the future risks that adhere in the status quo compared to the risks he believes are contained in some projected situation of change. In rejecting majority rule Pretoria, and the white South Africans who support it, are calculating that their futures will be at greater risk under a system of majority rule than they are within the political status-quo of white supremacy. In 1987 a survey revealed that over eighty percent of white urbanites believed majority rule, in which blacks could form the government, would threaten the property and physical safety of whites, produce a decline in white living standards, lead to discrimination against whites, escalate crime, and undermine law and order.[15] In other words, whites perceive that their material well being and physical security is at lower risk within the existing political arrangements than it would be under a majority rule system. Pretoria can be expected to undertake negotiations in which it is willing to contemplate a majority rule outcome only when its risk calculus, or that of the constituencies it relies on, is reversed; that is, when it calculates that whites will be poorer and less secure attempting to maintain a regime of white supremacy than they would be in a system in which whites might lose political control.

The implications of the above logic are clear -- that which reduces the material welfare of whites and/or threatens their physical security, and does so in a way that ties these costs to efforts to maintain minority control, will make a negotiated transition to majority rule more likely. A weakening economy and political unrest are the two primary mechanisms for producing this outcome. The former would result in declining material standards of life and a lack of confidence about future prospects; the latter, including insurrectionary activity (strikes, boycotts, demonstrations, 'riots'), armed conflict, and urban/rural sabotage would not only threaten physical safety but contribute in general to an overall decline in the quality of life. There is, admittedly a major and unelaborated assumption in all of this -- that an overall decline in the material, psychological, and physical quality of life for white South Africans and the resultant acceptance of the "risks" of majority rule will translate into a willingness on the part of governing authorities to negotiate an end to their rule.

Power transformations which are preceded by the collapse of the state's security forces, either through defeat in external war as in Russia in 1917, or at the hands of a revolutionary army as in China in 1949, or through internal divisions as in Cuba in 1959, Iran in 1979, and the Philippines in 1986, are relatively easy to comprehend. But if we assume that the security apparatus remains relatively loyal --and intact, as I think we must in the South African case, then the circumstances in which the governing group accepts a handing over of power are difficult to perceive. The best that one can say is that over time a situation of economic, physical, and psychological deterioration is likely to impact on constituencies that the governing group represents, eroding support for the political status quo among elements considered vital by the ruling elite, including elements of its security forces; that the costs of security will escalate beyond the financial capabilities of a deteriorating economy; and that the resources and policy options to turn the situation around are perceived as exhausted. The process of decline and disaffection would be accompanied by a gradual shift, over time, toward a position where negotiation for some form of majority rule is deemed acceptable.*

It is common for the reverse of above argument to be made; an environment of economic prosperity and free of violent threats is often seen as facilitating a negotiated solution to the South African situation. The economic growth argument holds that an expanding economic pie eases the process of change because it reduces the cost of change to whites by obviating the need for resource redistribution. Our discussion of the conditions necessary for a majority rule outcome pinpoints the fallacy in this line of thinking. The "change by way of growth" argument assumes that there already exists a predisposition on the part of the authorities to move toward majority rule; in the terms of our discussion, it implies that overlapping "zones of agreement" already exist. Expanding resources would simply facilitate movement within an already existing zone of agreement. When the commitment to majority rule on the part of the governing group does not exist, or when it is in fact committed in the opposite direction, as is the case, there is no reason for prosperity to produce a convergence of agreement in the direction of majority rule.   This is the pointed lesson, as is frequently noted, of the experience of the 1950s and 1960s.

---

*Defeat in war is improbable, and the race issue makes it unlikely that significant defections to the opposition will occur within the security apparatus, as they did for instance in the Philippines.

The counter-argument to the proposition that political violence will move South Africa in the direction of majority rule has a greater initial plausibility, than does the change through prosperity notion. Armed resistance and sabotage, particularly when they involve civilian casualties, are usually thought to harden attitudes within the target population, rallying support for the state. A specific version of this argument is frequently made about the ANC's commitment to armed struggle. The use of violent tactics, especially when they involve "soft" targets, are said to drive whites toward Pretoria; generating support for the government's harsh security measures; increasing white fears of the liberation movement; and, consequently, making it more difficult to break whites away from support for a system of white supremacy.

In respect to the short term there is little reason to question the proposition that the increased use of force by a liberation movement, particularly when it produces civilian casualties, increases resistance to change. There is a good deal of support in the South African situation for its validity. But the medium to long term response to armed resistance and political violence may well be quite different. The negative reaction that revolutionary violence produces in the target population presumes that the status quo forces are capable of providing increased security against the revolutionaries. But if it turns out that this presumption is misplaced; if, over time, security instead declines, if the physical dangers and psychological stress imposed by violence and sabotage increase despite the government's counter-measures, then the desire for personal security, for ending the continuing danger, can produce a willingness to consider coming to terms with the revolutionaries. This outcome, depends however, on the revolutionary organization being able to credibly project an ability and willingness to in fact stop the violence. If it lacks sufficient internal discipline, or does not appear to actually control the armed insurgents, then it is unlikely to appeal as a superior alternative to the government as a provider of security. Or, if its use of violence appears wanton and irrational, if its image is that of simply a "killing machine," then it is unlikely to be perceived as desiring to introduce security, with the result that it will not significantly erode support for the established authorities. This then is a crucial strategic dilemma for the South African liberation movement. How to undermine the sense of physical security of whites under a regime of white supremacy, while not appearing to the white population as an organization whose purpose is the physical annihilation of that population.

In sum, I have argued that the precondition for negotiations leading to majority rule is a period, probably an extended one, of economic decline and "political unrest." The international system has played, and I believe will continue to play, a role in contributing to this outcome in three basic ways: 1) by denying vital economic resources to the South African economy; 2) by providing financial and training resources to organizations of the opposition, and by offering these organizations diplomatic and moral support; and 3) by impeding, through its impact on the economy, the ability of the government to effectively impose its version of security through the elimination of opposition groups and leadership cadre. The specific manner in which these international "contributions" occur is a function of the dynamics of the South African domestic order and the particular way in which that dynamic interfaces with the global system.

DOMESTIC AND INTERNATIONAL LINKAGE

More than perhaps any other state in the contemporary world, South Africa's international situation and its domestic politics are inextricably linked. This is so because in its efforts to maintain white minority rule, the government of South Africa has, at least since the end of the Second World War, been challenged by a fundamental contradiction between its international and domestic requirements. Internationally, South Africa requires access to markets for the export of its minerals and, increasingly, for its manufactured goods, and it depends upon the importation of vital capital, technology, and producer goods. These are prerequisites for the health, growth, and development of its modern industrial economy. But the nature of South Africa's domestic system of white supremacy and the efforts government is required to make in order to maintain it, threaten such access to global markets and opportunities and thus directly place in jeopardy economic growth and development.

The contradiction between domestic and international requirements is a dynamic one: the greater the domestic black opposition and the more manifest the government's repressive response to it, the greater its problems with its international environment. Active political pressure by the majority and its counterpoint, repressive action by the minority government, render the nature of the South African system visible to the world and thus serve as a catalyst for international reactions. Conversely, in periods of relative political quiescence, Pretoria's international problem recedes. It is when the majority makes its political opposition felt and visible, and thus when the need of the white government to make its domination manifest is greatest, that the international threat becomes substantial.

In this dynamic the domestic situation is the active element, but the international reaction in respect to constraints on the South African economy is both real and consequential. Moreover, the internationally imposed constraints on the economy can have a "boosting effect" on the dynamic. They contribute to material conditions of life that produce intense political alienation; they deny government resources that can be used for policies of co-optation; and, they make the financing of repression more politically painful. In combination, the international constraints thus increase the likelihood of repeated episodes of internal political unrest. Each of these episodes, in turn, generates a greater international reaction and a higher level of economic constraint. Figure III summarizes this security contradication dynamic.

The international reactions to the Sharpeville massacre of 1960, the Soweto Uprising of 1976, and the township insurrection of 1984-1986, demonstrate the reality of Pretoria's security contradiction, as well as its dynamic quality. In March of 1960, the images of the police killings of anti-pass law demonstrators in Sharpeville, carried abroad by the news media, galvanized international attention on the South African system of apartheid, as well as on the resistance to it, and the government's repressive efforts to maintain and extend it. Pretoria quickly found itself diplomatically isolated, and faced with threats to its future security and economic growth. The first ever U.N. resolutions calling for diplomatic isolation, economic sanctions, and an arms embargo against South Africa were passed. On the international economic front, Sharpeville created a crisis in South Africa's access to foreign capital. Until 1960, there were only two years since the end of the Second World War that South Africa was not a net capital importer. But from 1960 to 1964, despite a healthy economic outlook and a favorable trade situation, huge annual net capital outflows were experienced. One result was a balance of payments crisis more severe than any experienced since 1932.[16]

Over time, the security measures adopted by Pretoria after Sharpeville had their intended effect. The organized internal opposition to white supremacy was broken, and a decade of political quiescence ensued. This laid the basis for Pretoria to overcome the international isolation it had suffered following Sharpeville. Diplomatically, the greatest gains were made in respect to the United States, where the Nixon/Kissinger administration initiated a 'tilt' toward the white regime. Washington stopped supporting U.N. resolutions condemning Pretoria, partially lifted its arms embargo, and encouraged U.S. business to increase its investments in the South African economy. The international capital markets can also be said to have 'tilted' toward South Africa once its domestic scene had become tranquil. In 1965 foreign capital began once more to flow into South Africa, initiating a ten year period of capital inflows whose extent was historically unprecedented.

In June of 1976 the political peace that had existed since Sharpeville was abruptly shattered. The rebellion that began in Soweto and rapidly spread to the black townships of South Africa's larger cities, lasting approximately six months, generated international repercussions that were a replay, in a more intense form, of what had followed the Sharpeville shootings. Pretoria experienced what was, until that point, the greatest diplomatic estrangement from the West in its modern history. The U.N.

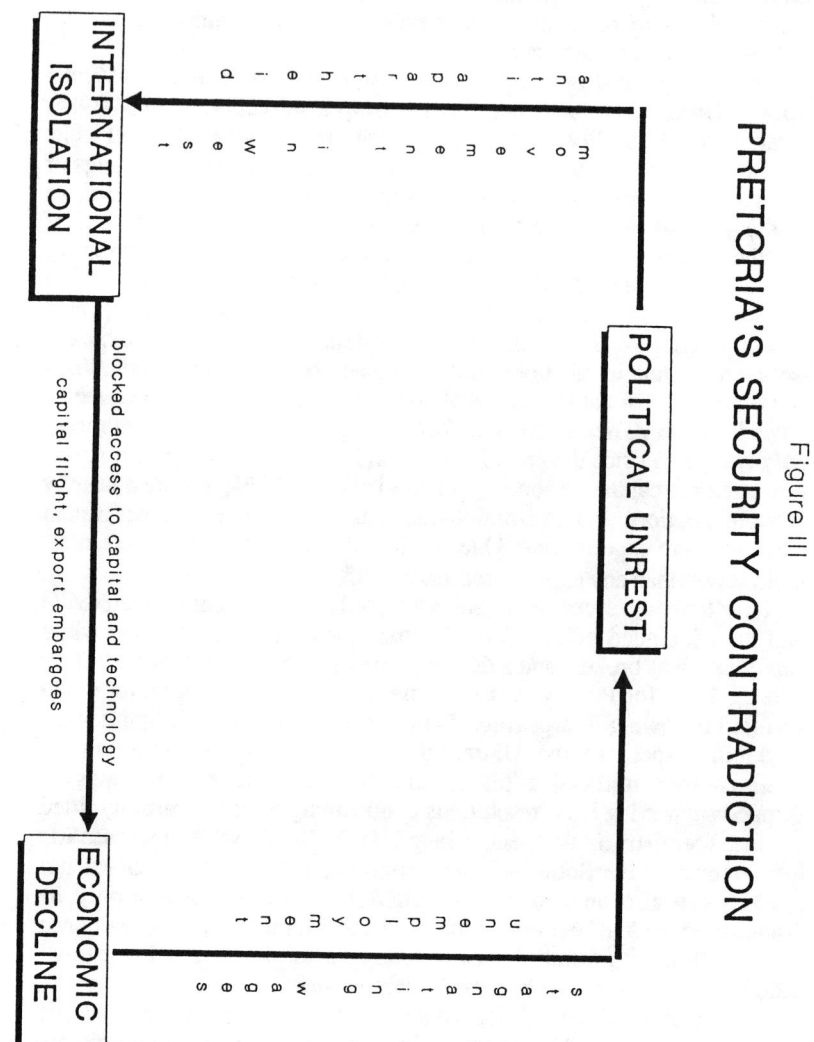

Figure III

PRETORIA'S SECURITY CONTRADICTION

arms embargo was expanded and made mandatory. The U.S. government, for the first time ever, demanded a system of majority rule in South Africa. On the international economic front, the flow of direct investment to South Africa slowed to a trickle. Multinational corporations, either because they had doubts about the long-term stability of the Republic, or because they were under pressure from their shareholders or their home government, or for a combination of these reasons, no longer considered South Africa a particularly attractive place for investment purposes. At the same time some of the largest international banks announced that they did not intend to increase their loan exposure in South Africa, and those loans that South Africa was able to obtain came with premium interest charges attached. As the flow of new capital into South Africa slowed, foreign-owned firms began to repatriate an unusually large proportion of their local earnings. As a result the country's capital flow experienced a dramatic turnabout. Within six months of Soweto, South Africa's capital account, which had recorded a positive net inflow each year for a decade, swung into reverse. In 1977 there was a net outflow of R810 million, and in 1978 an even more dramatic outflow of R1370 million.[17]

With the effective repression of the Soweto Uprising and the return of a surface peace to the townships, South Africa began a return to international capital markets, as it had after the crushing of opposition groups in the wake of Sharpeville a decade earlier. In 1982, South Africa once again experienced a positive net inflow of direct foreign investment after six continuous years of negative foreign investment flow.[18] At the same time, both the private and public sector were able to successfully turn to the international banking system as a source of foreign funds.

But unlike the period following the Sharpeville repression, after Soweto the return to the international economy and related economic growth could not be sustained. A number of things were different in the latter period. For one, despite the Government's banning of all Black Consciousness organizations, the period after Soweto was one of organizational effervescence in the black community. It was a time of the birth and expansion of numerous social organizations that were autonomous from the state, capable of mobilizing large numbers of people, and either explicitly or implicitly oriented to political opposition (*e.g.*, the trade unions, the civic associations in the larger townships, youth congresses, and the United Democratic Front, after 1982). For another, anti-apartheid constituencies and organizations in the countries of North America and Western Europe remained in place, despite a fall-off in their activities once the events of "Soweto" had passed and the media attention had moved away from South Africa. The first of these post-Soweto conditions was an important factor in contributing to another period of political unrest, and the second to a rapid and intense international reaction.

The insurrection that broke over South Africa's black townships in Fall of 1984, and continued through the Spring of 1986, constituted a form of militant mass political opposition more intense, widespread, violent, and explicitly radical, than anything in South African modern history. The international reaction was swift and more intense than had been generated previously by Sharpeville and Soweto. Through a combination of private decisions and governmental actions South Africa was, by the end of 1986, effectively cut off from international capital markets, and faced with selective embargoes against some important foreign exchange earning exports -- coal, steel, fresh vegetables and fruits. Even the availability of commercial credits to South African importers was drastically curtailed, despite the fact that such trade financing was generally exempt from the lending prohibitions of government imposed sanctions, such as the U.S. Comprehensive Anti-Apartheid Act of 1986 (Table 1, below).

	Letters of Credit (millions of dollars)	Nonbank Credits (millions of dollars)
1983	123	142
1984	110	128
1985	112	80
1986	42	50
1987	11	76

Source: United States General Accounting Office, Report to Congress, *South Africa: Trends in Trade , Lending and Investment* (1988), 28

TABLE 1
U.S. COMMERCIAL CREDIT TO SOUTH AFRICA

At the same time that South Africa's access to new capital was being drastically curtailed, foreign capital already within the South African economy began a quick exodus. A significant amount of disinvestment by foreign MNCs, especially ones of U.S. origin, took place between 1985 and 1988. Table 2, below, reveals the spurt of disinvestment by U.S. owned firms after the onset of the 1984 insurrection.

	1984	1985	1986	1987	1988	Total
Companies	7	40	50	55	25	177

Source: Investor Responsibility Research Center (GAO report, p. 30)

TABLE 2
DISINVESTMENT BY U.S. OWNED FIRMS

Of far greater consequence then disinvestment was the decision by major international banks to recall their outstanding short-term loans to South African borrowers. Given that the actions of foreign governments and the preferences of private actors precluded access to the kind of alternative sources of foreign capital that had been available once the impact of Soweto had subsided (in the early 80s), the impact on capital flows was devastating for the South African economy. Figure IV shows the effect of the 1984-86 insurrection on the net flow of loan capital. As can be seen, the cumulative loss to the economy between 1984 and 1987 -- the result of loan repayments, on the one hand, without the recourse to counterbalancing new lending, on the other -- has been over $4 billion. The total loss of capital from all sources during the same period was more than twice as large -- 25.2 billion rand, or approximately $10 billion at the 1989 rate of rand/dollar exchange (see Figure V).

Huge outflows of foreign capital, because they have taken place in the context of blocked access to new foreign capital, have undermined South Africa's prospects for economic growth. First, the economy has been denied the new capital required for economic expansion. Of course, domestic savings could, in principle, substitute for foreign capital as a source of new investment. But, under the circumstances of a hostile international economic environment, future economic prospects are rendered problematic, increasing the risks for investors whatever their nationality. In the 1980s, South African investors appear to have become reluctant to undertake the risk involved in gambling on South Africa's future, while at the same time they are investing billions of Rand abroad.[19] "We should be opening more mines, putting up more plants ...," the chairman of Gencor, South Africa's second largest mining-finance house, told *Leadership* magazine. "That we haven't ...is because uncertainty has produced a lack of confidence."[20] Data on domestic investment reveal a consistent decline since 1981. By 1985 real gross domestic fixed investment had slumped by sixteen percent. In the manufacturing sector the slide was fourteen percent between June 1984 and June 1986, alone.[21] One South African publication referred to the process as one of "domestic disinvestment."[22] "Companies are not ploughing money back into productive investment, and [are] reducing the value of their existing plant and stocks."[23] Thus, because of the psychological impact of international economic sanctions -- the sense of pessimism and risk they cast over the future -- the South African economy in the 1980s has not been able to adequately substitute domestic for lost foreign investment. The impact of sanctions that have blocked South Africa's access to international capital markets is consequently greater than just the loss of foreign capital.

MOVEMENT OF INTERNATIONAL LOAN CAPITAL

Figure IV

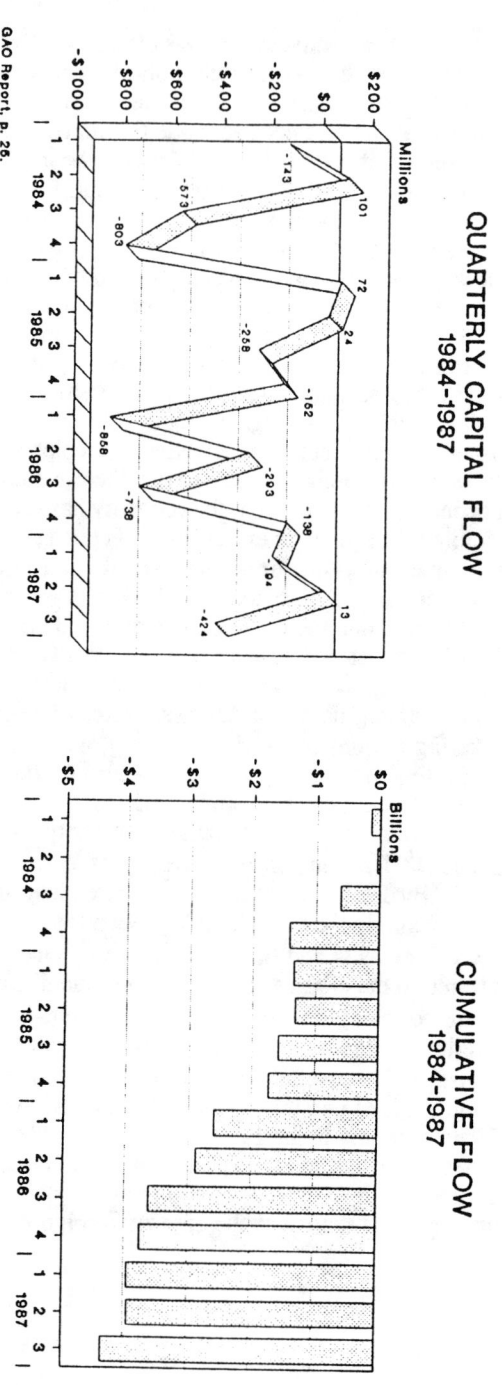

QUARTERLY CAPITAL FLOW
1984-1987

CUMULATIVE FLOW
1984-1987

GAO Report, p. 26.

FLOW OF CAPITAL FROM SOUTH AFRICA

Figure V

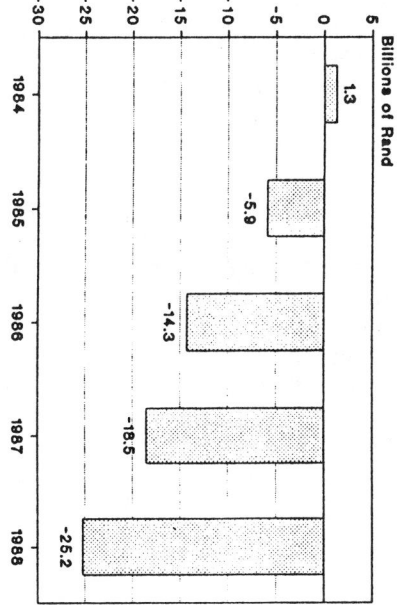

FLOW OF CAPITAL: ALL SOURCES
1984 - 1988

Billions of Rand

	1984	1985	1986	1987	1988
Series 1	1.3	-7.2	-8.4	-4.2	-6.7

Source: WEEKLY MAIL, December 2, 1988,
p. 19., and March 17, 1989, p. 18.

FLOW OF CAPITAL: ALL SOURCES
Cumulative: 1984-1988

Billions of Rand

1984   1.3
1985   -5.9
1986   -14.3
1987   -18.5
1988   -25.2

A second growth retarding consequence of economic sanctions in the 1980s has been the import constraint created by pressure on the balance of payments. The South African economy is heavily import dependent in the area of producer goods and industrial components. For economic growth to take place, therefore, the economy must have a surplus of foreign exchange with which to pay for these vital technology-embodied imports. Sanctions have struck at all of the mechanisms available to an economy to obtain foreign exchange -- new foreign direct investment, access to foreign loans, and earnings from exports. With its foreign exchange generating capacity limited by sanctions, the need to meet foreign bank demands for loan repayment has created an endemic balance of payments crises. Pretoria in the late 1980s has had difficulty simply meeting its foreign financial obligations; an available foreign exchange surplus to support the import requirements of sustained economic growth is thus absent.

The external economic squeeze, in combination with the structural characteristics of the South African economy, has produced a decade of economic stagnation, and decline. From 1982 to 1987 average annual growth in GDP was only one percent, considerably below the population growth rate of about 2.5 percent per annum. In three of these six years the economy actually shrunk, declining by more than two percent in 1985 alone.[24] The impact on personal incomes has been dramatic. As Figure VI indicates, disposable income has been on a downward slide since 1981, declining by 8.3 percent in real terms, by the end of 1987.[25] Economic stagnation also translates into unemployment. Among Whites, 'Coloureds' and Asians unemployment rates quintupled, while the number of unemployed among those of African descent reached over a million by the third quarter of 1986.[26]

Economic decline in the context of increasing international economic isolation has significant political implications, beyond affecting people's calculations about the future under a continuation of minority rule. The absence of economic growth has undermined Pretoria's reform effort, the financial cost of which was officially estimated to require an annual growth rate of from five to seven percent.[27] Specifically, the strategy of co-opting a black middle class as a buffer against the forces pushing for full majority rule has been nullified, as economic stagnation has denied Pretoria the funds for school construction, housing projects, township electrification, and the like. Likewise the plans to reduce the political alienation of the black urban masses through an amelioration of material conditions have been obliterated by unemployment and overcrowding. We can see here the interactive nature of Pretoria's security contradiction. Militant political opposition ("unrest") on the domestic front stimulates the introduction of international constraints, which through their impact

Figure VI

REAL PER CAPITA INCOME

Index: 1975 = 100

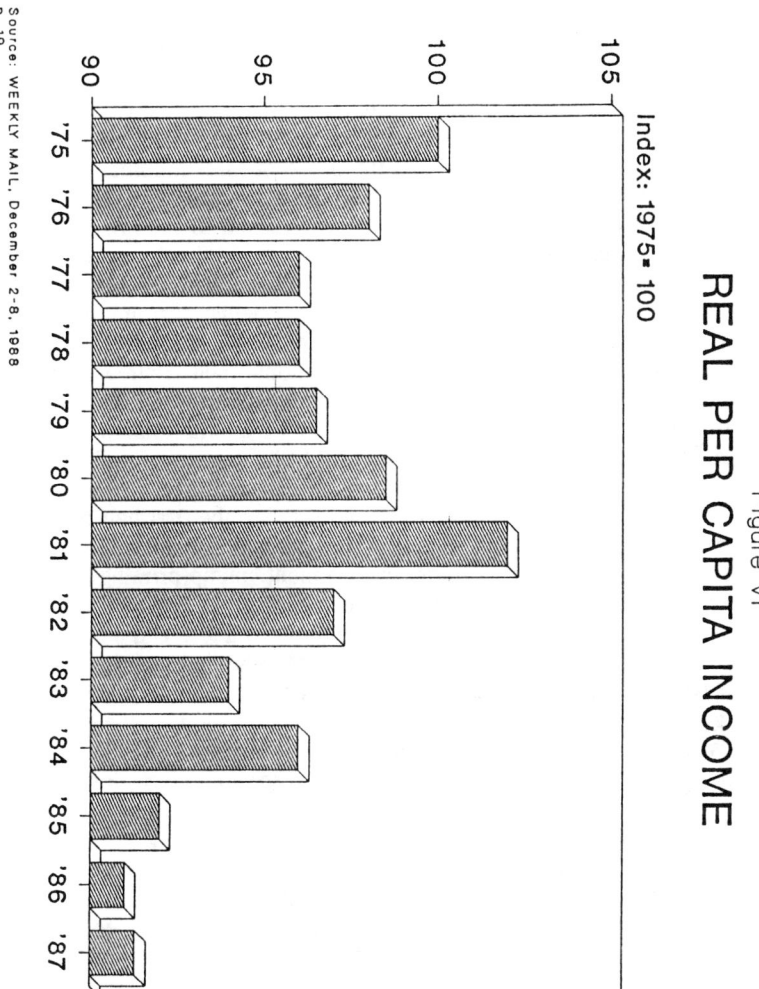

Source: WEEKLY MAIL, December 2-8, 1988
p. 19.

on the economy help perpetuate the conditions conducive to future
outbreaks of insurrectionary action.

STATE OF EMERGENCY, SANCTIONS AND GROWTH

Although the 1984 insurrection lasted considerably longer than had the
Soweto Uprising, under a "state of emergency" declared in June of 1986,
Pretoria was able to bring to an end the phase of mass mobilization and
mass organization that had characterized the urban townships for more
than twenty-two months. A surface calm returned to the urban areas.
Overt mass attacks on and resistance to authority declined sharply. The
visible political conflict and violence that still continued involved a kind
of civil war within the black townships; a battle between groups collabo-
rating with the state and those identified with the liberation or
"democratic" mass movement. The international media, already under
censorship from Pretoria, gradually lost interest in the South African
story. The stage was thus set for the erosion of international economic
isolation. But a very significant aspect of the situation since mid-1986 is
that except for some minor slippage in the banking area, international
pressure has held. True, during 1987 and through the first half of 1988
Pretoria spoke confidently of its ability to successfully withstand international economic pressure. Through government "pump-priming" and an
economic strategy termed inward industrialization, whereby import substituting industrialization would lessen foreign dependence and create economic growth, Pretoria proclaimed that the international sanctions threat
could be blunted. The end of the insurrection produced by the state of
emergency bolstered confidence within government and in some business
circles. Modest but real economic growth in 1987 and early 1988 fed optimism and encouraged a stance of bravura in respect to international pressure. Sanctions were not working, the South African population was
told, and many of those abroad who had opposed economic pressure on
Pretoria echoed this theme.

But by mid-1988 the growth potential of inward industrialization was
revealed as more apparent than real, and the long-term economic
prognosis from South African business as well as from Pretoria turned
decidedly gloomy. Most significantly, a wide array of influential
economic actors for the first time acknowledged that sanctions had
extracted significant costs and that a sanctions-filled future was one of
economic decline. Thus, in mid-1988 Henri de Villiers, chairman of the
Standard Bank Investment Corporation, warned the South African public
and government:

In this day and age there is no such thing as economic self-sufficiency and we delude our-
selves if we think we are different. ... South Africa needs the world. It needs markets, it
needs skills, it needs technology, and above all it needs capital.[28]

At about the same time Chris van Wyk, managing director of the Trust
Bank of Africa Ltd., echoed the thoughts of the chairman of Standard
Bank: "I'm fed up with the feeling that we can go it alone...We can't ignore what sanctions and disinvestment have done."[29] According to van
Wyk, as a result of sanctions-induced capital outflows and a loss of export
earnings of nearly five billion dollars, "South Africans will be five to ten
percent poorer by 1990." This type of analysis also found its way into
the annual reports for 1988 of a number of South Africa's largest financial
and industrial institutions. Thus the report of Rand Mines Ltd. declared --

...[S]anctions are beginning to have an adverse effect on the economy ... The
expansion of the South African economy is being restricted by the continued absence of
substantial capital inflows. There is a consensus that the confidence of overseas
investors must be restored, before adequate funds from that source will again be
available.[30]

The key to the business community's turnabout regarding the impact
of sanctions lay in collapse of the mini-boom of 1987. Because its cause
was embedded firmly in the relationship between sanctions and the structure of the South African economy, it revealed clearly the political and
economic dilemma facing Pretoria. In the late 1980s Pretoria sought to
meet its foreign debt obligations by spurring economic growth, and
boosting exports, so as to build its reserves of foreign exchange. But because of the economy's import dependence, economic expansion translated
rapidly into increased imports and thus greater claims on foreign exchange
reserves. By mid-1988 it had become apparent that under conditions of
international financial isolation and forced debt repayment, the import
costs of sustaining a growth rate of only two percent exceeded earnings
from exports. Economic expansion in the sanctions environment meant a
short period of growth, followed by a balance of payments crisis,
followed by decline. The irony of this situation, as well as its political
lesson, was outlined by Johan Louw, chief economist for SANLAM,
South Africa's second largest financial conglomerate and the largest
Afrikaner financial institution:

We can't afford a growth rate of more than two percent [because of pressure on the bal-
ance-of-payments]. Normally a developing country should be importing capital, but we
are exporting capital in order to repay debt. Unless we get certain reforms here we won't
get foreign capital again. We have to at least show the outside world that we are moving
in the right direction.[31]

Of all the comments emerging out of the economic difficulties
encountered in late 1988, the most interesting and significant are those by

Pretoria's Minister of Finance, Bernard Du Plessis. Addressing the South African Parliament in his 1989 Budget Speech, Du Plessis observed: "How ironic that we are now forced to label a modest growth rate of three percent in our economy as 'overheating.'" Sounding more like a spokesperson for the ANC than Pretoria's official spokesman on financial matters, Du Plessis declared that for South Africa the main question is not whether any progress can be made, but whether there can be "economic survival in the face of an internationally organized assault on the economy." "The answer for us," he stated, "clearly lies in the full-scale effort to break the isolation imposed on us, by dynamic expansion of our trade with the outside world and a restoration of our creditworthiness by means of the correct economic measures and political progress."[32]

Du Plessis's acknowledgement of the costs of sanctions and his prescription -- a "full-scale effort to break the isolation imposed on us" -- illuminates the context for Pretoria's most ambitious foreign policy gambit -- agreeing to the Namibia/Angola Accord in summer 1988. Once before Pretoria had entered into a diplomatic agreement to bring regional "peace and security," the Nkomati Accord of March 1984. At the time of the treaty with Mozambique, a South African newspaper commented that Nkomati represented "the beginning of a new road which would, if followed ... lead South Africa back into Africa and through Africa back into the world."[33] And, the road back to the world was also presumably a road away from sanctions. The Nkomati Accord, the commentary continued, "will have a valuable spin-off benefit in the international arena by making the prospect of economic sanctions against South Africa -- ever present for two decades -- more remote."

From Pretoria's vantage point the Angola/Namibia Agreement represents "Nkomati II"; it is a replay of the 1984 scenario whereby a regional posture of diplomacy and compromise is supposed to pave the way back from international isolation and economic sanctions. But the 1984 experience also indicates the limits of a regional or foreign policy in achieving the international acceptance that Pretoria requires. Within a month of the Nkomati agreement Pretoria's strategy began to bear fruit. P.W. Botha undertook a six nation European trip, the first time in twenty years that a South Africa head of government had paid an official visit to Europe. But this apparent "road back to the world" turned out to be a *cul de sac*, for Western governments were primarily attuned to South Africa's domestic situation rather than to its foreign policy. When in September of 1984 insurrection erupted in the townships of the Vaal triangle the Nkomati strategy was foiled, and the stage was set for further international isolation and an escalation in sanctions pressure.

The 1984 experience indicates that in order for Pretoria to realize the hoped for gains out of the 1988 Angola/Namibia peace accord it will have to match its regional overture with some dramatic domestic policy change. This much is generally realized by many in South African high policy circles. Thus the chief economist for SANLAM, Johan Louw continued, "We have to at least show the outside world that we are moving in the right direction. Perhaps under a new state president things will get moving."[34] The divisions that characterized the National Party elite in mid-1989 were rooted, to a significant degree, in the recognition of the validity of this type of assessment. While the risks attached to a new domestic political initiative loom as prohibitive to those concerned primarily with security, there is considerable support for some dramatic new gesture to the black majority. Such a move might include one or all of the following -- the release of Nelson Mandela, the lifting of the State of Emergency, and the introduction of a new power sharing arrangement that would allow for representation of the black population in a consociational/federal system.[35]

Would the introduction of steps like the above solve Pretoria's problem *vis a vis* the international system? Only if they would lead to a substantial portion of black opinion that is now associated with the "democratic mass movement," the UDF/ANC, accepting Pretoria's new power sharing arrangement. But given the current political atmosphere in the black community, and the limited perspective of the National Party on how much power it can afford to relinquish, such an outcome seems highly unlikely. Even after three years of repression, there is no sign that the center of gravity of black politics has moved substantially away from the demand for majority rule. And, the level of material hardship that characterizes the townships suggests the continued existence of a tinderbox of easily politicized alienation. That is probably what Minister of Law and Order, Adrian Vlok, has in mind when he says that in the urban townships "a climate of revolution still boils beneath the surface."[36] There is also little sign that the cost imposed by sanctions has yet led the South African ruling group to conclude that political control by the white minority is no longer viable.

Under these circumstances the most likely effect of an effort to build on the international good-will generated by the Angola/Namibia Accords by introducing the type of domestic changes mentioned above would be the reverse of what Pretoria sought to achieve. Lifting the state of emergency, releasing Mandela, and offering yet another formula for sharing power without giving up control is likely to both stimulate and facilitate a new wave of insurrectionary activity, which, in turn, will produce a ratcheting up of international sanctions. This is, of course, precisely the pattern that followed the introduction of apartheid reforms in the late 1970s.

The situation in early 1989 illuminates the very essence of a ruling group caught in the vise of irreconcilable contradictions. On the one hand, it is required to make domestic changes in order to placate an international audience upon which it is vitally dependent. On the other hand, its commitment to maintain the power and privilege of the white group at home so limits the changes it can make, that all of its policy options lead to political unrest and further estrangement from the international audience. Over time, with a weakening economy, declining standards of living, and an erosion of state resources, there occurs a series of incremental domestic adjustments toward the power demands of the black majority. In essence this describes the process of change experienced by South Africa since the mid-1970s. A transition to majority rule is likely to be made only if the interactive process of domestic unrest and international pressure continues into the future until the point is reach at which the ruling group views the risks inherent in clinging to minority rule as greater than those attending a system based on majority power.

SUMMARY

The dynamic quality of Pretoria's fundamental security contradiction -- its commitment to maintaining white rule at home while preserving access to markets abroad -- is revealed by the events of 1960 to the present. Both the contradiction and its dynamic interaction have become especially intense since 1976. Isolated internationally because of its system of racial rule, Pretoria finds that when its domestic situation is characterized by visible black resistance, Western governments are unwilling or unable to resist taking steps against it. Likewise, under these circumstances, multinational corporations and international banks come to recognize significant costs in an expanded, or even continued, presence in or relationship to South Africa.

International isolation is transposed into withdrawal from South Africa and blocked access to markets for new capital and technology. Difficulty in obtaining new direct investment from abroad, in importing the latest technology, in finding export markets, and in gaining access to international bank loans threatens South Africa's long-term economic growth. Without economic growth, the prospects for domestic tranquility and security decline, for unemployment and downward pressure on wages serve to increase black anger and to make militant political responses more likely.

A violent and seemingly unstable domestic situation, in circumstances of diplomatic isolation and hostility, serves to undermine South Africa's economic relations further, by increasing the likelihood of sanctions and by reducing the attractiveness of South Africa's investment climate. Such developments in South African foreign economic relations, in turn, threaten economic growth, jobs, and income, producing more alienation and threats to domestic security, in a continuing downward spiral of inter-

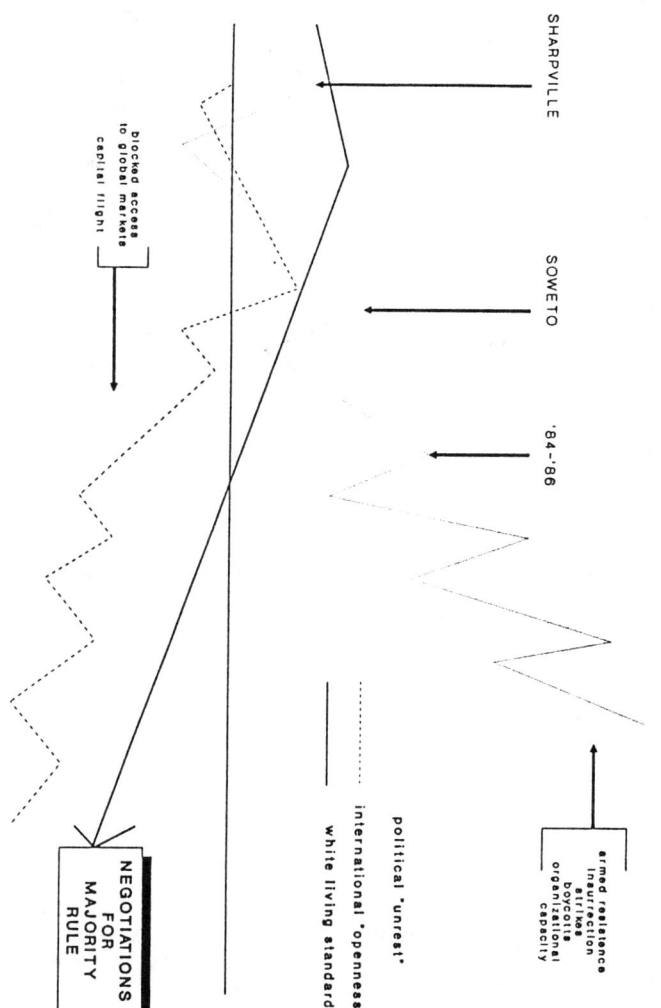

Figure VII

PATH TO NEGOTIATIONS

SHARPVILLE

SOWETO

'84-'86

blocked access
to global markets
capital flight

NEGOTIATIONS
FOR
MAJORITY
RULE

political "unrest"
international "openness"
white living standards

armed resistance
insurrection
strikes
boycotts
organizational
capacity

national isolation, political unrest, and economic decline. (See Figure III).

Figure VII presents a "model" which adds the dimension of timing to the above notion of a downward spiral. Political unrest and international isolation interact in a series of 'peak episodes', with increased international pressure following shortly after an upsurge in militant political opposition. Observing the three peak episodes that South Africa has thus far experienced -- Sharpeville, Soweto, and the 1984-1986 insurrection -- we can see an interesting pattern. Each successive episode had a larger mass base, was more politically radical, lasted for a longer period, and produced more costly international isolation. The episodes also follow more quickly upon each other, and they have a 'plateau effect.' While political unrest and international isolation recede after each peak episode, South Africa's internal political order and its international situation do not return to the *status quo ante*. Instead, the level of political militancy and radical political organization, as well as the level of international pressure remain higher than prior to the previous peak episode, creating a kind of plateau from which the next episode of unrest and isolation take off.

Projecting the model based upon the last decade and a half into the future, one would expect to see a series of peak episodes of increasing frequency and intensity. Coinciding with this dynamic, and caused by it, a gradual erosion in the standard and quality of white life takes place, until at some point in the future negotiations for majority rule appear as an attractive alternative to a continuation of the spiral of decline. Predicting precisely when that will occur requires a crystal ball, not a model.

Notes

1. A.N. Pelzer, ed., *Veroerd Speaks*, (Johannesburg: APB Publishers, 1966), 361-362.
2. *Ibid.*, 362-363.
3. Quoted from a speech to the South African House of Assembly, January 27, 1959.
4. *Ibid.*
5. Verwoerd, quoted in Andre du Toit, "Ideological Change, Afrikaner Nationalism and Pragmatic Racial Domination in South Africa," in Leonard Thompson and Jeffrey Butler, eds., *Change in Comtemporary South Africa* (Berkeley: University of California Press, 1976), 41.
6. N.E. Wiehahn, *The Complete Wiehahn Report* (Johannesburg: Lex Patria Publishers, 1982), para. 3.34, p. 32 .
7. Gerrit Olivier, "Recent developments in South African Foreign Policy," *Optima*, (December 1988), 203.
8. Leon Trotsky, *1905* (New York: Random House, 1971), 326.
9. Theda Skocpol, *States & Social Revolutions* (Cambridge: Cambridge University Press, 1979), 32.
10. Republic of South Africa, *First Report of the Constitutional Committee of the President's Council* (1982), 3.

11. *Ibid., 9.*
12. P.W. Botha's quotation from *Citizen* (May 1, 1987).
13. "South Africa's National Party Government" in Peter C. Berger and Bobby Godsell, eds., *A Future South Africa* (Boulder: Westview Press, 1988) 29
14. *The Economist* (January 26, 1985).
15. *Financial Mail (SA)* (October 7, 1988).
16. D. Hobart Houghton, *The South African Economy* (Cape Town: Oxford University Press, 1973), 180-184, 277.
17. *South Africa, Barclay's Country Report*, 3 (May, 1979). See also, Africa Research Bulletin (15 August - 14 August 1977), 4402.
18. *International Financial Statistics* (various issues, 1977-85).
19. *Weekly Mail* (May 5-May 12, 1988), 16.
20. *Leadership*, 7(6) (1988), 32.
21. *Weekly Mail* (January 16-22, 1987), 13.
22. In 1988 total fixed investment grew by about five percent, reversing a trend in which gross domestic fixed investment fell in real terms every year since 1981. Despite this increase, the level of real domestic investment spending was still twenty-seven percent lower in 1988 than it had been in 1981. Moreover, a substantial portion of the new investment spending during 1989 was in residential buildings-- especially "black housing"-- rather than in the directly productive area of new plant and equipment. *Weekly Mail* (February 17, 1989).
23. *Ibid.*
24. *Weekly Mail* (March 31-April 7, 1988), 16.
25. *Weekly Mail* (December 2-December 8, 1988).
26. Stephen R. Lewis, *Apartheid Economics* (New York: Council on Foreign Relations, forthcoming), 1.
27. Estimate by Jan Lombard, Deputy Governor of the South African Reserve Bank, quoted in Mark Swilling and March Phillips, "The X Factor," *Weekly Mail* (September 2, 1988), 9.
28. Quoted by Roger Thurow, *Wall Street Journal* (August 1, 1988).
29. *Ibid.*
30. Rand Mines Ltd., 1988 Annual Report in *Leadership*, 7(6) (reprint., 1988). See also Nedbank and the First National Bank, Annual Reports in *Leadership*, 7(6) (reprint., 1988).
31. *Weekly Mail* (March 17-22, 1989), 16.
32. *Ibid.*
33. Sunday Times (Johannesburg, 18 March 1984), in *South African Digest*, (March 18, 1984), 19.
34. Johan Louw, quoted in *Weekly Mail* (March 17-22, 1989), 16.
35. Willem de Klerk, "South Africa Is Poised for Leaps Toward a New Beginning," *International Herald Tribune* (April 17, 1989).
36. *Citizen* (November 2, 1988).

Popular Support for Armed Struggle: A Comment

Moeletsi Mbeki

I begin with the model of escalating conflict in South Africa. I want to emphasize the position, because in the few months I have been in the U.S.A., I have been struck by the depth of perception here that somehow the world's problems can just be talked away. The only ones that cannot be talked away are the ones that involve American national security. When it comes to our rights in South Africa, this should be negotiated and talked about until everybody has agreed. But when it comes to America's influence over Western Europe, in maintaining capitalism in Western Europe, in maintaining capitalism in Japan, we have to have arms to influence them, we have to have nuclear weapons to maintain the influence of the United States. We have to have armed soldiers stationed in Panama to maintain peace in Latin America, et cetera, et cetera. The point which I want to make about South Africa is that the core of the strategy for South Africa comes from the students, the rank and file workers, and so on. So I want to get across to students here that this model of the USA which is what I have been learning, is that America is entitled to solve problems of its own concern by force, but the rest of the world is not permitted to do so.

The problem of South Africa is one of those issues, one of the instances, which have to be solved through armed conflict. How far the war will actually go and what shape it will take, in many respects, is not the key issue. The fact is, for the blacks in South Africa to reconquer their freedom, to reconquer their self-determination (which was, after all, seized from them by military force and is kept away from them through military force), they have to use armed force. This is, I think, an axiom about the situation in South Africa. How much armed force, how to use it, when, what will the South African regime do in return? -- those are details. Whether our use of force destabilizes Southern Africa or not in the process, those really are details.

Since 1960 there has been this spiralling of conflict in South Africa. I want to add some background. When the white regime or the whites took over South Africa, they disrupted with such a thorough disruption over a period of about two hundred years, that for about fifty years there was a period of relative peace, fifty years from say the First World War to the 1960s. There was relative peace because of the disruption of the African social cohesion that the whites had successfully imposed over the black community. There were pockets of resistance, but they could not cohere, and they could not be sustained over the long term. The beginning of the twentieth century is really when the total conquest and subjugation of black South Africa was finalized. (The last area to be conquered was in 1898, subdued by the Transvaal Republic.) Sporadic modern resistance starts from the First World War when you have the setting up of the Industrial and Commercial Worker's Union and a few strikes here and there. Then it peters out and re-emerges in the late 1920s and again the regime crashes on it. It re-emerges during the Second World War in the squatters' movement, and so on. The main pattern begins to emerge in 1950 with the Defiance Campaign. You can see that between 1950 and Sharpeville in 1960, you have a relatively longer wait.

Why is it we are getting this continuing resistance now? It is a reflection of the long-term evolution of South African society. South African blacks have become urbanized. We now have two, three, four generations of urbanized communities. They have become an established proletariat, despite migratory labor. The end result is that we are establishing a set of values and cohesiveness in the black community, which makes it possible for coherent organization to develop.

The working class in South Africa, the black working class, was constructed not just from the tribes of South Africa, but was constructed out of practically the whole world. We have Chinese in South Africa, we have Indians in South Africa, we have just about everybody. When you look at the population that makes up so-called Coloured, we have people descended from Madagascar, who descended from Java, who descended from West Africa, Mozambique, etc. So this was the society or the working class that was put together by the industrialization process of South Africa. This is what made is possible for relative peace to obtain in South Africa for the greater part of the twentieth century -- lack of social cohesion among of the blacks. That "honeymoon" is now over. There is now a recurrence of social conflict; a continuing and sustained conflict of self-determination.

Now whether we get support from the United States government, or whether the Conservatives in Britain, or Republicans in America support the South African regime or try to comfort the South African regime, essentially it won't change things. Now we have the kind of society that is beginning to be able to mount an effective armed insurrection. We will get the arms. Incidentally, the point that always gets forgotten is that we fought against whites in South Africa for practically two hundred years with no one arming us. The question of whether Moscow will continue to provide aid is not the big question. Whether the Russians become more friendly to the South African regime or more friendly to us (I say they are more friendly to us) will not change the direction of the struggle.

There are two important elements missing in these pages: the element of armed struggle and discussion of what has happened to the armed struggle. There is too much concentration on economic pressure. Yes, economic pressure has had a strong effect on the South African economy. I have been in the Commonwealth Secretariat Study Group that is looking into the question of sanctions and is preparing a report for the Commonwealth Heads of State. It is very clear from all the evidence we have looked at that sanctions have hit the South African regime very hard. Other measures, especially the United States' sanctions, have hit the South African economy very hard. So we would like those to continue. We accept the emphasis on them.

But a point which has to be emphasized, which is missing in Robert Price's chapter, is that the greatest part of the support for the struggle in South Africa and Southern Africa is from socialist countries. It comes in the form of military training in the introduction of Africans to military science and to the use of modern weapons. This is the part of the international community's pressure on the South African regime which should be brought to our attention. What they are going to do in future in the communist countries, I do not know.

A second component of this armed struggle is the support from the independent African countries. This is another item that is missing from Prices' chapter. Many of us -- African refugees, exiles, our armed wing -- have to go through the independent countries. This is the secret of the guerrillas you can read about in the trials in South Africa. You can see they get support form Angola, they get support from Ethiopia, from all over Africa.

Then there is the question of popular support for the struggle in South Africa by the mass of the population in Western countries. It has to be specified that the conservatives in Western Europe and in the United States are looking for ways of working with the South African regime and preserving the socio-economic system in South Africa practically intact, with a few modifications here and there. So for them the question of majority rule is not priority. But the great mass of people, who have compelled Reagan to sign in 1986 the Anti-Apartheid Act, support majority rule in South Africa. The great mass of American people support majority rule. This is another item that needs emphasizing in Robert Price's chapter.

5
South Africa:
Possibilities and Impossibilities

Conor Cruise O'Brien

"Towards Peace and Security in Southern Africa...." I think that may be a long haul. I think from the part of the conference I was able to attend that the tone appeared to be rather more optimistic than I myself would find probable for the short and middle term of the future of South Africa. I'm going to confine myself here to the core area, to South Africa itself, rather than try to spread myself over something that would prove too wide.

It the title, I refer to "possibilities and impossibilities." The judgements on what is possible or impossible of course are subjective and personal. And you will probably differ from me, many of you, on two of my three "impossibilities." Continuation of the status quo is impossible. Major reform is impossible. Revolution is impossible.

Most of you will agree about the status quo. Some of you certainly will differ either about reform or about revolution. But I do not think I need to labor the reasons why I believe those to be impossible, because you have been going over this ground, and you are certainly aware that even if either revolution or reform is not impossible, there are very formidable barriers in the way of either. So you can see how someone might conclude that they were impossible.

Robert Price identifies some interesting *possibilities*. Let me read, by way of reminder, relevant parts:

That which reduces the material welfare of whites and/or threatens their physical security and does so in a way that ties these costs to efforts to maintain minority control will

This is a slightly revised and edited version of the closing Address to the Conference at Haverford College, "Toward Peace and Security in Southern Africa," April 30, 1989, deliberately retaining the informal tone of a speech, rather than a formal paper. Its position in this selection is dictated by its relevance to the preceding discussion of political change in South Africa. [Editor's Note.]

make a negotiated transition to majority rule more likely. A weakening economy and political unrest are the two primary mechanisms for producing this outcome. There is admittedly a major and unelaborated assumption in all this, that an overall decline in the material, psychological and physical quality of life for white South Africans, and the resultant acceptance of the risks of majority rule, will translate into a willingness on the part of governing authorities to negotiate an end to their rule.[1]

He says later:

The best that one can say is that over time a situation of economic, physical and psychological deterioration is likely to impact on constituencies that the governing group represents, eroding support for the political *status quo* among elements considered vital by the ruling elite, [*etc.*][2]

I think the Price analysis is very interesting, very instructive, and I would like to think about it further. At the present stage, however, I have some questions about it. I think that there may be difficulties about part of that analysis. I have two main questions here -- questions only. One question is about the effectiveness of economic pressure. I think this analysis may perhaps exaggerate the effectiveness of that factor. There are, I think, two main reasons why this may be the case. One is that political and economic power are more separate in South Africa than is the case perhaps in any other state. Among the many pernicious varieties of apartheid is a kind of apartheid or near-apartheid between the public and the private sector in South Africa. The public sector is now exclusively controlled by Afrikaners. They call the political shots in every sense of the term. They feel, of course, indirectly the squeeze on the economy, and to some extent they feel it directly, too. They do not feel it with anything like the intensity that the business community -- which is still largely, though by no means exclusively, English-speaking -- feels it, but they feel it. I think if real power in South Africa were in the hands of the business community, the transition to one-man one-vote would happen quite quickly. but power, political power, is not in those hands. It's in the hands of the Afrikaner and that's a different proposition. Remember also that one of the benefits which the Afrikaners have had from their coming to power in 1948, and staying there, is a virtual monopoly of the public service. They were able to "Afrikanerize" the public service, by the neat device of making it bi-lingual. As English speakers generally do not speak Afrikaans, and Afrikaners always speak some English, that had the effect desired, especially when civil service selection boards had a majority of Afrikaners. So the public service is now "Afrikanerized." A new government, in majority-ruled conditions, would "de-Afrikanerize" and then "Africanize" it to a very great extent. Afrikaners have a lot more to lose than English-speakers have in the event of that transfer. And that's one of the reasons why I am a bit skeptical about the effectiveness in this context of economic pressure.

Another point, of course, is that among the major resources of South Africa are gold and diamonds. A power which possesses as much wealth in that form as South Africa does has some means of resisting economic pressure. There is no difficulty in finding access to markets for those particular commodities. They make their own way to a great extent. I'm not denying, however, that the economic erosion is serious and it is well-documented in the Price chapter.

I have a second question about the effectiveness of political violence. We're not talking about the morality of it here, simply about the effectiveness. I agree that in the short term, as Price acknowledges, violence increases resistance to change, but that in the longer term it may produce willingness to negotiate. In that much I agree with Price, but here is my most significant difference with him, and it radically changes, if you agree with my view, the perspective opened up by that analysis. That is the consideration that there is also a middle term to be considered. The Afrikaner leadership may someday resort to negotiations, I agree, but in my opinion the Afrikaner leadership is not going to resort to negotiations until they are altogether convinced that they have fully exhausted the possibilities of drastically increased repression. This is not a very pleasant thought, but I think we are obliged to look at it. Black violence is likely to increase, whether in revolutionary or anarchic forms, with the demographic explosion and with expanding unemployment referred to in the Price chapter. And that violence is likely to splash over increasingly into the white areas, irrespective of what the opinion of the ANC leadership in Lusaka may be about that. I think it is possible to exaggerate the influence of Lusaka over developments in South Africa, even among the blacks.

The Afrikaner leaders and their security forces are likely to respond to that, at first at least, with something closely resembling a veritable reign of terror -- collective punishment of disaffected areas and communities, reckless use of firepower against the inhabitants of such areas. Such tactics can work for a time and if they do work for a time, they will be tried again when the next challenge arises. And I think we all have seen that this is an undulating thing -- there are periods of violent unrest, followed by a lull, followed by a new period of violence, and the lulls seem to be getting shorter. "Anarchy kept at bay by fascism" might come to be quite an accurate description of the politics of South Africa in the middle term, which I have in mind.

I know that some of you, perhaps many of you, will regard this part of my analysis as excessively pessimistic, just as you may regard the final part of it as excessively optimistic. I do not know. Some people are quite impressed by the movement of Afikaner intellectuals in an opposite direction to the direction I have been talking about -- about their willingness to talk about majority rule and peace, to meet the ANC, and so on. I think, however, it would be a mistake to overestimate, in present circumstances, the influence of Afrikaner intellectuals. They were indeed very influential at one stage in the history of this matter. In the 1930s it was a group of Afrikaner intellectuals which had the distinction of inventing apartheid, which is an intellectual artifact. But those were intellectuals who were working in the sense of their tribe, who reflected the values of their tribe, and were looked up to as leaders of their tribe. The modern intellectuals, to their credit, have broken with the values of their tribe and as a result they have, in my opinion, now little or no influence over it. Price cites eighty percent *of whites* as opposing transit to majority rule. I think the figure would probably be larger for the Afrikaner community.

I am tempted to say, then, that things will have to get worse before they get better, but I am not even convinced that things *will* get better, if South Africa is left to itself. I do not personally believe that South Africa left to itself can rid itself of apartheid. It is too deeply ingrained by now in the culture of the Afrikaners, who are the political masters of South Africa. I don't think that blacks can force that transition, not for a very long time. And I do not think the Afrikaners are psychologically capable of accepting it, unless they are brought under a degree and kind of international pressure which no power at present contemplates.

Price at one point refers to "challenging Pretoria's regional hegemony." He says "[it] is a very different matter than invading South Africa and forcing its unconditional surrender. This remains an extremely implausible occurrence for the foreseeable future."[3] Foreseeable future, of course, is always arguable. There generally is not much of the future that you can foresee. There are exceptions. A person who jumps off the top of a high-rise building will foresee the future with great clarity for a very short time. But in other conditions it is not generally given to us to foresee the future. We can guess about it; we ought to guess about it, and we ought to sharpen our guesses off one another, as you might say, as much as we can. I am trying to contribute here to that. And my guess, at this point, approximates to, but is not the same as, the outcome that Price considers to be "implausible for the foreseeable future." Anything like that, anything like invasion, is certainly implausible, if things remain much as they are now. But that's a large "if." If, as I believe, the situation in South Africa deteriorates drastically, perhaps around the beginning of the next century, then I think the major powers may have to reassess their position, also drastically. The Western powers in particular will not wish to be seen as opposing, under these conditions, measures recommended by Third World countries, and those measures under those circumstances are also likely to be drastic. Even so, I agree invasion remains a very unlikely option.

Perhaps the most likely option, under those drastically deteriorated circumstances, is mandatory and general economic sanctions proclaimed by the Security Council of the United Nations and enforced by means of a blockade by land and sea with the participation of both superpowers.

Participation of the superpowers in a United Nations enforcement action was regarded as very unlikely when I first offered this possible scenario, about two and a half years ago. It may seem perhaps a shade less unlikely now, as we have seen support of the Soviet Union for the United Nations develop quite strongly, amid unprecedented harmony among the permanent members of the Security council, particularly over the U.N.-mediated ending of the Gulf War and developments of that kind. However, I agree that what I have in mind is remote, inconceivable at present, and conceivable only after a drastic deterioration inside South Africa.

I believe that "recurring black violence met by increasingly drastic white repression" is likely to prove a good guess. What happens next is harder to guess. An international response of the kind I have indicated, and would hope for in those circumstances, is possible, only possible. It is also possible that the world, even in those terrible circumstances, would leave South Africa to stew horribly in its own juice, more or less as it has left Lebanon to do. As against that, South Africa is of much more consequence to the world's economy, and of much more significance in the world's politics, that Lebanon ever was. So I would ask you at least to entertain this possibility. For me, it represents the only tolerable outcome to this situation that I can conceive of as plausible, in certain circumstances which have not dawned. Short of that, I do not see any way in which South Africa can get out of its difficulties. I think you will have that "anarchy tempered by fascism" syndrome unless there is international action. I'm not of course speaking in the perspective of the Bush Administration, but a much longer perspective, certainly stretching into the next century. And unless your Constitution is amended, the Bush Administration cannot last into that. So we are looking a fair distance ahead, I would say, into the first and second decades of the next century.

Let us take the more benign hypotheses that I would offer -- that is to say the possibility of international action. Assuming the advent of international blockade -- blockade, remember, by land and sea and backed by both superpowers -- that is, effective siege of South Africa, combined with an ultimatum that the siege will not be ended until the institutions are changed and there will be non-racial elections under United Nations supervision. That is a hopeful scenario in my view. Assuming that, what would be the response of the rulers of South Africa to that? I know some of the *broederbond*, people whom you might rightly call the political rulers of South Africa, and I have discussed this with some of them. Interestingly, they do not rule it out. They see this as a possibility, no more, for the fairly distant future. Some of them hinted to me that South Africa, under those circumstances, would use the nuclear weapons which it has at its disposition now and would have increased by then. That, of course, would be the *Götterdämmerung* of the Afrikaner *volk*. Would they do it? I doubt it. Or would they capitulate?

I think that we have a precedent here in the conclusion of the Anglo-Boer War, as it is called in South Africa, the Boer War as they call it in Britain, 1899-1902. By 1902 the Boer commanders, grandfathers of the present establishment, were divided into two groups known in Afrikaans as the *bittereinders* and the *hensoppers*. *Bittereinders,* I think, is self-explanatory: people who would fight to the bitter end. And *hensoppers* were, of course, greatly despised by the *bittereinders,* but at the end of that hard-fought war, it was the *hensoppers* who prevailed. And my own hunch is that if it did come to that, if they were faced with real action, not just rhetoric, but real action from the world community, they would feel that they could give in with honor. And their honor, their concept of honor, is very dear to them. As they might see it, "just as it had taken the forces of a world empire to bring us down in 1902, so it takes the world again in arms to prevail over these otherwise indomitable Boers," and they would hope in some way to come back as they did come back between 1902 and 1948. They are rather a formidable people and I think in our prognoses about South Africa we should not ignore *either* how formidable they are or that in certain circumstances, when the pressure is overwhelming, and they can regard their honor as satisfied; they can give in.

How would the capitulation come about? I have discussed that question also with a former editor of *Die Burger* and member of the *broederbond* who, I was rather surprised to find, has actually considered this topic. I asked him, "If it comes to the eleventh hour and it is in the interest of your people, then, to give in and have a transit to majority rule, how would it be done?" He said,

The white electorate will never agree to that, they haven't got the brains to do it. Even if it was staring them in the face that this was the thing to do, they still wouldn't do it. And however often you ask them to vote, it would always go against it. the only way of doing this is by martial law, military rule. You would put the white electorate to sleep, they would wake up in a black country.

That is the remarkable utterance of that particular gentleman.

Calling for an even larger crystal ball, what would South Africa be like after its first non-racial elections? On the right, of course, the prophecy is always that you would have a one-shot election followed by dictatorship, as elsewhere in Africa. That is not necessarily so. I do not believe it would be so if elections were held under international auspices. South Africa is a far more complex society than the countries to the North. I think the Parliament resulting from that election would be very diverse, both ethnically and in terms of class interests. And I belive that a coalition government, involving whites as well as blacks, trade unionists as well as capitalists, might emerge. There would be a strong collective interest in the new South Africa on the part of people with anything to lose -- and all people with jobs have something to lose -- against the threat of anarchy arising from mass unemployment. The problems facing any such government would be daunting in the extreme. Even after apartheid is gone, South Africa will still have enormous social problems. But it is surely better, and I think we will probably all agree at least on this much, surely better that those problems should be dealt with by a government that has a wide degree of popular confidence than by a regime that is execrated by the overwhelming majority of those over whom it dominates, solely by force and the threat of force.

Notes

1. Robert M. Price, "Majority Rule in South Africa: The Role of Global Pressure," in this volume, p. 79
2. *Ibid.*, 79.
3. *Ibid.*, 73.

PART TWO

INTERNATIONAL AND
REGIONAL PRESSURES

6
U.N. Efforts in International Cooperation toward Political Change in Southern Africa

J.V. Gbeho

It is double pleasure for me to participate in your conference because of the honor that it brings to me personally and my country, Ghana, and also because Southern Africa is, at this time, a very important, if not critical, area of focus for the international community. I have no pretensions of expertise, neither do I believe that even the international community has all the answers to the bizarre and often tragic events that are occurring there. I am convinced, however, that it is in the best interest of the international community to continue studies, discussions and negotiations concerning the sub-region, with the view to achieving the best decisions possible on the threat to international peace and security in the whole area. It is for this reason that I am delighted to associate myself with your Conference entitled, "Toward Peace and Security in Southern Africa."

The Conference is proceeding on the assumption that "the continuing conflict in Southern Africa represents a threat to world peace, sufficient to require renewed exploration of ways to reduce and indeed resolve that conflict." Perhaps with the exception of South Africa and a few of its allies, most members of the international community, certainly the overwhelming majority of the United Nations member states, would concur in that assessment because *apartheid* is a threat to world peace and has been rightly condemned by resolutions of both the Security Council and the General Assembly of the United Nations.

In order to understand why the policies of apartheid of the Government of South Africa are at the root of the conflict that has engulfed the Southern Africa sub-region, extending from Mozambique around the Cape of Good Hope up to Angola, it is necessary to step back a little into the history of the area in order to determine the origins of the conflict as well as the attachment of the racist Pretoria regime to its present policies.

This is a slightly edited version of an address to the Conference at Haverford College, "Toward Peace and Security in Southern Africa," April 29, 1989. [Editor's Note.]

Ever since explorers, navigators and immigrants from Western Europe set foot on the soil of South Africa hundreds of years ago, the economic lure of that part of Africa has proved too great to resist. The geo-political importance of the location, connecting the Atlantic and Indian oceans, and its wealth in natural resources, ranging from fresh water for sailors in the early years to the highly valued strategic minerals needed by the most powerful of modern industrial states, have been the reasons for the deep and sustained interest in the sub-region.

Southern Africa is incredibly rich in mineral resources that are of strategic, military and industrial interest. It is a significant producer of coal, gold, diamonds (gem and industrial), uranium, chrome, platinum, vanadium, vermiculite and oil, to name only the significant ones. South Africa and Zimbabwe together have about ninety-five percent of the world's resources of chromium; South Africa is one of the leading producers of gold and diamonds. Zambia is the world's fifth largest producer of copper; while Zambia and Zaire contain two-thirds of the world's resources of cobalt. Zimbabwe is rich in forty different minerals (including chromium, nickel, copper, coal, gold and asbestos) and Botswana is the world's third largest producer of diamonds. Added to these are very fertile land, water resources, good climate and contrived cheap labor. These were the conditions that dictated Dutch or Boer settlement of the area in the seventeenth century; these were the conditions that inspired the great British colonialist, Cecil Rhodes, to dream of ceding the Cape to Cairo to Anglo-Saxon colonial subjugation; and these were the conditions that have prompted the modern government of South Africa to devise the intricate and controversial system called *apartheid* based on the racial domination of whites.

The Boer mentality of racial superiority or exclusivity could not be effectively overcome when the Union of South Africa was established in 1910 under the South Africa Act (1909). In the Constitution that was agreed upon at the National Convention at Durban, Natal in 1908 and attended by only white delegates, racial discrimination as a basis of government was enshrined. It finally became a fact in 1948. A historical imperative of the South African situation therefore, is that *apartheid* is not just a basis for the organization of society. It is also, and more importantly, *a way of thinking, a way of life.*

The myth in South African history is that the Dutch settlers claim to be the first to have settled in the country and therefore are as entitled to it as any black African. This is of course far from the truth since history and archeology prove that indigenous tribes lived, undertook crop farming and raised cattle in the area thousands of years before the advent of the European. It is, therefore, only natural that settler efforts to dispossess the indigenous people of the area of their land and other assets and the imposition of racist laws and policies on them should be resisted from the beginning until now. In the other colonies of Mozambique, the

Rhodesias, South West Africa, the former high commission Territories, and Angola this conjoined in the last fifty years with the fight against colonialism, while in South Africa, opposition has steadily coalesced into the anti-apartheid struggle as we know it today. The violent clashes, the geo-political interest and intrigue of outside powers in the conflict and the racist Pretoria regime's assisted acquisition of nuclear capability are all elements in the threat to international peace and security in the sub-region.

The subject of my talk today, "International Co-operation toward Political Change in Southern Africa," is reassuring because it indicated that there is a need for a political change there, in the general interest of Southern Africa and the world. I shall therefore not waste time in arguing the case for change but will proceed to give you some information on what the international community, as represented by the United Nations, is doing to bring about that much needed change.

The historical and economic imperatives have determined, in diverse ways, the attitudes of Member States of the United Nations towards the apartheid policies of the Government of South Africa in the region. These attitudes can be classified in the context of the following fundamental principles of the United Nations:

   i)   the principles of equal rights and self-determination (Art. 1 para. 2 and Art. 73b);
   ii) the principle of non-interference in the domestic (internal) affairs of Member States (Art. 2 para. 7);
   iii) the principle of respect for human rights and fundamental freedoms (Art. 55 and 56).

EQUAL RIGHTS AND SELF-DETERMINATION

These principles have all been seriously undermined in Southern Africa by the introduction and maintenance of the policies of *apartheid* and other destabilization policies flowing therefrom.

Under Art. 1(2) of the United Nations Charter, relations among nations are based on the principles of sovereign and equal rights, and the self-determination of peoples. Art 73(b) requires Member States of the United Nations which are administering territories to develop self-government, based on the political aspirations of all peoples and the particular circumstances of the territory. For Africans who have been excluded from the government of their own country, the South African situation was a classic colonial case which fell under these Articles. At the level of the Organization of African Unity (OAU), the issue was conclusively resolved when the organization adopted the Lusaka Manifesto which determined that South Africa is an independent state since there was no external administering power and that the struggle was for the eradication of apartheid.

When all the sovereign and independent countries of the sub-region attained freedom from colonial domination, their example and friendship with the National Liberation Movements of South Africa, notably the African National Congress and the Pan Africanist Congress of Azania, attracted the wrath of the racist Pretoria regime which has since then pursued a policy of military aggression and destabilization against them, thereby endangering international peace and security in addition to undermining fundamental principles of the Charter.

NON-INTERFERENCE

South Africa's massive interference in the internal affairs of its neighbors is typified by its activities in Angola and Mozambique. The support that it gives to terrorist groups to spread death and destruction as a means of inducing change in the policies of its neighbors constitutes interference in their internal affairs.

HUMAN RIGHTS

Among the countries of Western Europe, Austria, Canada, Denmark, Ireland, Israel, Norway and the United States have considered the South African issue in the context of Art. 55 and 56, which enjoins member states to promote, *inter alia*, universal respect for and observance of human rights and fundamental freedoms for all without distinction as to race, sex, language or religion. By Art. 56, member states pledged themselves to take joint and separate action in cooperation with the United Nations to achieve this objective. The continued reluctance of the Pretoria regime to enfranchise the black majority or to permit people to live and work wherever they pleased is without doubt, therefore, the denial of their fundamental human rights.

ACTION

Under the guise of the seeming contradictions in the Charter, the United Nations found it difficult from 1952 to 1958 to agree on a particular form of action it should take to end race conflict in South Africa. The colonial powers and others persisted in their view that any action by the organization would constitute a violation of Art. 2 para. 7 on domestic jurisdiction. Even countries like the United States which saw the need for the Assembly to discuss the issue doubted the propriety and effectiveness

of the Assembly taking any action on the issue. Several countries, including those in Africa and Eastern Europe and Ceylon, Costa Rica, and
Yugoslavia, argued that it was the duty of the General Assembly to re-
mind the Union Government of its pledge under Art. 56 and the principles
at stake in the implementation of apartheid. Within this period, United
Nations efforts were limited to the adoption of Resolutions in favor of
equality, freedom and justice, calling upon the Government of the Union
of South Africa to reconsider its position and revise its policies in the
light of its Charter obligations and inviting the Government to cooperate
in a "constructive approach" to the question.

The efforts of the United Nations entered a new phase in 1958 and
lasted until 1961. Within this period the Assembly agreed on the inscrip-
tion of the item, over the objection of the Union of South Africa, and
adopted Resolutions, by voting, to deplore the failure of the South
African Government to comply with its repeated requests and demands,
strongly deprecating the continued and total disregard by the South African
Government of its Charter obligations, condemning policies based on racial superiority and urging all States to *take such separate and collective
action as is open to them in conformity with the Charter*. A significant
observation of this period was that the United States, Canada and New
Zealand which had previously questioned the propriety and desirability of
adopting new resolutions on the matter were willing to consider with favor, resolutions on racial situation in South Africa. In fact, the United
States voted in favor of all resolutions within this period.

It is also significant to note that it was during this period, to be precise on March 25, 1960, that the Security Council first considered the
issue of race conflict in South Africa following the large-scale killings at
Sharpeville of unarmed and peaceful demonstrators against racial discrimination and segregation in the Union of South Africa on March 21, 1960.
By its Resolution S/134 of April 1, 1960, the Security Council, *inter
alia*, recognized that the situation in the Union was one that had led to
international friction and, if continued, might endanger international peace
and security.

AFRICAN PRESSURE

With the emergence of a number of colonies in Africa into independence in 1960, the pressure on the United Nations to take specific action
increased. At the sixteenth Session of the General Assembly in 1961, a
group of twenty-five African Member States in concert with Iraq, Cuba,
Indonesia, Saudi Arabia and Syria made a serious effort to have the
Assembly adopt a resolution which, among others, would have led to the
expulsion of South Africa from the United Nations and the application of
sanctions against South Africa. The resolution was adopted by the

Special Political Committee by fifty-five votes to twenty-six, with twenty abstentions. It, however, failed to pass the Plenary when votes were taken on the three operative paragraphs relating to the expulsion, sanctions and drawing the attention of the Security Council to the recommendations in accordance with Art. II, para. 2 of the Charter.

The seventeenth Session in 1962 marked a watershed in the efforts of the United Nations to induce the Government of South Africa to abandon apartheid. Thirty-four Member States comprising twenty-seven African countries and India, Indonesia, Iraq, Mongolia, Pakistan, Saudi Arabia and Syria successfully piloted through the Special Committee and the Plenary, a resolution [1761(XVIII)] that requested member states to apply limited sanctions including breaking off diplomatic relations with the Government of South Africa boycotting South African goods. The Resolution also established the Special Committee Against Apartheid to (a) keep the racial policies of the Government of South Africa under review when the Assembly is not in session and (b) to report either to the Assembly or to the Security Council or both, as appropriate, from time to time. The Security Council was also requested to take appropriate measures, including sanctions, to secure South Africa's compliance with the resolutions of the General Assembly.

From 1962 to date, discussions at the U.N. have centered around the action that could be taken to induce South Africa to abandon apartheid. It is now universally accepted that apartheid is evil and should be eliminated. If the regime attempts to perpetuate apartheid through repression, armed struggle would be the only optional reaction. However, if it chooses to remove apartheid through reforms, dialogue would be the logical process.

The experience of the United Nations would seem to suggest that armed struggle would be the most effective means to secure political change. However, it is obvious from the historical and economic imperatives I have set out that it is not a means that could now enjoy consensus support within the organization. Peaceful means therefore is the option that imposes itself. Among the armory of peaceful means could be identified dialogue and pressure. Dialogue, which ruled as a policy in late 1960s and early 1970s, expressed its failure in the activities of the so-called Contact Group of Western states, Canada, Federal Republic of Germany, France, the United Kingdom and United States, over Namibia. Similarly, constructive engagement, heir to dialogue, has also failed. It took a humiliating defeat on the battlefield recently, at the hands of Angolan and Cuban forces whose objective was to force racist South Africa to negotiate -- to agree on an arrangement under which Namibia would hopefully achieve independence in 1990.

Dialogue and, for that matter, constructive engagement, have failed because the Afrikaners have refused to voluntarily alter their stand on white racial superiority. At the 1961 session of the Assembly, the Foreign Minister explained apartheid as an abbreviated form of "aparte untwikkeling" -- a separate development, a traditional policy of South Africa designed to equally serve the interest of the whites and the Bantus. The Policy was also to safeguard what had been built over the centuries by the whites and, at the same time, to take into account the political aspirations, traditions, culture and material needs of the Bantus. These sentiments were adjudged such an insult to every African and to every man of intelligence that the Assembly passed a Motion of Censure on 11th October, 1961 against the regime. In 1962 the Foreign Minister again defended apartheid as the "elemental human urge to survive." In 1964 the racist regime took advantage of the international situation that was dominated by the Cuban missile crisis to justify apartheid as a bulwalk against communism in Africa.

Nowhere has the racist regime publicly declared its intention to abandon apartheid. Pronouncements have been limited to reforms. However, as Francis Wilson and Mamphele Ramphele have noted in their recent book *Uprooting Poverty: The South African Challenge:*

Renewal of South African Society is not possible without the defeat of the racist ideology which sustains the ruling elite...It [apartheid] is a way of thinking about human beings and their social relationship which, like Nazism, has to be rooted out of both individual and collective consciousness so that society can grow along entirely different lines.

The half-hearted attempt made in November 1983 at reform ended at the grant of limited political rights to the "coloured" and the Asian minorities. The tri-cameral parliament assures the perpetuity of the traditional policy of separate development since it has separate chambers for Whites, Coloured and Asians. Each House has power to legislate for its own affairs, including housing, social welfare, education and local government. Little wonder therefore, that the black majority contemptuously rejected these so-called reforms and have insisted on their enfranchisement in a democratic, non-racial and equal South Africa.

The history of South Africa speaks persuasively for pressure as the most effective means to force South Africa to review its way of thinking. Military defeat forced them to review their continued occupation in Namibia. The combined effect of the Security Council arms embargo and the voluntary oil embargo and the sanctions recommended by the Security Council has finally prompted the recognition of the injustice of apartheid in South Africa. It is a matter of record that the twelve months following the decision of the banks in 1985 to call in their loans were a period of negative economic growth for South Africa and the most significant political reforms made in South Africa, which in turn could be said to have represented a review of thinking. These reforms included the abolition of the pass laws, the recognition of Trade Unions and the granting of property rights to the black majority.

It should be obvious from my submission that the route to peace in Southern Africa lies in the maximization of pressure on the regime to abandon apartheid. That pressure should take the form of effectively isolating the regime from the world. Hence the need for comprehensive and mandatory sanctions -- comprehensive in range and mandatory in extent of applicability. Sanctions alone will not defeat apartheid. The defeat of apartheid will of course be achieved through the strength of the opposition of democratic forces inside the country but international pressure, especially sanctions, will help those forces eradicate apartheid in a shorter period of time.

As far as the sub-region as a whole is concerned, the actions of the United Nations, representing the international community, must be supplemented and buttressed by measures of individual governments and nongovernmental bodies, if peace and stability are to be achieved. Collaboration by many countries with South Africa ought to be reviewed with a view to curbing their desire and capacity of the racist regime to forment conflict in the area. Decrease in assistance to the guerilla bandits in Mozambique and Angola as well as ensuring that current plans for Namibia to become independent are not scuttled by South Africa, will all go a long way in restoring conditions to normalcy. Moral and material assistance to the oppressed to set up a free, democratic and non-racial society in South Africa and to create a peaceful and viable sub-region should also be the objective of all.

7

The Front Line States, Regional Interstate Relations, and Institution Building in Southern Africa

Gilbert M. Khadiagala

For the weak, survival is success.
--Julius K. Nyerere

INTRODUCTION

Since the 1970s, regional cooperation among the Front Line States (FLS) -- Angola, Botswana, Mozambique, Tanzania, Zambia, and Zimbabwe -- has reflected the structural changes produced by the decolonization process in southern Africa. Beginning with the independence of Angola and Mozambique in the mid-1970s, and Zimbabwe in 1980, these changes led to a search for closer political interaction. By the early 1980s, this interaction formed the basis for a larger economic arrangement, the Southern African Coordination Conference (SADCC) embracing all independent states in the region.

Underlying this process of regional aggregation has been the need to manage the asymmetries in power relationships between them and South Africa. Exercised historically through an elaborate set of interlocking economic relations, South Africa's dominance in the 1980s assumed an aggressive posture through political and military intervention within the region. Reflecting both the internal and external pressures on its domestic apartheid policies, South Africa's regional intervention became the primary source of instability in the region. Apart from the deleterious impact on the stability of regimes, destabilization also cast doubt on the ability of South Africa's neighbors to sustain the momentum for regional cooperation. The contest between an emerging Front Line security system and a receding South African-dominated system -- constituting the dynamic interplay of conflict and cooperation in southern Africa -- serves as the background for analysis of peace and security in the 1980s and projections for the future.

This chapter suggests that regional collaboration and the concomitant process of institution building by the FLS and SADCC are partial mechanisms for problem-solving and self-maintenance. Providing these states with an organizational framework for meeting some of their politico-security and economic needs, these mechanisms are, more significantly, avenues for alternative external access to the region. Constrained both by limited domestic means and the multiple dependencies on South Africa, regional institutions facilitate external multilateral and bilateral intervention to strengthen their economic capacity and contain the conflicts stemming from South Africa's intervention. Further, I argue that since South Africa's dominance continues to inhibit the ability of the FLS and SADCC to build self-sufficient institutions for coping with the demands of decolonization and statehood, their medium-term effectiveness will depend on the willingness of external actors to support them, and, in the long-term, on the transition to a post-apartheid South Africa.

I begin with an analysis of the individual and collective efforts by the FLS and SADCC to meet the challenges posed by South Africa's regional policy in the 1980s. While appraised primarily from the prism of southern Africa's most vulnerable states, Angola and Mozambique, these efforts are discussed in the larger context of the limits and possibilities of regional states in meeting their objectives. Here I also discuss the critical role of external actors in contributing to the transformation of regional interstate relations. Finally, with an eye to the recent changes in regional relations, I lay out scenarios possible in the 1990s and beyond.

REGIONAL INTERSTATE RELATIONS IN THE 1980s: PRESSURE FROM PRETORIA

Throughout the 1980s, three major goals dominated the FLS' perceptions of security: regime stability; black majority rule; and creation of regional economic institutions to reduce their dependence on South Africa. The salience of apartheid South Africa at the regional level compelled them to be conscious of the interrelated nature of these goals; thus, while they differed in their level of commitment to black majority, there emerged a realization that, for most of them, regime survival and economic cooperation hinge on movement toward majority rule in Namibia and South Africa.

Despite the optimism that greeted Zimbabwe's independence in 1980, the regional setting in which the FLS operated imposed severe limits on their ability to meet effectively all these goals. At the heart of these limits was South Africa's projection of its military and economic power through the adoption of a "total national strategy" designed to thwart what Pretoria considered to be a "total onslaught" from neighboring countries. This tendency toward regional intervention, Kenneth Grundy and Philip Frankel have argued, corresponded to the increasing militarization of South African society and the use of the Defense Force as an instrument in its regional relations.[1] Apart from the practice of blunting the domestic and internal pressure on the white regime, this strategy found ideological rationalization in the need to fight the purported encroachment of communism in southern Africa. A 1982 government *White Paper on Defense and Armaments Supply* explicitly stated:

The ultimate aim of the Soviet Union and its allies is to overthrow the present body politic in the RSA and to replace it with a Marxist-oriented form of government to further the objectives of the U.S.S.R., therefore all possible methods and means are used to attain this objective...This onslaught is supported by a worldwide propaganda campaign and the involvement of various front organization and leaders.[2]

In addition to South Africa's strategy, the policy options of the FLS were constrained by what they saw as a realignment of Western interests -- primarily those of the United States -- and South Africa with respect to peace and security in the region. In most of the 1970s, the United States and her allies had been at the forefront of exerting pressure on Pretoria to change its domestic system and facilitate the decolonization of Namibia and Zimbabwe. At the start of the 1980s, the Reagan Administration's sympathy and compatibility with South Africa in the global campaign against communism invariably strengthened the latter's regional agenda.[3]

The experience of Angola and Mozambique mirrors the broader problems the FLS faced in dealing with South Africa's destabilization. While their independence set in motion the transformation of regional relations culminating in the geopolitical sphere that became the basis for the FLS alliance, Angola and Mozambique emerged in the 1980s as the weakest links in this alliance. From the inception of the FLS alliance in the mid-1970s, independent states expected that these two states would constitute the cornerstones of what Tanzania's Julius Nyerere called a sphere of "economically independent countries stretching from the Indian Ocean to the Atlantic, that would be a really powerful challenge and deterrent to South Africa."[4] As the targets of South Africa's sustained destabilization policies, Angola and Mozambique became the sick men of southern Africa.

Compared with other FLS members, Angola and Mozambique have the advantage of not being landlocked. They, however, inherited fragmented political systems that attracted external intervention and complicated the process of national consolidation.[5] In Angola, the civil war between the Popular Movement for the Liberation of Angola (MPLA) supported by Cuban troops and Eastern bloc advisers and the Union for the Total Independence of Angola (UNITA) supported by South Africa, and later the United States, remained a source of instability in the region. Far from destroying UNITA's insurgency in the immediate post-independence period, the MPLA government in Luanda faced the difficult task of consolidating its hold over most of southern Angola.[6] In Mozambique, while the Front for the Liberation of Mozambique (FRELIMO) government had a smooth transition to independence, in the late 1970s a rebel movement, the Mozambique National Resistance Movement (RENAMO)

grew under the patronage of Rhodesia's security forces, and was adopted by
the South Africans in the early 1980s.[7]

More than other members of the, Angola and Mozambique bore a dis-
proportionate portion of the burdens of decolonization in southern Africa.
Angola permitted the South West African Peoples' Organization
(SWAPO) and the African National Congress (ANC) to establish training
camps and supply routes. Its geographic proximity to Namibia facilitated
SWAPO's incursions into the territory. In the struggle for Zimbabwe,
Mozambique opened its 750-mile frontier with Rhodesia to the most significant nationalist movement, Zimbabwe African National Union
(ZANU), inviting it to establish military bases, and resettled more than
150,000 Zimbabweans in refugee camps. Economically, Mozambique
supported the United Nations sanctions against the Rhodesian government
by closing its borders with Rhodesia, an action that cost it more than
$500 million in rail and transit fees.[8] With Zimbabwe's independence,
the FRELIMO government gave the ANC access for infiltration into the
Transvaal and other areas adjacent to Mozambique.

Buttressed by their socialist orientation and post-independent alliances
with Soviet-bloc countries, Angola and Mozambique's consistent support
for the ANC and SWAPO exposed them to South Africa's regional strategy. According to Thomas Callaghy, Pretoria developed a distinctly bleak
view of these states as "puppet socialist states, propped up by the Soviet
block" whose aim was to "support, train, and harbor 'terrorist organizations' that sought to question the South African government."[9] In light
of this perceived threat, a critical facet of South African regional strategy
was to ensure that:

neighboring states are not used as springboards for guerrilla or terrorist attacks on
South Africa. South Africa clearly not only wants to give undertaking to this effect but
also wants them to implement it effectively, thus ensuring that unauthorized incursions
do not take place. Furthermore, South Africa would wish that black states in the region
(not merely neighboring countries) would not provide training facilities for anti-South
African liberation movements and, ideally, would not allow the movements to establish
offices in their countries.[10]

In implementing this strategy, the South African Defense Force
(SADF) launched a series of well-orchestrated military invasions into
southern Angola in the early 1980s. Ostensibly meant to eliminate
SWAPO's military activities, the intensity of these attacks became inexorably linked with the broader campaign to dislodge the MPLA government from power and destroy Angola's economic infrastructure. In alliance
with Jonas Savimbi's UNITA forces, SADF's virtual occupation of
Angola succeeded in preventing the economic reconstruction of Angola.[11]
Explaining the parameters of this strategy, South Africa's Defense Minister, Magnus Malan, said in October 1982:

South West Africa's war is your war. If you withdraw from South-West Africa, then you are busy extending the front, bringing it 1,500 kilometers closer to the Republic of South Africa. You will shift the operational area from the Cunene in south Angola, where the struggle is actually taking place, to the Orange River, to the Northern Cape. If South-West Africa is communist, I see Botswana going in the same direction because it will be subject to pressure. And Zimbabwe will have no hesitation in becoming totally Marxist. Then there is Mozambique, which is already Communist. Then you will have the red belt pulled tight on our borders.[12]

By the end of 1983 the Angolan government estimated the costs of South African destabilization at over $10 billion; over half of its budget was devoted to defense-related expenditures.[13]

Pretoria's two-pronged onslaught in Angola coincided with the impasse in the efforts to reach a Namibian settlement. In the mid-1970s, the Western powers, under the rubric of the Contact Group, had negotiated a settlement plan, United Nations Resolution 435, under which South Africa would withdraw from the territory. While South Africa had long claimed to have accepted this plan, since 1978 its strategy had been to delay the implementation process as it sought to build an internal alternative to SWAPO. International pressure on South Africa was reduced by the Reagan Administration's insistence that Namibia's independence be linked to the withdrawal of Cuban troops from Angola. This linkage afforded South Africa the opportunity of pulling together another possible alternative to SWAPO after the collapse of the Democratic Turnhalle Alliance (DTA) administration in January 1983.[14]

Faced with the pressure of occupation, the Angolan government began exploring the possibilities for a peace agreement with South Africa using American and Zambian mediation. In February 1984, South Africa and Angola reached the Lusaka Agreement; in return for South Africa's withdrawal from southern Angola and the implementation of the UN independence plan, Angola agreed to limit SWAPO infiltration from its sanctuary bases in southern Angola.[15] As part of the agreement, a joint military commission was established to monitor the ceasefire. Although the ceasefire agreement and the partial withdrawal of SADF units in April 1985 considerably lessened the external military pressure on Angola, the war against UNITA continued. By August 1984, Savimbi's forces had extended their activities beyond their stronghold in southeastern Angola and had succeeded in infiltrating saboteurs into Luanda.[16] To stem the tide of UNITA's offensive, the Angolan army mounted a major operation against UNITA's strongholds in August-September 1985. Although they overran and recaptured the Cazombo salient that projects into Zambia and inflicted heavy casualties on UNITA, the Angolan forces failed to capture UNITA's strongholds of Mavinga and Jamba. SADF's re-entry into the war saved Savimbi from annihilation.[17] On 20 September 1985 Malan appealed for Western intervention to bolster SADF-UNITA offensive: "If these [MPLA] forces should wipe out Savimbi, then South Africa will be able to say that she did her best to sustain this anti-Marxist force. The West will have to accept that it did not do its duty and that, as a result, a potent anticommunist force has been lost to us and the West."[18]

After the appeal, the Reagan Administration, following closely on the Congressional repeal of the 1976 Clark Amendment which had prohibited military assistance to Angolan opposition groups, began supplying $15 million per year in covert military aid to Savimbi.[19] Coming on the heels of South Africa's failure to honor the Lusaka agreement, Angolan officials in early 1986 accused Washington of entering into a strategic alliance with South Africa.[20] To counter this alliance, the Luanda government became increasingly dependent on Soviet and Cuban support, the consequences of which I will address shortly.

In a similar concerted campaign of destabilization in the early 1980s, South Africa targeted the vulnerable Mozambique regime. Afraid of the growing strength of the ANC and its ability to attack strategic points in South Africa, Pretoria embarked on a campaign to compel Mozambique to oust the ANC. South African retaliation took two forms. First, it carried out commando raids on ANC headquarters in Maputo in 1981-83. Second, it strengthened the military capacity of RENAMO to sabotage economic targets in Mozambique. In addition to this pressure, Mozambique's economy was ravaged by drought which killed an estimated 100,000 people and left another four million threatened by starvation in 1983. Further, in January 1984, cyclones destroyed agricultural projects, swept bridges away, and inundated whole villages. In February 1984, Mozambique estimated the costs of Pretoria's policy at $2.6 billion.[21] As the destabilization campaign took its toll, Mozambican leaders admitted that they had inadequate military capacity to counteract South Africa's aggression, and that the Soviet-bloc countries were unable to provide military assistance to blunt the escalating attacks.[22]

Against this background, Samora Machel embarked on a European tour of the Britain, France, the Netherlands, and Portugal to improve relations with the West in October 1983. Although promising increased economic aid and extended trade, the West counseled Machel to seek an accommodation with South Africa to reduce tensions in the region.[23] For the United States, the Deputy Assistant Secretary of State for African affairs, Frank Wisner, noted in January 1984:

In Mozambique we have opened a dialogue with the government of President Samora Machel on the problems of the region in general and the neuralgic relationship between Pretoria and Maputo. In that regard we have urged both sides to discuss their problems in a realistic manner.[24]

Prodded by Western support, Mozambique signed an agreement with South Africa, the Nkomati Accord, in March 1984. Under the terms of the agreement, each party promised not to allow its territory to be used for acts of war, aggression, or violence against the other; a Joint Security Commission was set up to monitor the agreement.[25]

Machel's description of the Nkomati Accord as a "victory for African diplomacy...a triumph over the forces of violence and militarism" initially caused consternation among the FLS.[26] With the exception of Angola, all the FLS saw Nkomati as a setback to the liberation struggle. Nyerere was blunt in his criticism: "There is nothing to be gained by pretending that a defeat was in fact victory."[27] But although critical of Machel's claims for Nkomati, they all appreciated Mozambique's difficult situation and hoped that South Africa would honor the agreement. Acknowledging that Machel had to bend over backwards to obtain an agreement that would end Mozambique's insecurity, Zimbabwe's Prime Minister, Robert Mugabe, suggested that independent states in the region "were too weak to provide the ANC with the external bases it needed."[28]

From the outset, Mozambique vigorously implemented its side of the bargain by expelling the ANC from its territory. Pretoria, however, violated the spirit and substance of the Accord; shortly before the signing of the agreement, SADF provided RENAMO with sufficient arms to continue its offensive. Far from withering away, RENAMO made even harder attacks on critical economic targets and brought the war to Maputo. By August 1984, RENAMO had launched an offensive in the northern province of Cabo Delgado, a region that had once been FRELIMO's backbone during the liberation war.[29] In the face of Mozambique's accusations and threats to abrogate Nkomati, South Africa arranged a series of peace talks between RENAMO and FRELIMO leading to the Pretoria Declaration of October 1984. Under the terms of this agreement, both parties agreed to a ceasefire and asked South Africa to police it.[30] Conflicting interpretations of this agreement, however, doomed South African attempts to arrange a ceasefire. Of critical significance was that from Pretoria's perspective, this agreement legitimized RENAMO's political position.[31]

Subsequent to Nkomati and the public disclosure of an earlier agreement with Swaziland, South Africa attempted to interest Botswana, Lesotho, Zambia, and Zimbabwe in non-aggression pacts. Except for the overthrow of the Lesotho government in January 1986 through a virtual economic blockade, SADF's military raids on the ANC in Gaborone, Harare, and Lusaka did not translate into new nonaggression pacts.[32] But while eschewing formal security pacts, Botswana and Zimbabwe made it clear that they would not be used as a base for attacking South Africa.[33] Furthermore, to deter South African aggression, the FLS sought to mobilize international support; in this respect, after SADF's raid on Gaborone in June 1985, Botswana took her case to the UN Security Council; the United States, in a show of support, recalled its ambassador from Pretoria.[34]

Pretoria's efforts to use the Nkomati Accord as the key to reducing its international isolation was shattered by the domestic opposition that followed. Although the government had succeeded in convincing Western governments that domestic reforms would be accompanied by regional peace, the outbreak of violence in the black townships of the Vaal Triangle in September 1984 altered this image. The next fifteen months witnessed an unprecedented degree of black opposition, making black townships ungovernable. The decision to declare a state of emergency, first in July 1985 and then in June 1986 contributed to a worldwide campaign for divestment and economic sanctions against Pretoria. More important, despite repeated attacks on the ANC in neighboring countries, the ANC was able to establish itself as a legitimate actor in South African politics.[35]

South Africa's failure to comply with the terms of the Accord galvanized regional efforts by the FLS to provide security assistance to Mozambique. At a FLS summit in Lusaka in March 1985, called because of the deteriorating security in Mozambique, the six heads of state resolved to give all necessary support to Mozambique. In May 1985, Nyerere said his country would not hesitate to provide a rear base in a new war to liberate Mozambique if South Africa toppled the Machel government. A joint multilateral security arrangement building on the 1980 Zimbabwe-Mozambique security agreement was agreed upon at a meeting between Nyerere, Mugabe, and Machel in June 1985.[36] To the FLS, the defense of Mozambique represented not only the sustaining of the FRELIMO regime, but was also inextricably linked to economic liberation of the FLS from South Africa through SADCC.

TOWARD ECONOMIC LIBERATION: THE SOUTHERN AFRICAN COORDINATION CONFERENCE

The creation of SADCC was a direct attempt to counter the economic pressure of South Africa's Total Strategy: the Constellation of Southern African States (CONSAS). South Africa's Foreign Minister, Roelef F. Botha, first raised the idea of CONSAS in March 1979, and P.W. Botha formally announced it that November.[37] From the time of its adoption, the promotion of CONSAS was seen by Pretoria as an effort to expand its economic links with independent states in southern Africa. As P.W. Botha noted:

We, and the other countries of southern Africa are confronted by the challenge and the opportunity to consolidate, in an evolutionary way, the undeniable economic interdependence between us to each other's mutual advantage and towards a logical economic grouping.[38]

Apart from independent states, CONSAS was to include South Africa's homelands. Tied to South Africa's domestic politics, this idea was supposed to achieve two aims. First, it would create the institutions to regulate relations between southern African states at Pretoria's behest. Second, by including the homelands in an association with independent African states, it would provide the means of finally assuring them a measure of international recognition.[39]

Since one of the major pillars of CONSAS was to be an independent Zimbabwe under a favorably disposed government, the rise of Mugabe dealt a blow to South Africa's regional policy.   Encouraged by Zimbabwe's newly gained independence and their enhanced stature in southern Africa, the FLS decided in July 1979 to take measures that would reduce their economic dependence on South Africa. Lesotho, Malawi, Swaziland, and Zimbabwe joined in these efforts. At a formal launching of SADCC in Lusaka in April 1980, the leaders approved the Lusaka Declaration, which defined the objectives of SADCC as follows:

a. the reduction of economic dependence, particularly, but not only, on the Republic of South Africa.
b. the forging of links to create a genuine and equitable regional integration;
c. the mobilization of national, interstate, and regional policies;
d. concerted action to secure international cooperation within the framework of the strategy for economic liberation.[40]

Embracing the goals of SADCC, the Lusaka Declaration became a symbol of the determination of African states to create independent regional institutions that would mitigate the effects of increasing contacts with South Africa.[41] Specifically, they saw SADCC as both a short- and long-term vehicle for fostering development. To Nyerere:

Our purposes are not simply greater independence from South Africa. If South Africa's apartheid rule ended tomorrow, there would still be need for the states of southern Africa to cooperate, to coordinate their transport systems, to fight food and mouth disease together, to rationalize industrial development.[42]

As an instrument of managing the asymmetries in power relations within southern Africa, SADCC represents the continuous efforts by African states to widen the parameters of their economic independence and political leverage by revising pre-existing structural relations. From the outset, these efforts were dependent not only on how each member pursued their goals collectively, but also on their ability to generate external support in meeting these goals.

In their attempts to meet the interrelated goals of economic development and disengagement from South Africa, the founders of SADCC sought to avoid the shortcomings of prior regional integration schemes in Africa, particularly the defunct East African Community (ECA). Since these experiments faltered because of a lack of political will, overambitious development programs, and inequities in the distribution of benefits, SADCC deliberately established a limited and flexible regional organization. Hence two features of SADCC's *modus operandi* are distinctive: the emphasis on sectoral coordination and the primacy conceded to national decision making.[43]

Eschewing the grandiose schemes of integrating diverse national economies under a supranational economic entity, SADCC founders opted for a step-by-step approach to specific projects.[44] They devised a regional division of labor in which each one was responsible for coordinating a specific sector. The purpose of this voluntarist approach to regional harmonization was to minimize potential conflict among members with differing political, ideological, and economic systems. In the words of SADCC's Executive Secretary Simba Makoni:

This mode of operation guarantees us a direct involvement by our governments and their functionaries in the activities of the organization. It places primary responsibility and accountability for the organizations's policies, programmes and projects on the member Government rather than on a distant, faceless and impersonal bureaucracy. Such a decentralized system demands of its members maximum political commitment to the ideals and objectives being pursued, as well as maximum confidence and trust in each other. These two attributes ... are the hallmarks of SADCC: the explanation and vindication of how Marxist Mozambique and capitalist Malawi or Republican Tanzania and Traditional Monarchist Swaziland can work so well and effectively together.[45]

At a meeting in Blantyre, Malawi, in 1981, SADCC assigned each state its own sector for coordination: Angola is responsible for energy; Botswana, crop research and animal control; Lesotho, soil conversation and land utilization; Malawi, fisheries, wildlife and forests; Mozambique, transport and communications; Swaziland, manpower; Tanzania, industrial development; Zambia, development funding and mining; and Zimbabwe, food security and security printing. This division of labor underlined the importance of a loose structure for coordination and intraregional development, while at the same time, eliminating the fear of smaller non-FLS states of domination by the FLS. Rather than fostering inequalities, regional specialization had the potential of creating new constructive forms of interdependence among SADCC members.[46] According to the late President of Botswana, Seretse Khama:

Among equals there is a very real role for specialization and division of labor. None need to be exploited by it. All may benefit from it. No independent southern African state is large enough to pursue economic autarky. Among genuine partners acting in agreed coordination, there is nothing wrong with mutual interdependence. It is the one-sided dependence of the weak upon the strong which destroys self-reliance, corrodes initiative and distorts development.[47]

Studies on regional cooperation among developing countries have emphasized the necessity of reducing areas of contention to sustain momentum for coordination in limited areas.[48] Constantine Vaitsos has, for instance, contended that "economic integration should not -- at least in the foreseeable future -- contemplate all-embracing schemes. Instead, it needs to concentrate sectorally or inter-sectorally on the functional fulfillment of specific goals and tasks."[49] Specifically, emphasis should be placed on those policies and projects which have significant and measurable results so as to induce domestic forces to support the process of regional cooperation. Reginald Green, an economic advisor to SADCC, has argued that in light of the dismal failure of the common market approach to developing country economic integration, the novelty of SADCC lies in the ability of its members to identify common interests as the basis for cooperation.[50] Furthermore, SADCC states perceive the structural weakness and fragmentation of their political economies as constraints as well as opportunities. To Green:

The weakness of national economies does make resources hard to provide for new initiatives, but it also underlines the need to reshape economic development strategy in ways which require common or coordinated action, e.g., industrialization, food security and transport improvement.[51]

In choosing a decentralized and limited regional organization which reflects the economic and political diversity among the nine states, SADCC's approach more critically took into account the asymmetry of economic power between them and South Africa. Recognition of the structures of dependence, especially the differences in the levels of dependence on South Africa among the SADCC states, was the most compelling factor in their choice of a selective disengagement strategy.[52]

The SADCC states have a total GDP of $23 billion, an area of over four million square kilometers and a population of about seventy-two million. In contrast, South Africa with a population of thirty-two million has a GDP of $56 billion, the highest per capita consumption of energy and two-thirds of the region's exports (roughly $18 billion of $25 billion in 1986).[53] Despite the wide differentials in per capita GNP within the SADCC region -- from Botswana's $840 to Malawi's $160 -- South Africa's per capita GNP at $1860 dwarfs that of all SADCC states.[54] Furthermore, given that a bulk of South Africa's income is controlled by the minority whites, only about five percent of the population of southern Africa controls at least half of the region's income.[55]

One of the central elements of South Africa's dominance relates to trade relations in the region. At the most extreme are Botswana, Lesotho, and Swaziland which, as members of the South African Custom Union (SACU) are firmly integrated into South Africa's trading orbit. Except for Angola and Tanzania, which have no economic relations with South

Africa, the rest of SADCC members obtain half of their total imports from South Africa. In 1984, Botswana, Lesotho, Swaziland, and Zambia ran trade deficits of over $100 million vis-a-vis South Africa. Although Zimbabwe had a trade balance with South Africa in the same year, the latter is its largest trading partner, and the largest single market for its manufactured exports.[56] This structure of trade relations greatly inhibits intra-SADCC trade: compared to total SADCC trade of $1.3 billion with South Africa, intra-SADCC was only $245 million in 1984.[57]

As in trade relations, the SADCC states depend on South African investment -- in mining, manufacturing, distribution, and tourism. In alliance with foreign capital, South African companies are involved in mining and manufacturing in Botswana, Lesotho, Malawi, Zambia, and Zimbabwe. Most foreign investment in the SADCC region is concentrated in Zimbabwe, which holds about one-third of the total capital stock of SADCC. Over half of Zimbabwe's capital is foreign-owned, with South African interests holding about twenty-five percent.[58] South Africans have also invested in physical infrastructure such as the Cahora Bassa and Ruacana hydro-electric schemes in Mozambique and Angola respectively.

The movement of labor from southern African states to South Africa is another important characteristic of the asymmetrical relationships. With the exception of Angola and Tanzania, South Africa recruited about 300,000 mine workers from SADCC states in 1984.[59] Although the number of foreign workers used as migrant laborers was reduced in the mid-1980s, non-South African workers made up over forty percent of the total mining work force. The estimated number of migrant workers from SADCC states in 1984 was as follows: Lesotho, 140,000; Mozambique, 60,000; Malawi, 30,000; Botswana 25,000; Swaziland, 20,000; and Zimbabwe, 7,000.[60] Lesotho's dependence on work in South Africa makes it the most vulnerable of SADCC states; Stephen Lewis Jr. has estimated that in 1984, worker remittances were 507 million Maloti (about $350 million), as compared to a GDP of M401 million; these remittances accounted for seventy percent of the cost, insurance, and freight value of Lesotho's imports.[61]

Of all the areas of SADCC's dependence on South Africa, transport and communications is the most significant. The extent of dependence on the South African Transport Services (SATS) is underscored by the fact that six of the nine states -- Botswana, Lesotho, Malawi, Swaziland, Zambia, and Zimbabwe -- are landlocked; only Tanzania, Angola, and Mozambique have usable port and harbor facilities. South Africa has seventy-five percent of the subcontinental rail network and the most efficient ports. Furthermore, although the transport system embracing SADCC states is sizeable by African standards, it has suffered deterioration since the 1970s as a result of economic mismanagement and sabotage by South African-supported rebels. In 1981, fifty percent of the regional overseas trade passed through South Africa; by 1985 this figure reached eighty-five percent.[62]

But while the problems confronting SADCC states with respect to dependence on SATS posed the most formidable challenge to regional cooperation, they not only became the rallying point for SADCC's strategy of limited disengagement, but also served as the basis for increased external support for SADCC's goals. Thus, from the outset, SADCC understood that economic cooperation depended on the creation of an efficient transport and communications system. To coordinate regional efforts in this sector, the founders of SADCC established the Southern African Transport and Communications Commission (SATCC) based in Maputo. SATCC's objectives are:

    a) to provide coordination in overcoming transport and communication problems in the region;

    b) to provide economic and efficient means of transport and communications;

    c) to achieve self-sufficiency in the maintenance of equipment and plants;

    d) to encourage the efficient utilization of available resources for the betterment of transport and communications.[63]

By focusing attention on transport and communication as the key to the economic liberation, SADCC sought two primary objectives: mobilization of external funds for the rehabilitation and upgrading of existing transport infrastructure; and providing security for these routes. The first goal entailed making SATCC a credible institutional conduit for multilateral access to the region. In addition, SATCC developed, beginning in 1980, an overall strategy and concept of transport corridors which integrate all transport systems connected with the five regional ports of Dar es Salaam in Tanzania, Lobito in Angola, and Beira, Maputo, and Nacala in Mozambique. The second required the military coordination of the FLS' defense policies for the support of Mozambique, the center of SADCC's transport networks.

Since the first meeting at Maputo between SADCC and donor countries as well as multilateral development agencies in November 1980 -- at which the latter pledged $650 million for projects in the transport sector -- SADCC has attracted considerable donor interest in its regional efforts.[64] By 1987, SADCC estimated that of the $3.7 billion cost of the 158 main projects in the transport program, $1.1 billion -- or thirty-seven percent -- had been fully secured. A further $278 million, or nine percent, was under negotiations.[65]

SADCC's initial success was improving Zambia's access to the Tazara railway. Constructed with Chinese aid amounting to $494 million in an interest-free loan, it opened in 1976 with a capacity of two million tons. The Tazara railway, however, encountered operational and management problems from the beginning; traffic declined from a peak of 1.3 million tons in 1977-78 to barely half that in 1982. At a SADCC-donor meeting in Lusaka in March 1983, the European Economic Community (EEC) provided $10.2 million for its rehabilitation.[66] In 1987, the annual capacity of the Tazara railway rose to 1.5 billion tons, enabling the export of seventy percent of Zambia's copper and cobalt and twenty percent of Zaire's copper.[67]

The development of alternative transport routes through the Mozambican ports of Beira, Maputo, and Nacala was regarded both by SADCC and external donors as critical to restoring and increasing self-sufficiency in transport and to create a viable regional network to facilitate trade expansion. At the center of these efforts was the rehabilitation of the 170-mile long Beira corridor, a vital road, rail, and oil pipeline from eastern Zimbabwe to Beira. As the shortest access port for Zimbabwe's trade, Beira also has the potential of serving Zambia and Malawi. In the mid-1960s, it handled 4.3 million tons a year; in 1985-86, its capacity averaged 1.3 million tons. The railway's capacity was 2,500 tons a day in 1986; SADCC's aim was to triple it to 8,000 tons a day over a three-year period at a cost of $500 million.[68] At the donors' conference in Brussels in October 1986, the EEC, the World Bank, and the African Development Bank (ADB), committed a bulk of the $185 million aid package for the initial phase of the program.[69]

To assist in rehabilitating the corridor, SADCC established the Beira Corridor Group (BCG), a consortium of private and public companies from Botswana, Malawi, Zambia, and Zimbabwe. Apart from improving the physical infrastructures, BCG explores the potential for investment along the corridor. By 1987, the BCG had organized 246 businesses to invest $147 million in the corridor over the next four years; the Zimbabweans had contributed over $5 million in investment.[70] Since its formation in 1985, the BCG has expanded its functions to other SADCC corridors with the aim of attracting local and foreign investment in the region.

The link between road, rail, and pipeline increased the importance of the Beira Corridor, making it the most visible front in the attempts by the FLS, especially Zimbabwe, to secure it against RENAMO sabotage. In July 1985 Zimbabwe deployed between ten thousand and fifteen thousand troops to Mozambique, and in joint operations in August 1985 captured the RENAMO headquarters at Gorongosa. After this operation, South African officials publicly admitted that the SADF had wilfully flouted the Nkomati Accord. At the time of the worst RENAMO activity in mid-1986, Mugabe increased his troops to about twelve thousand at an estimated cost of $500,000 per day.[71] Subsequent to Machel's death in October 1986, Mugabe pledged to fight to the last man, at any cost, to prevent RENAMO's takeover of Maputo.[72]

With the marked improvement of the security situation on the Beira Corridor, Zimbabwe agreed to increase its military assistance to help stabilize the 300-mile Limpopo Corridor.[73] Running through Maputo, the Limpopo route serves Zimbabwe, Zambia, Swaziland, Zaire, and South Africa. Since the Beira and Nacala cannot carry more than half the region's bulky traffic, the Limpopo railway is an essential part of the strategy for transport independence.[74] Due to the importance attached to this corridor, Zimbabwe began part of the rehabilitation using its own resources; and in the first major intraregional mobilization of resources, Botswana provided 5.8 million pula in August 1988 toward the Limpopo railway.[75] Spurred by these efforts, international donors pledged $60 million in late 1988 to the first phase of the estimated $200 million rehabilitation program.[76]

From a security perspective, however, the Limpopo Corridor is the most vulnerable of Mozambican trade routes. Twice as long as the Beira, it is less than fifty miles from the South African border. Thus, although a joint Zimbabwe-Mozambique offensive succeeded in mid-1987 in securing part of the railway, a SADCC report noted that:

Even if additional troops from within the region could be found to secure the Limpopo line against the RENAMO threat (as they do successfully in the Beira corridor), there is no practical way of defending it against a concerted campaign of sabotage by South African regular commandos should Pretoria decide to mount one. The security question, still unresolved, is the key to whether the Limpopo line develops into a major project or not.[77]

One of the most successful FLS attempts to isolate RENAMO involved pressure on Malawi in the fall of 1986. Since the early 1980s, Maputo had repeatedly accused Malawi of allowing the RENAMO and SADF to use its territory to provide logistical support for rebel attacks in north and central Mozambique. In September 1986, Kaunda, Mugabe, and Machel threatened to close their borders with Malawi. Banda finally expelled thousands of RENAMO forces, and in December 1986 established a security commission with Maputo to monitor the borders.[78] In the wake of Malawi's expulsion, however, Mozambique faced a more severe RENAMO incursion; they captured towns along the Zambezi river, in an attempt to cut the country in two. As a result of this deteriorating situation, Tanzania increased its troop levels in Mozambique from three thousand in November 1986 to five thousand in February 1987.[79] In March 1987, Malawi also sent a contingent of three hundred to assist in Mozambique's defense. The *Indian Ocean Newsletter* noted the significance of Malawi's decision:

Malawi, South Africa's only public friend on the African continent, has given Pretoria a slap in the face by sending troops to help the Front Line States in the war against the MNR rebels in Mozambique. The aid is token, as Malawi's army is only five thousand strong, but it signals a realization by president Banda that his future lies in cultivating stronger ties with its neighbors and the Organization of African Unity rather than with South Africa inspite of aid from Pretoria.[80]

The commitment of the FLS to Mozambique's defense was largely instrumental in swaying Britain, Spain, Portugal, and France to provide other security assistance to Mozambique. Starting in late 1986, the British government provided training to an elite force of six hundred Mozambican troops in Zimbabwe to protect the Nacala railway.[81] In February 1987, Christopher Polten, the British Overseas Development Minister announced that Britain would double the number of Mozambican soldiers in training to provide security for the Limpopo line. As Joaquim Chissano, Mozambique's President, noted after a visit to Britain: "We have friends in the West as well as the East ... [who] now also speak of the need to support Mozambique militarily."[82]

At the January 1988 SADCC summit in Arusha, Tanzania, the issue of security and development received prominence. For the first time SADCC and external donors examined seriously the security necessary to safeguard development projects. According to Luis Barnuevo, Spain's Secretary of International Cooperation:

It is obvious that the continuous aggression of which these countries are victims makes the urgent tasks of economic development and the attainment of better living conditions for their people even more difficult, since it diverts men and scant resources into the military effort. Therefore, in our opinion, an attempt should be made to reach a formula whereby the financing of development projects likewise includes the necessary security factor for guaranteeing their defense.[83]

Nine years after the formation of SADCC, the most visible progress has been made in the transport sector. Mozambique's Transport Minister Armando Guebuza noted at the SADCC summit in February 1989 that the decision to make this sector a priority was a correct one since the share of trade via South Africa began to decrease due to efforts made on the regional corridors.[84] As of December 1988, 6.85 million tons of SADCC trade passed through SADCC ports. While this was below the 8.23 million tons handled in 1981, it nonetheless represented sixty-three percent of the region's annual overseas trade of 10.2 million tons.[85] Overall, the $2 billion development plan for SADCC corridors represents one of Africa's most concentrated investment programs this decade. SADCC's success, Guebuza added, arose from their strategy of "playing on the consciences of Western nations which hesitate to take stronger measures against south Africa."[86] It was partly due to the success of the four corridors that SADCC shifted its attention in early 1989 to the rehabilitation of the Lobito Corridor in Angola.

THE ANGOLA-NAMIBIAN FRONT

Unlike Mozambique where the FLS attempted, with some success, to coordinate a common approach in dealing with RENAMO rebels, their room for maneuver was sharply curtailed in the conventional military confrontation between Angola and South Africa. Despite their vociferous condemnation of the Reagan Administration's two-pronged strategy of linking Namibian independence with Cuban withdrawal from Angola and covert military support for Savimbi, Angola's African allies had no real means by which they could influence the events in that conflict.

Prior to the unraveling of the Lusaka Agreement, Angolan President Jose Eduardo Dos Santos had in November 1984, for the first time, conceded to the concept of linkage by proposing the withdrawal of twenty thousand Cuban troops from southern Angola over a four-year period in return for cessation of South African aggression, an end to aid to UNITA, and implementation of the U.N. Namibian plan. South Africa responded by demanding not only that all the Cuban troops be withdrawn, but also that this should be accomplished within six months.[87]

Subsequent to the U.S. decision to support Savimbi, the Angolans suspended talks conducted by Chester Crocker, the U.S. Assistant Secretary of State for African Affairs. The diplomatic stalemate that ensued was to be broken only after war weariness began to consume the parties.

To counter the joint SADF-UNITA offensive in southern Angola, the Cubans and Soviets significantly increased military aid to Angola in early 1986. Estimated by U.S. sources at $2 billion, these weapons included anti-aircraft missiles, MIG-23's, T-54 and T-55 tanks, and mobile radar units.[88] Armed with these weapons, the Angolan army decided to launch a major conventional offensive against UNITA's outpost of Mavinga in the southeast. In what Angolan army Chief of Staff, Antonio dos Santos Franca, described as one of the fiercest battles ever fought in southern Africa, UNITA's forces, armed with U.S. stinger missiles, and backed by South African air power and four thousand troops, reacted swiftly and by surprise. The Angolan army was forced to retreat toward its regional base at Cuito Cuanavale, leaving over three thousand dead.[89]

Meeting in Luanda on November 15, 1987 to show their solidarity with Angola, the Front Line Presidents urged the Angolan government not to deploy Cuban troops against the South Africans because the latter wanted "to draw the Cubans into the conflict so as to be able to ask the West for increased aid."[90] But on precisely the same day, Fidel Castro, after having met dos Santos early in November, decided upon a new strategy involving sending additional troops who would have a role in combat rather than being restricted to logistical support as before. As Castro later indicated:

The first thing we did was to send the most experienced pilots of our air force to Angola ... So that they [could] begin to conduct air strikes against South African troops that besieged Cuito Cuanavale. We also sent our best anti-aircraft weapons. We reinforced our air combat. The Government of Angola [gave] us the responsibility of Cuito Cuanavale's defense ... the Cuban-Angolan strategy was not merely to stop the enemy in Cuito Cuanavale but to concentrate enough forces to the south to seriously threaten places of strategic importance for South Africa.[91]

Cuba's deployment of forty thousand troops in Angola in early January 1988 shifted the region's strategic balance, causing the South African military deep consternation. In the battle for Cuito Cuanavale in early 1988, South Africa not only lost its air superiority but also suffered significant casualties in its four thousand-man expeditionary army. By April 1988, Cuban-Angolan-SWAPO forces started air raids on South African military positions in northern Namibia.[92]

This shift in the military balance in southern Angola coincided with a weakening resolve on the part of South Africa, Angola, and Cuba on the utility of military confrontation. To the South Africans, there were a range of constraints on the economy, deriving from low foreign exchange reserves, denial of access to international loans and finance, and sharply decreasing state revenues for socio-economic development. The Director of Econometrics, Azar Jammine, estimated in July 1988 that the Angolan war was costing South Africa a crippling $1.72 billion a year.[93] Furthermore, there was growing frustration among white South Africans about the military's involvement in Angola: an editorial in *Kerkbode*, the official journal of the largest Dutch Reform Church, in June 1988 expressed disquiet over the "more or less" permanent presence of the SADF in Angola.[94]

For Angola, the country faced enormous economic problems. Since 1985 nearly half of Angola's 8.5 million had been uprooted by war. Agricultural production the central highlands had almost ground to a halt. By early 1988, Angola ran an external debt of $4 billion, much of it owed to the Soviets and Cubans. The cost of maintaining Cubans imposed a $400-500 million burden on the annual state budget. Battered by war, by the decline in oil prices, and mounting debt, Angola embarked on an economic liberalization program and applied for membership in the International Monetary Fund (IMF).[95] To the Cubans, an Angolan stalemate meant increasing financial and human costs. In the battle for Cuito Cuanavale, Cuban forces sustained direct casualties. Further, in the face of the decline in the Angolan economy, Cuba had to bear some of the costs for maintaining its presence in Angola.[96]

The improvement in Soviet-American relations since 1985 was a significant contribution to facilitating the attempts toward a negotiated settlement. In a series of meetings with Soviet officials in 1987 and 1988 culminating in his visit to Moscow in April 1988, Crocker developed an understanding with the Soviets about establishing peace in Angola.[97]

This understanding inevitably limited the room for maneuvers previously held by South Africa, the MPLA, and Cuba, thereby making possible the achievement of an agreement.

In March 1988, Angola, Cuba, and South Africa, under Crocker's mediation, began what Gillian Gunn has described as a process of negotiation from stalemate through diversionary tactics and massive retaliations to a willingness to sit down and discuss real issues.[98] Between March and July 1988, Crocker's task was to separate two agendas in the belief that mixing them would impede the negotiating process: one, implementation of the UN Settlement Plan and the withdrawal of Cuban troops from Angola; and two, Angolan domestic politics. Thus, he could maintain partiality while not bargaining away U.S. support for UNITA. On July 13, 1988, in New York, the parties achieved this goal when they agreed upon a series of principles. The achievements of this meeting represented an important step on the road toward a negotiated solution for the region by reaffirming the U.N. plan for Namibia, South African withdrawal from Angola, as well as the willingness of Angola and Cuba to deploy to the north and later evacuate to Cuba the entire Cuban military contingent.[99]

With South Africa's completion of its withdrawal from Angola in late August, the stage was set for discussions of the timetable for Cuban withdrawal and Namibian independence. An Angolan official witnessing South Africa's withdrawal commented that it provided confirmation that the region's governments had become "partners in peace."[100] Close to the end of December 1988, the parties had considerably narrowed their differences culminating in the signing of the Tripartite Agreement in New York. Apart from the provisions of Namibian independence and Cuban withdrawal, the agreement required Angola to shut down the training camps of the ANC in return for South Africa's pledge to stop supporting UNITA.[101]

PROSPECTS AND POLICY IMPLICATIONS FOR THE 1990s

Namibia's decolonization fulfills one of the central objectives of the FLS and SADCC. Apart from removing the threat to Angola's security, an independent Namibia should take its place in the amity of the FLS, hence consolidating the geopolitical arch of South Africa's neighbors. Since the *raison d'etre* of the Front Line alliance was to facilitate majority rule in southern Africa, Namibian independence will allow the FLS to shift the focus by strengthening economic cooperation under SADCC. In the short-term, however, the agenda of domestic stability in Angola and Mozambique remains a critical issue for the FLS. What role might the FLS play with respect to these two conflicts?

Domestic stability in Angola is inextricably tied to the relations between the FLS and Zaire, and American policy toward Savimbi. For some time the Angolan government has offered to negotiate with UNITA without Savimbi. In March 1989, Savimbi offered to exclude himself from any potential reconciliation talks with the Angolan government.[102] The other proposal Savimbi made to encourage national reconciliation was a unilateral moratorium on offensive military operations until July 1989. Ravaged by war and unable to defeat UNITA militarily, Luanda began to move beyond the amnesty granted to UNITA to engage in serious negotiations in June 1989.

Pressures on the MPLA will likely come from SADCC's need to rehabilitate the Lobito corridor, providing easy access for Zambia, Zimbabwe, and Zaire to the Atlantic Ocean. At a donors' meeting in Luanda in January 1989, Western countries pledged $90 million toward the first phase of an estimated $400 million development program to rehabilitate the Benguela railway and modernize the Lobito port. The Lobito project is a major new departure for SADCC in two respects. First, it involves a non-member -- Zaire -- as a major beneficiary. Second, it will be the first infrastructure program to involve private enterprises as an integral element from the beginning.[103]

Since the 1970s, Zaire has been regarded by the FLS as a pariah because of the corruption of the Mobutu regime and its willingness to serve as a conduit for American military aid to Savimbi. In addition, Mobutu's unabashedly pro-South Africa stance contributed to his alienation. In November 1986, the FLS issued warnings to Mobutu against continuing support for UNITA and threatened to cut off Zaire's only trade routes to South Africa through Zambia and Zimbabwe.[104] Yet at the time, SADCC states were making efforts to reopen the Benguela railway, Zaire assumed the position of Savimbi's major regional ally.

Zaire's elevation to this role, however, is largely a function of U.S. southern African policy. Since military aid to UNITA places Zaire in the role of a destabilizer, it postpones Mobutu's realignment with Front Line neighbors. Improvement in American-Angolan relations would therefore provide Luanda with the ultimate incentive of reaching a negotiated settlement with UNITA and by extension, removing a source of conflict between Mobutu and his neighbors. Even though the Bush administration reaffirmed its support for Savimbi, Luanda muted its criticism. Pedro de Castro Van Dunem, Angola's Foreign Minister, said in January 1989 that "Angola hoped the Bush administration will continue to review this question and will try to take steps in better directions."[105]

As part of the reappraisal of superpower relations in southern Africa, the Bush administration would enhance the chances for a negotiated settlement in Angola by adopting an evenhanded approach to both parties. Deprived of $80 million a year in South African support, and facing the prospects of dependence on an uncertain Zaire, Savimbi would be more amenable to negotiations in a climate of increased Angolan-American diplomatic contacts. Pointing to Savimbi's vulnerability, Van Dunem observed: "Zaire can never be as solid a base for Savimbi as South Africa unless there is a level of U.S. involvement that we do not believe will happen."[106]

More critically, American carrots to Luanda such as facilitating its membership in the IMF and World Bank would enhance efforts by the FLS and other African countries to contribute to domestic reconciliation in Angola. In this respect, Angola hosted an eight-nation meeting in May 1989 attended by leaders from Gabon, Congo, Sao Tome and Principe, Zaire, Zambia, Zimbabwe, and Mozambique at which Dos Santos unveiled his proposals for national reconciliation.[107] The gist of these proposals entail eventual incorporation of UNITA in the MPLA government. Inclusion of Zaire in these deliberations served to underscore the seriousness Luanda attaches to this question. Announcing these proposals, Dos Santos hoped the "summit will help our people and governments to see their way to fully reaching the goals of peace, stability, good neighborliness, peaceful coexistence, and cooperation."[108] Strengthening these regional initiatives along the lines of the Contadora process in Central America is an option for the Bush Administration.

As for the Mozambican conflict, Pretoria and Maputo agreed in September 1988 to revive the joint monitoring commission of the Nkomati Accord. Two months following South Africa's promises to stop supporting RENAMO, more than 600 power pylons, stretching from the Cahora Bassa dam in northwest Mozambique to the South African border were sabotaged by RENAMO. The chairman of the Mozambican parliament, Marcelino dos Santos, stated that it was unlikely that RENAMO had the technical capacity to carry out such systematic destruction in so short a time.[109] Furthermore, in early 1989, U.S. Deputy Assistant Secretary of State for African Affairs, Alison Rosenberg, confirmed that South Africa is continuing to supply RENAMO.[110]

Against this background of continuing South African destabilization of Mozambique, Pik Botha unilaterally invited the superpowers to mediate between RENAMO and FRELIMO.[111] Since the State Department's report documenting RENAMO's atrocities, there has been some progress in isolating it diplomatically.[112] In the face of this isolation, South Africa's peace offensive is likely motivated by two considerations. First, Pretoria would benefit from a shift in international energies away from apartheid to another regional 'problem area.' Such a move would also assist in breaking South Africa's isolation as it presents itself, once again, as a regional problem solver. Second, it might be attempting to win for RENAMO at the negotiating table what it has failed to win on the battlefield. The cautious response from Maputo, Washington, and Moscow to South Africa's peace offensive is indicative of the underlying apprehension with which South Africa's intentions are viewed. But perhaps, the most interesting response was from RENAMO which refused the idea of Pretoria's mediation because the latter has become "the ally of communist Mozambique."[113]

Despite the uncertainties in Pretoria's long-term policy toward Mozambique, there is increasing regional and international pressure on Chissano to reach some accommodation with RENAMO. At the end of 1988, Tanzanian troops, which had been defending most of central and northern Mozambique for twenty-three months, withdrew citing the mounting costs, both in casualties and money.[114] While Mozambique indicated that its armed forces could contain RENAMO, the marked increase in the number of Mozambican refugees in Malawi subsequent to Tanzania's withdrawal points to the gloomy military situation. Zimbabwe is also beginning to show signs of exhaustion in its military involvement in Mozambique. In February, a number of Zimbabwean members of parliament asked the government to push for a negotiated solution in Mozambique; pressure too is building from Zimbabwean investors in the BCG concerned about the rising cost of their investment due to the continuing civil war.[115] Internationally, Margaret Thatcher, on a visit to Zimbabwe in March, told both Mugabe and Chissano that while she would offer more military aid to Mozambique, negotiations should be considered. In what appeared to be a partial response to Botha's invitation she said: "We are ready to take part in any political initiative which has the support and Mozambique and other countries in the region to end the conflict."[116]

Like Angola, the FLS, especially Zimbabwe, has a critical role in the future resolution of Mozambique's conflict. Toward this end, the *Economist* has noted: "Zimbabwe could do itself and regional stability a good turn by making its military support for the Mozambican government conditional on that government seeking an accommodation with the MNR guerrillas, whose resilience is plainly not due solely to South African support."[117] Whatever role Zimbabwe plays in this conflict the critical question will remain: would Pretoria be willing to rein in RENAMO?

Stability in Angola and Mozambique will be central to SADCC's long-term regional objectives. Endowed with natural resources that neighbors would tap from, both countries might contribute not only to regional transport self-sufficiency but also energy. Since 1987, SADCC has explored ways in which its past priority of infrastructure development could be linked to a focus on production and investment promotion in the region. As the SADCC executive report pointed out, "viable and sustainable infrastructure needs to be underpinned by investment in productive activities and by increased intraregional trade."[118] This new emphasis reflects not only the progress made since 1980 in the transport sector, but also recognition of the need to overcome the poor economic performance of most members. Although for the first time in fifteen years economic growth exceeded population growth in SADCC countries in 1988 -- 4.5 percent GDP versus 3.3 percent population growth -- a majority of them continue to be overwhelmed by problems of debt and unemployment.[119]

To improve the investment climate, SADCC states have embarked on major structural adjustment measures, including new investment codes and easing unnecessary controls on the economy.[120] In the 1990s, these reforms might not only strengthen member economies and restore intraregional trade, but also provide more regional access to external actors. The 1986 Nordic-SADCC Accords in which the two regions cooperate in trade, technology transfers, and investment might serve as a model for this kind of access. As a 1988 SADCC report stressed:

The Nordic/SADCC Initiative currently provides the only vehicle outside the [SADCC] annual consultative conference for formal consultations between SADCC and a group of its cooperating partners on matters specific to investment, production and trade. It is hoped that this kind of forum will be broadened...[121]

What might be the FLS and SADCC's role toward change in South Africa? At the height of the international campaign for sanctions against South Africa in mid-1986, Zambia and Zimbabwe committed themselves to imposing sanctions under the framework of the Commonwealth plan. Subsequently, Kaunda and Mugabe failed to generate support from the rest of the SADCC members. At a SADCC summit in Luanda in August 1986, southern African leaders reaffirmed their long-established position that their economic dependence upon South Africa leaves them in no position to initiate sanctions.[122] Botswana's *Daily News* seemed to capture this broad consensus: "the survival of Botswana is of paramount importance...self-preservation is the first law of nature."[123]

To demonstrate its neighbor's vulnerability, Pretoria introduced time-consuming customs checks on the Beitbridge border crossing to Zimbabwe and a system of cash deposits for Zambian imports passing through South Africa. Mugabe's description of these measures as a "declaration of economic war" underscored SADCC's predicament.[124] Unable to impose sanctions itself, SADCC has, however, called on other countries to do so. According to Makoni:

Although we recognize that individual member states may not be in a position to impose sanctions, SADCC supports the imposition of sanctions against South Africa by those within the organization and outside who are in a position to do so. The vulnerability of SADCC countries cannot be used as an excuse by those in a position to impose not to do so. SADCC member states will cooperate to minimize the effects on their economies of the imposition of sanctions.[125]

In one of many inconsistencies surrounding calls for economic sanctions, Zambia in April 1988 launched a new air route that effectively sidestepped an American ban on direct air links with South Africa. At the same time, when the Australian airline severed its air links to South Africa, it was replaced by Zimbabwe's.[126] In addition, SADCC countries have, on many occasions, encouraged foreign companies divesting from South Africa to invest in their countries. The ambivalence of SADCC toward sanctions thus removes this option as a future course of action on their part.

Angola's decision to close down the ANC's training camps as part of the Namibian agreement was a setback to the guerrilla struggle. Yet, for the most part, it confirmed the reality set in motion by the Nkomati Accord that the FLS cannot afford to use their territories for infiltration into South Africa. As the ANC is pushed further away from the battle lines, its strategy for liberation of South Africa will certainly change. Just as the Nkomati Accord led the ANC's mobilization of support within South Africa, the recent changes might lead to a reaffirmation of this strategy.

In a post-Namibian independence southern Africa, external engagement might reflect a form of condominium in the partnership among superpowers. One of the results of the Namibian settlement is that it afforded the superpowers a potential vehicle for military disengagement from the region. Anchored in the need to reduce entanglements in regional trouble spots, this partnership might have two implications for regional relations. First, it might entail more superpower interest in strengthening the economic capacity of SADCC. Recent Soviet and American interest in SADCC programs points to this possibility. Of critical importance in this respect is that the middle European powers have laid the basis for enhanced multilateral involvement in southern Africa's economic future through their vigorous participation in SADCC. Reflecting what Harvey Glickman has aptly called a "Cooperative Reconstructionist Initiative," such an approach might also serve as a deterrence to South Africa's destabilization.[127] By helping to contain Pretoria's predatory policies, this partnership would contribute to long-term viability of regional institutions.

The impact of such superpower partnership on South Africa's domestic politics is, however, limited in the medium-term by two transitions in southern Africa -- the Namibian independence process and the transition to a post-Botha South Africa. Since superpower relations with South Africa are now, in particular, dependent on Pretoria's behavior in Namibia, coordinated pressure for internal change is unlikely. But one would hope that the resolution of these issues should pave the way for greater cooperation between the West and the Soviet Union in tackling the problem of apartheid. Such cooperation might avoid the basic flaw of constructive engagement which, while initially formulated to address the sources of conflict in southern Africa, in the end became hostage to South Africa's regional policies.

Second, it is possible to envisage a superpower partnership that reduces the leverage of regional states. The most recent was the unanimous decision by the U.N. Security Council to scale down the United Nations' Transition Group (UNTAG) for Namibia's independence. Causing considerable disquiet among the FLS and other nonaligned states, this move was an indication of how superpower unity would threaten their influence. As Theo Ben-Gurirab, SWAPO's U.N. representative, poignantly observed: "The big powers [now] have found a way of striking deals. The smaller powers have become chips on the chessboards."[128] The confrontation between SWAPO and South African forces on the eve of the implementation plan which resulted partly because of an inadequate U.N. team points to the dangers of such partnerships.

The problem with this second scenario, however, lies not in the short-term and expedient convergence between superpower interests, but rather in the potential for long-term total disengagement from the region. As southern Africa becomes marginal in superpower strategic objectives, there is a possibility of their disengagement. Such disengagement might follow the lines of Nixon's Guam Doctrine which envisaged medium powers playing the role as guardians of regional peace and security. In the present configuration of regional power, Pretoria would stand to gain. It is instructive to note here that one of the most ominous changes in the pattern of external intervention is the evolving rapprochement between Pretoria and Moscow.[129] Nurtured during the Angola-Namibia negotiations, this relationship has developed to the extent that the Soviets have indicated their intention to stop supplying arms to the ANC. In December 1988, Karen Khachaturov, the deputy chairman of the Novosti News Agency advised African countries "to seek political victories, not total victory...The old talk of destroying imperialism was a noble goal but not a realistic one. [Today] we do not seek an all-out settlement. We want small but significant results."[130] From my perspective, the Soviet "discovery" that the ANC cannot militarily dislodge the apartheid regime would seem less than honest. Perhaps the only positive aspect to this relationship might be to destroy one of the central tenets of Botha's Total Strategy -- regional intervention to stem the tide of a communist onslaught. In this respect, former SWAPO Information Secretary, Peter Katjivivi, has argued that Pretoria would be more amenable to surrendering Walvis Bay -- Namibia's only port -- in a climate of improved South African-Soviet relations.[131] As it is now articulated, however, Soviet policy is reminiscent of Crocker's constructive engagement policy in which the FLS were urged to address Pretoria's regional security concerns.

CONCLUSION

Coping with destabilization has been the dominant theme in the FLS' and SADCC's relations with South Africa in the 1980s. Formulated to create a regional environment congenial to South Africa's security needs, destabilization reduced the ability of independent states to fulfill their objectives. At its worst, it impeded the process of nation building in Angola and Mozambique, the critical actors in the FLS-based security system. To deal with Pretoria's dominance, independent states opted to mobilize local and external efforts through SADCC. Limited in its objectives, SADCC has emerged over nine years as a mechanism for multilateral problem-solving and goal fulfillment. By strengthening their economic capacities in a cooperative structure of their own, the SADCC countries might reach a stage of development that would enable them to interact with South Africa from a position of greater strength. More critical, since economic cooperation engenders a habit of mutual interaction, it in the long run contributes to dampening political conflicts. The revision of economic policies away from state-centered to market-centered models within SADCC might presage an era in which such uniformity places their cooperation on a more sound basis.

From the outset, this chapter has argued that institution building in southern Africa will continue to reflect the extant inequalities of power relations. As long as apartheid informs South Africa's domestic policies, neighboring states will strive to mitigate the effects of these inequalities. That they are willing to accomplish this goal at the price of dependence on external actors is testimony to this determination. The political integration of SADCC into a South African economic system or, alternatively, South Africa's integration into SADCC will await the resolution of South Africa's internal conflict. Commenting on the response of South Africans to the Namibian settlement, a South African scholar had a message which has broad implications for the future of southern Africa:

There are already signs that we may be falling back on the tried and tested myth -- now considerably less valid than before -- that the primary requirement in our regional policy is military preparedness against the threat of Soviet destabilization. If this is to be the basis of the government's defense against right-wing criticism of a settlement, we run the risk of falling into the twin traps of "feeding the crocodile" and "believing our own propaganda." Southern Africa deserves better.[132]

Notes

The author gratefully acknowledges the McArthur Foundation for a fellowship in International Peace and Security.
   1. Kenneth W. Grundy, *The Militarization of South African Politics* (Bloomington: Indiana University Press, 1986); Philip H. Frankel, *Pretoria's Praetorians: Civil-Military Relations in South Africa* (London: Cambridge University Press, 1984).

2. Grundy, *op. cit.*, 11.
3. *Ibid.*, 13.
4. Interview with Julius K. Nyerere, *Third World Quarterly* 6 (October, 1984), 836. For analysis of the FLS, see Gilbert Khadiagala, "The Frontline States in Southern Africa's International Politics Since 1975," Ph.D. Dissertation, The Paul Nitze School of Advanced International Studies, The Johns Hopkins University. [Forthcoming.]
5. Roger Martin, "Regional Security in Southern Africa: More Angolas, Mozambiques or Neutrals?" *Survival* (September-October, 1987), 387.
6. *Ibid.*
7. Colin Legum, "The Nkomati Accord and Its Implications for the Frontline States and South Africa" in Ibrahim Msabaha and Timothy M. Shaw, eds., *Confrontation and Liberation in Southern Africa: Regional Directions After the Nkomati Accord* (Gower: Westview, 1987), 90. See also Steven Metz, "The Mozambique National Resistence and South African Foreign Policy," *African Affairs* 85 (October, 1986), 491-508.
8. Allen Isaacman and Barbara Isaacman. "Mozambique: In Pursuit of Nonalignment," *Africa Report* (May-June, 1983), 48.
9. Thomas M. Callaghy. "Apartheid and Socialism: South Africa's Relations with Angola and Mozambique" in Thomas M. Callaghy , ed., *South Africa in Southern Africa: The Intensifying Vortex of Violence* (New York: Praeger, 1983), 278.
10. Cited in Robert Davies and Dan O'Meara, "Total Strategy in Southern Africa: An Analysis of South African Regional Policy Since 1978" in Ibrahim Msabaha and Timothy M. Shaw , *op. cit.*, 248.
11. Grundy, *op. cit.*, 11.
12. Cited in Barry Streek, "Namibia: South Africa's Stakes in the Border War," *Africa Report* (March-April, 1984), 59.
13. Callaghy, *op. cit.*, 279.
14. *Ibid.*
15. Colin Legum, *Battlefronts of Southern Africa* (New York: Africana Publishing House, 1988), 345.
16. *Ibid.*
17. John A. Marcum, "Regional Security in Southern Africa: Angola," *Survival* (London) (January-February 1988), 11.
18. Cited by Marga Holness, "Angola: The Struggle Continues" in Phyllis Johnson and David Martin, eds., *Destructive Engagement: Southern Africa at War* (Harare: Zimbabwe Publishing House, 1986), 107.
19. *Ibid.*
20. Colin Legum, *Battlefronts of Southern Africa*, 391-393.
21. Joanmarie Kalter, "Mozambique's Peace with South Africa: The Economics of Desperation," *Africa Report* (May-June, 1984), 19. See also J. Gus Liebenow, "South African Hegemony. Part I: The Impact of the Nkomati Accord," *UFSI Reports* 24 (September, 1984), 1-9.
22. Legum, "The Nkomati Accord and Its Implications," 94.
23. *Ibid.*
24. Frank Wisner, "An American Perspective Today," *South Africa International* (January, 1984), 472.
25. Legum, "The Nkomati Accord and Its Implications," 95.
26. Cited in J. Gus Liebenow, "South African Hegemony. Part II: The Impact of the Nkomati Accord," *UFSI Reports* 25 (November, 1984), 2.
27. *Ibid.*
28. *Ibid.*
29. *Ibid.*, 3.

30.   *Africa Research Bulletin* (October 1-31, 1984), 7397.
31.   I. William Zartman, "Deadlock in Namibia," *SAIS Review* 5 (Fall, 1985), 263.
32.   Richard Dale, "Not Always So Placid a Place: Botswana Under Attack," *African Affairs* 86 (January, 1987), 73-91. See also Robert M. Price, "Pretoria's Southern African Strategy," *African Affairs* 83 (January, 1984), 11-32.
33.   Richard Dale, *op. cit.*, 76.
34.   *Ibid.*
35.   Martin Murray, *South Africa: Time of Agony, Time of Destiny: The Upsurge of Protest* (London: Verso, 1987), 264-265.
36.   *Africa Research Bulletin* (July 15, 1985), 7683.
37.   Davies and O'Meara, *op. cit.*, 265.
38.   Cited in Christopher Hill, "Regional Cooperation in Southern Africa," *African Affairs* 82 (January, 1983), 215.
39.   *Ibid.*
40.   Southern African Development Coordination Conference (SADCC), "A Declaration by the Governments of Independent States of Southern Africa made at Lusaka on 1 April 1980" (Lusaka: Government Printer, 1980), 4.
41.   Kenneth W. Grundy, "South Africa and the Political Economy of Southern Africa" in Gwendolen M. Carter and Patrick O'Meara, eds., *International Politics in Southern Africa* (Bloomington: Indiana University Press, 1982), 160-161.
42.   Cited in SADCC, "The Proceedings of the Second Southern African Development Coordination Conference held in Maputo on 27-28 November 1980" (London: SADCC, 1981), 8.
43.   Roger Leys and Arne Tostensen, "Regional Cooperation in Southern Africa: The Southern African Development Coordination Conference," *Review of African Political Economy* 23 (January-April, 1982), 52-71. See also Barron J. Boyd, "A Subsystemic Analysis of the Southern African Development Coordination Conference," *African Studies Review* 28 (4), 46-61.
44.   Clever Mumbengegwi, "The Political Economy of a Small-Farmer Agricultural Strategy in SADCC" in Coralie Bryant, ed., *Poverty, Policy, and Food Security in Southern Africa* (Boulder, Lynne Rienner Publishers, 1988), 160; Richard F. Weisfelder, "The Southern African Development Coordination Conference. A New Factor in the Liberation Process" in Thomas M. Callaghy, *op. cit*, 237-266.
45.   Cited in Ibbo Mandaza, "Perspectives on Economic Cooperation and Autonomous Development in Southern Africa" in Samir Amin, Derrick Chitala and Ibbo Mandaza, eds., *SADCC Prospects for Disengagement and Development In Southern Africa* (London: Zed Press, 1987), 213.
46.   Wolfgang Zehender, *Cooperation versus Integration: The Prospects of the Southern African Development Coordination Conference* (Berlin: German Development Institute, 1983). See also Weisfelder, *op. cit.*, 242.
47.   Cited in Amon J. Nsekela, ed., *Southern Africa: Toward Economic Liberation* (London: Rex Callings, 1981), xvi.
48.   Constantine V. Vaitsos, "Crisis in Regional Economic Cooperation (Integration) Among Developing Countries: A Survey," *World Development* 6 (June, 1978), 719-769; Carol Thompson, "Self-Sufficiency and Regional Coordination: Formulating New Theories in Southern Africa," Paper prepared for the African Studies Association Annual Meeting, (Chicago, October 29, 1988).
49.   Vaitsos, *op. cit.*, 750.
50.   Reginald H. Green, "SADCC: From Dependence and Poverty Toward Economic Liberation," in Colin Legum, ed., *Africa Contemporary Record: Annual Survey and Documents 1982-83* (New York: African Publishing Company, 1981), A97-A98.

51. *Ibid.*, A97.
52. Michael Clough and John Ravenhill, "Regional Cooperation in Southern Africa" in Michael Clough ,ed., *Changing Realities in Southern Africa: Implications for American Policy* (Berkeley: Institute for International Studies, 1982), 123-60. Also see Douglas G. Anglin, "SADCC After Nkomati," *African Affairs* (January 1985), 163-182.
53. *World Development Report 1988* (New York: Oxford Press, 1988), 222.
54. *Ibid.*
55. Stephen R. Lewis Jr., "Some Economic Realities in Southern Africa: One Hundred Million Futures" in Coralie Bryant, *op. cit.*, 41.
56. *Southern Africa: Opportunities for Investment and Trade* (Gaborone: SADCC 1988), 114-5.
57. Lewis, *op. cit.*, 44-45.
58. D.G. Clarke, *Foreign Companies and International Investment in Zimbabwe* (Gwelo: Mambo Press, 1980); Joseph Hanlon, *Beggar Your Neighbor* (London: Penguin Books).
59. Gavin Maasdorp, "Squaring Up to Economic Dominance: Regional Patterns" in Robert I. Rotberg, ed., *South Africa and Its Neighbors: Regional Security and Self-Interest* (Lexington: D.C. Heath, 1985), 91-136.
60. Lewis, *op. cit.*, 52.
61. *Ibid.*
62. Bernard T.G. Chidzero, "Challenges to Development in Southern Africa" in Coralie Bryant, ed., *Poverty, Policy and Food Security in Southern Africa* (Boulder: Lynne Rienner Publishers, 1988), 127.
63. SADCC, 1988, 54.
64. Douglas G. Anglin, "SADCC After Nkomati," *African Affairs* 84 (April, 1985), 180.
65. *Africa Economic Digest* (February 14, 1987), 3.
66. *Africa Research Bulletin* (January 15-February 14, 1983), 6717.
67. Foreign and Commonwealth Office (London), "Southern Africa Transport Routes," (Mimeo, March, 1987), 4.
68. Reginald H. Green, "The SADCC on the Front Line: *Breakdown or Breakthrough?" in Colin Legum, ed., African Contemporary Record: Annual Survey and Documents, 1986-87* (New York: Africana Publishing Company, 1988), A88.
69. *Africa Economic Digest* (November 11, 1986), 17.
70. Thompson,"Self-Sufficiency and Regional Coordination," 22; See also "Corridors of Commerce," *African Review of Commerce and Technology* (March, 1989), 33-34.
71. Hasu H. Patel, "Regional Security in Southern Africa, Zimbabwe," *Survival* (London, January-February, 1988), 52; See also Margaret A. Novicki, "Mozambique: A Permanent Emergency," *Africa Report* (March-April, 1989), 17-22.
72. *Africa Research Bulletin* (November 15, 1986), 8260.
73. *Africa Research Bulletin* (February 1-15, 1987), 8357.
74. SADCC, 1988, 132.
75. *Africa Research Bulletin* (August 31, 1988), 9207.
76. *Ibid.*
77. SADCC, 1988, 132.
78. *Africa Economic Digest* (September 20, 1986), 13; *AED* 27 (January 27, 1987), 3; Diana Cammack, "The 'Human Face' of Destabilization: The War in Mozambique," *Review of African Political Economy* 1 (February-March, 1989), 64-75.

79.   Kenneth Good, "Zambia and the Liberation of Southern Africa," *Journal of Modern African Studies* 25 (September, 1987), 539-540.
80.   Cited in *Africa Research Bulletin* (April 15, 1987), 8439.
81.   *Times* (London, February 12, 1987). See also Allen Isaacman, *op. cit.*, 33.
82.   Cited in Allen Isaacman, *op. cit.*, 33.
83.   *Southern African Economist* (Harare, February-March, 1988), 12.
84.   *Africa Research Bulletin* (February 28, 1989), 9420.
85.   *Ibid.*, 9419.
86.   *Ibid.*, 9420.
87.   Colin Legum, "The Southern African Crisis: An Embattled South Africa Faces a Future of Increasing Isolation" in Colin Legum, ed., *Africa Contemporary Record, Annual Survey and Documents* (New York: Africana Publishing Company, 1985), A15.
88.   John A. Marcum, *op. cit.*, 10.
89.   Godwin Matatu, "Angola Blows the Myth of South African Invincibility," *Southern Africa: Political and Economic Monthly* 3 (Harare, May, 1988), 19.
90.   *Africa Economic Digest* (November 20, 1987), 16.
91.   *Foreign Broadcast Information Service Daily Report, Latin America* (December 12, 1988), 10.
92.   "FAPLA: A Force to Reckon With," *Southern African Economist* (Harare, October, 1988), 20-21.
93.   Cited in J. Gus Liebenow, "Southern Africa: Not Yet Quiet on the Western Front," *UFSI Reports* 3 (September, 1988), 7.
94.   *Ibid.*
95.   John A. Marcum, *op. cit.*, 10.
96   Gillian Gunn, "A Guide to the Intricacies of the Angolan- Namibia Negotiations," *CSIS Africa Notes* 90 (September, 1988), 6.
97.   Sean Cleary. "Impact of the Independence of Namibia on South Africa," *South Africa International* 19 (January, 1989), 125.
98.   Gillian Gunn, *op. cit.*, 1-16.
99.   *Ibid.*, 12. See also J. Gus Liebenow, "Southern Africa: Not Yet Quiet on the Western Front," 12-14.
100. *African Economic Digest* (September 3, 1988), 6.
101. James Brooke, "Angolan Sanctuary Closing to Rebels," *New York Times* (January 10, 1989), 4.
102. David B. Ottaway, "U.S. Hails Savimbi's Proposals to Sit Out UNITA-Angolan Talks," *Washington Post* (March 28, 1989), A16.
103. *African Economic Digest* (February 13, 1989), 3.
104. *African Economic Digest* (November 29, 1986), 19.
105. Jim Hoagland, "Angola Vows to Work With U.S. Despite Bush Commitment to Savimbi," *Washington Post* (January 14, 1989), A15.
106. *Ibid.*
107. *Financial Times* (May 18, 1989), 4.
108. *Ibid.*
109. Karl Maier, "Mozambique: The Battle for Zambezia," *Africa Report* (March-April, 1989), 22.
110. *Ibid.*
111. William Claiborne, "Mozambique Role for U.S. Still Unclear," *Washington Post* (February 11, 1989), A14.
112. Robert Gersony, "Summary of Mozambican Refugee Accounts of Principally Conflict-Related Experience in Mozambique," Bureau for Refugee Programs, Department of State, (Washington, D.C., April, 1988).
113. *Africa Research Bulletin* (March 15, 1989), 75.
114. Karl Maier, *op. cit.*, 15.

115. *African Research Bulletin* (February 15, 1989), 54.
116. *Financial Times* (March 31, 1989), 4.
117. *Economist* (April 2-28, 1989), 23.
118. *Africa Research Bulletin* (February 29, 1988), 8893.
119. *Africa Research Bulletin* (February 28, 1989), 9421.
120. *Ibid.*
121. Thompson, "Self-Sufficiency and Regional Coordination," 31.
122. *Africa Economic Digest* (August 30, 1986), 25.
123. *Ibid.*
124. *Africa Research Bulletin* (August 31, 1986), 8307.
125. *Southern African Economist* (February-March, 1988), 31.
126. *Africa Research Bulletin* (April 15, 1988), 8904.
127. Harvey Glickman, "Reconstructionist Strategies in Mozambique: Crisis Intervention and Beyond," *Issue* 17 (Winter, 1988), 21-24.
128. Cited by Ethan Schwartz, "U.N. Council Votes Peace Force for Namibia," *Washington Post*, (February 17, 1985), A35.
129. Lally Weymouth, "A Moscow-Pretoria Axis? Why Two Enemies are Beginning to Talk," *Washington Post*, (December 18, 1988), C1-C2.
130. *Ibid.*
131. Personal communication, (April 30, 1989).
132. Cleary, *op. cit.*, 128.

The SADCC and the Front Line States; Viewing Their Performance: A Comment

W. Ofuatey-Kodjoe.

The Southern Africa Development Coordinating Conference (SADCC) and the Front Line States (FLS) represent two sectors of a single collective response of the black states of Southern Africa to the attempts of the Republic of South Africa (RSA) to maintain *apartheid* at home and to establish a political, economic and military hegemony over the region. In the short term, the primary objectives of the two organizations are to reduce their economic dependence on, and their military vulnerability to the Republic of South Africa.[1] In the middle term, their objectives are to assist the liberation movements in the dismantling of *apartheid*, and to reduce their general international dependency.[2] Finally, in the long term, they seek to establish balanced, equitable collective development in a post-*apartheid* Southern Africa.[3] Considered together, therefore, the FLS and the SADCC have as their *raison d'etre* the collective security and collective development of their members; objectives that are considered by the members to be complementary and mutually reinforcing.[4]

Khadiagala sets out to answer the question whether they will be able to achieve their objectives. His response is that the hostile actions of the Republic of South Africa and their own internal weaknesses have seriously inhibited and will continue to inhibit the ability of the FLS and the SADCC to succeed on their own, and that their success will depend on. the support of external actors. He supports his conclusion by analyzing the activities of the members of these organizations, particularly Mozambique and Angola, the two countries that have borne the brunt of South Africa's aggression. He also projects the most likely scenarios of conditions in the region in the 1990s.

Khadiagala concentrates on three features of the SADCC: the novel sectoral approach of the organization; the priority given to transportation as the key sector in the strategy of dependence reduction; and the fact that the overwhelming proportion of the resources needed for funding SADCC projects and providing security has come from external donors such as the European Economic Community (EEC), the World Bank, the African Development Bank (ADB), Britain, Cuba and the Scandinavian countries.

Khadiagala observes that the pursuit of the objectives of the FLS and the SADCC have been severely constrained by South Africa's "total strategy" of destabilizing the SADCC countries, and the support given South Africa by the NATO powers, particularly the United States, presumably for the purpose of thwarting communist encroachments in the region. On the basis of these patterns, he develops a scenario of conditions in the region in the 1990s that is characterized by a) continued destabilization by South Africa, exemplified by Botha's 1988 visit to Zaire where such intentions were explicitly expressed, b) the emergence of "national conciliation" in Mozambique and Angola, due *inter alia* to war weariness; c) pressure from external actors; d) the preference of the U.S.A. and the U.S.S.R. for a negotiated settlement in the region as shown in the United Nations Security Council resolution on Namibia; and e) the emerging possibility of a Moscow-Pretoria rapprochement. In Khadiagala's view such a 'conciliation' is worthy of approval and endorsement as a situation that will permit Mozambique and Angola to make more significant contributions to the politics of dependence reduction, as well as increase the possibility of attracting foreign aid to the region.

On the whole Khadiagala presents an accurate account of the objectives and some of the activities of the FLS and the SADCC countries. The scenarios of national conciliation in Mozambique and Angola are supported by events that have unfolded in the region in May and June 1989. Several important aspects of the activities of the FLS and the SADCC require further exploration. First, without denying the importance of Mozambique and Angola in the politics of Southern Africa, a consideration of the inter-state relations of the region must include an examination of the activities of other key actors in the region, such as Zimbabwe, Zambia and Tanzania. The activities of these countries have had a profound effect on the politics of the region, as well as on the eventual viability of the SADCC itself, especially with regard to the provision of security for the "corridors" of the Southern Africa Transport and Communications Corporation (SATCC). Furthermore, the activities of individual countries, even important countries, cannot be considered as representing the positions and activities of the organizations under investigation. For instance, although the FLS has taken a position favoring the application of sanctions against South Africa, support for this position was far from unanimous. At the 1985 Arusha Summit, seven members, including Lesotho supported sanctions while two other members disagreed, although they decided not to block the collective decision.[5] Therefore, a thorough understanding of the functioning of these organizations requires an examination of the dynamic relations among the members.

Second, given the centrality of apartheid as a key factor in the political economy of the region, it is necessary to analyze the "total strategy" of

South Africa, especially the South African decision-makers' perceptions of changing international conditions which may require different tactical responses. Such analysis permits us to assess elements of flexibility and rigidity in the strategies of the Republic of South Africa. For instance, it might also be useful to determine the extent to which South Africa will actually carry out its threats to retaliate against the SADCC in the event of the implementation of comprehensive sanctions against it, and how such retaliation would actually affect the ability of the FLS to achieve their objectives of reducing their dependence on South Africa.

Third, the analysis requires an evaluation of the performance of the FLS and the SADCC in relation to their own declared objectives, and in relation to their potential to help in bringing about peace and security in the region. We need to examine the problems which they have had to face, how they have tried to cope with these problems, some of the contradictions in the performance of these organizations, as well as situational exigencies. It should then be possible to identify the major factors that have affected the failures and successes of the FLS and the SADCC in the past and thus be able to suggest what their prospects might be regarding the achievement of their basic objectives of dependence reduction and security

An evaluation of the performance record of the SADCC and the FLS shows a mixture of successes and failures. The SADCC operations got off to an impressive start. By 1984 over 250 projects had been identified and approved. Much of the estimated cost of over $4.6 billion had been negotiated and many of the projects were well under way.[6] In particular, the performance of the SATCC in the rehabilitation of rail links and port facilities was such that it was estimated that by mid 1989 the road, rail and port facilities would be able to handle virtually all the trade of the SADCC countries.[7] In addition, SADCC had recorded some successes in regard to the connection of its members with air links, satellite communications, and a regional microwave network, so that there was "some growth in the total level of intra-regional transactions."[8]

Yet, with regard to the short term objectives of dependence reduction and security, the SADCC has been less successful. Economic performance in the region has been disappointing. There has been general stagnation, leading to decreases in production, trade and gross domestic product, acute shortages of foreign exchange, and serious problems of debt service. It is estimated that the average SADCC citizen is ten percent poorer since 1980.[9] Most important, the majority of SADCC countries are not only economically weaker, but they are also more dependent than ever on the Republic of South Africa.[10]

In the area of security, the FLS have had a great deal of difficulty in coping with the South African campaign of sabotage, terror and aggression. The most dramatic evidence of this was the capitulation of Mozambique and Angola in the Nkomati and Lusaka Accords, respectively. In spite of these agreements, the aggression of South Africa continued, so that by 1986 the FLS seemed to be on the brink of collapse. A year later they seemed to have turned the situation around and they were able to provide some security for the rehabilitated rail links.[11] This development has led Reginald Green to note, "This literally is the SADCC's war, and at last, the SADCC has been able to move off the defensive and is winning."[12] While South Africa has reduced the pressure on the FLS, this is due more to the success than the failure of the "total strategy". Indeed, the "reconciliations" that South Africa has been able to instigate are really major concessions by FRELIMO and MPLA, one of the costs of which has been an even further abandonment of the African National Congress (ANC).

The performance of the SADCC and the FLS may be analyzed in terms of two factors: the structures, strategies and resources of the organizations, and the situational exigencies with which they have had to contend. A great deal has been made of the novel SADCC approach to regional integration, emphasizing sectoral coordination and the primacy of national decision-making.[13] These strategies have had some effect on the development of projects and the securing of funding. However, in terms of actual performance, the effect of these structures and strategies has been relatively minor.[14] The factor that has proved to be most decisive has been the lack of financial and military capability.

The lack of capital in the region is so acute that SADCC has had to depend on outside donors for more than eighty percent of the funding for its projects.[15] The effect is to increase the dependence of SADCC on the Western powers. Apart from increasing the possibility of donor manipulation, this imposes a pattern of investment and trade which will lock them into the role of producers of raw materials and importers of manufactured goods.[16] In terms of the SADCC objective of reducing their dependence on South Africa, the economies of the Western powers are so integrated with that of South Africa that SADCC's increased dependence on Europe in fact *increases* their dependence on South Africa.[17] The view that substituting dependence on Europe for dependence on South Africa is a step in the right direction turns out to be just so much wishful thinking.

The fact that the SADCC and the FLS suffer from military insufficiency in the face of South African aggression is an undisputable fact. The South African Defense forces maintain superiority over all the defense forces in the region. The South Africans demonstrated the ability to use these forces with skill and flexibility, commando raids in support of their surrogates in neighboring countries, and in repeated invasions and acts of sabotage.[18] Cuban forces in Angola were able to keep that country from being overrun. Their departure from the scene could have serious consequences for the security of the region, if South African adherence to previous agreements is any guide.

The institutional and resource problems of the SADCC and the FLS have also left them vulnerable to a variety of situational exigencies. The prolonged drought severely curtailed food production. The global recession which exacerbated problems of declining industrial output and external debt.

An external factor of some significance for the performance of SADCC has been the policies of foreign countries. The most active external actors in Southern Africa have been the European countries. The Arab countries have shown little interest. Cuba has has had troops in Angola since that country became independent. There is some doubt as to whether the MPLA regime would have survived without the Cubans. The Soviet Union has traditionally provided some support for the national liberation movements in southern Africa. The role of the Western powers, the most active group in the region, has been the subject of some controversy. Their activities seems to be simultaneously supportive of South Africa's *apartheid* regime and its enemies. The Western powers seem to support SADCC projects because of their own economic interests and "as a soft option, a face saving commitment, a dubious counter balance to their involvement with South Africa."[19] The NATO powers seem receptive to the dismantling of *apartheid*, but only if can be accomplished peacefully, and in a way that would leave intact the capitalist nature of the country and the interests of the white minority. Consistent with these interests, the NATO powers have been willing to give tacit support to South Africa's attempt to establish a political, economic and military hegemony over the whole area.[20] The behavior of the detente-minded Soviet Union in the Namibian negotiations may reflect its unwillingness to support armed struggle unconditionally in Southern Africa and its readiness to concede the region to the West.

Another group of interested actors are the African countries. These countries are on record in the United Nations and other international fora to be unequivocally opposed to *apartheid*. This may be so in rhetorical terms. However, the reality is that on the question of how to deal with South Africa, the African community is beset with ambivalence and ambiguity. In any case, the African opposition to apartheid decided at the inception of the Organization of African Unity (OAU) that their support for national liberation in southern Africa will mainly be in the area of diplomatic activity. Few, if any, African countries have the inclination or the ability to engage South Africa in armed conflict.

What are the prospects of the SADCC and the FLS achieving their objectives in the near term? What are the opportunities and constraints facing these organizations? The most important factors are the objectives and the capabilities of the Republic of South Africa, and the reactions of interested actors. At the present time, the objectives of South Africa are to maintain *apartheid* at home, and to establish a political, economic and military hegemony in the region, as it is articulated in the concept of the

Constellation of Southern African States (CONSAS). It has demonstrated
in its "total strategy" that it has the capability to achieve this objective if
there is no interference from the larger international community. As long
as this objective and capability are maintained, the only peace that is
possible in Southern Africa is one that is imposed by South Africa. Such
a 'pacification' will be a racialist, capitalist political-economic order
involving the "homelands" and the SADCC countries under the
domination of South Africa.

Whether the maintenance of *apartheid* will continue to be the objective
of the Republic of South Africa depends primarily on the balance of
internal political forces. It may be that the liberal opposition, the
nationalist hardliners, the anti-*apartheid* coalitions, the labor movements
and others might eventually produce a leadership which would be willing
to move toward a negotiated agreement of the Zimbabwe type.

In the event that South Africa continues to maintain *apartheid*, the
SADCC and the FLS will have no option but to adopt a confrontational
posture, even if only rhetorically. The FLS have a responsibility to be
seen as the vanguard of the anti-*apartheid* movement; a major deviation
would undermine their legitimacy. Such confrontation will probably be
limited to diplomatic efforts. It is clear, since Nkomati, that active
support of armed conflict has been abandoned as a viable option for the
FLS.[21] What is left is a policy of dependent development, with South
Africa as the core. In this situation the amount of hostility between the
SADCC and South Africa will depend on the extent that confrontation is
perceived by South Africa as a threat to the stability of the region. The
more hostility there is, the more police actions will be undertaken by
South Africa. Under such circumstances the ability of the SADCC and the
FLS to provide security or to reduce its dependency will be severely
limited.

In the event that South Africa decides to abandon *apartheid*, the policy
of dependent development will still an the option open to the SADCC.
Under such conditions, however, there would be no grounds for hostility
between South Africa and the SADCC. Therefore, there will be
incentives on both sides for more harmonious relations and higher
economic integration. Here the opportunity exists for the SADCC to
work out relations with a post-*apartheid* South Africa which would grant
to its members some possibility of economic growth and development.
Such a policy is in fact consistent with the bourgeois aspirations of the
political and economic elites in Southern Africa. Such a policy is also
consistent with the desire of the NATO powers to develop the same type
of patron-client relations in the region that exist between the EEC and the
African, Caribbean and Pacific (ACP) countries.

This analysis suggests that neither the option of confrontation or
dependent development provide a solution to the problem of the SADCC
and the FLS. As we have seen, the policy of confrontation cannot

succeed unless conditions within the Republic of South Africa are fortuitous, and unless the Western powers support it. In the meantime, South Africa can be expected to retaliate vigorously. On the other hand, the policy of dependent development is more appropriately called "underdevelopment" unless *apartheid* is dismantled. If the root cause of this dilemma is *apartheid*, and if no solution is viable if *apartheid* persists, then the SADCC and the FLS might do well to consider adopting the policy of confrontation as the most appropriate.

This may seem paradoxical because of the limited probability of success and the high probability of South African reprisals. However, if it is true that the objectives of security and dependence reduction cannot be achieved without dismantling *apartheid*, then the elimination of *apartheid* should be the main target of these organizations. They have to go back to the original idea of the elimination of *apartheid* as their *raison d'etre*. Furthermore, by taking a strong confrontational posture, and giving full support to the ANC, they would make a most important contribution to activating two sources of action that are indispensable for the destruction of *apartheid*, namely, the Western powers, who, history has shown, will become involved against *apartheid* only when their global and local interests are jeopardized by extreme instability; and the anti-*apartheid* forces within South Africa, without whom the entire enterprise has no meaning.

Notes

1. D. Anglin, "SADCC After Nkomati" *African Affairs*, 84(335) (April, 1985), 163.
2. J. Amon Nsekela, ed., *Southern Africa: Toward Economic Liberation* (London: Rex Collings, 1984), 2-3.
3. Reginald Green, "The SADCC on the Frontline: Breakdown or Breakthrough?" in Colin Legum, ed. *Africa Contemporary Record* (New York: Africana Publishing Co., 1988), A83.
4. Reginald Green and Carol B. Thompson, "Political Economies in Conflict: SADCC, South Africa and Sanctions," in Phyllis Johnson and David Martin, eds., *Destructive Engagement: Southern Africa at War* (Harare: Zimbabwe Publishing House, 1986), 246. Also see Christopher Hill, "Regional Cooperation in Southern Africa" *African Affairs*, 82(327) (April, 1983), 217.
5. Green and Thompson, *op. cit.*, 275.
6. Stein Rossen, "Aspects of Economic Integration Policies in Africa, with Special Reference to the Southern African Development Conference" in Tore Rose, ed., *Crisis and Recovery in Subsaharan Africa* (Paris: OECD, 1985), 282.
7. Green, *op. cit.*, A84.
8. Anglin, *op. cit.*, 173.
9. Rossen, *op. cit.*, 285.
10. Anglin, *op. cit.*,170; and Derrick Chitala, "The Political Economy of SADCC and Imperialism's Response" in Samir Amin, Derrick Chitala and Ibbo Mandaza, eds., *SADCC: Prospects for Disengagement and Development in Southern Africa* (London: Zed Books Ltd., 1987), 221. Also see Ibbo Mandaza, "Perspectives on Economic Cooperation and Autonomous Development in Southern Africa" in Samir Amin *et al.*, eds., *op. cit.*, 214.

11. Green, *op. cit.*, A89
12. *Ibid.*, A90.
13. Rossen, *op. cit.*, 28.
14. Hill ,*op. cit.*, 227.
15. Anglin, *op. cit.*,176.
16. Green and Thompson, *op. cit.*, 268. Also see W. Ofuatey-Kodjoe, 'The Economic Policies of the OECD Countries toward Africa" presented at a Conference entitled *What Cooperation With Africa*, at the Instituto Italo Africano in Rome, Italy (April 2-5, 1989),.26
17. Mandaza, "Perspectives on Economic Cooperation," 214.
18. Green and Thompson, *op. cit.*, 251.
19. Ibbo Mandaza, "Conflict in Southern Africa" in Emmanuel Hansen, ed., *Africa: Perspectives on Peace and Development* (London: Zed Books Ltd., 1987), 112.
20. Hill, *op. cit.*, 236. See also Chitala, *op. cit.*, 15.
21. Anglin, *op. cit.*, 181.

8
Namibia:
Reflections on Relative Independence

Joseph B. Diescho

INTRODUCTION

When British Prime Minister Harold Macmillan politely warned South Africa on February 3, 1960, that the "winds of change" were blowing across the African Continent, the case of Namibia was pending before the International Court of Justice (ICJ). Many people assumed that the territory of South West Africa, like other colonial territories, would be free soon. That was thirteen years after the South African government had submitted its last report to the United Nations, in accordance with the mandate it has been given by the League of Nations in 1920 to develop the indigenous peoples of Namibia materially, socially, economically and politically.[1] Even after the ICJ itself ruled in favor of South West Africa in 1966, the South African regime continued to administer the territory. Only in 1969 did the United Nations finally declare South Africa's occupation of Namibia illegal and ask South Africa to leave.

In the ensuing years, South Africa refused to give up Namibia despite numerous United Nations resolutions condemning South Africa's presence there. While the U.N. Council for Namibia and the United Nations Commissioner for Namibia have been Namibia's *de jure* administrators, South Africa has been its *de facto* ruler. As soon as South Africa took over the administration from the defeated Germans in 1915, discriminatory laws were imposed and the Namibian people were excluded from the political and economic life of the country. In 1959, in response to growing repression of the African people, Namibians began to organize resistance on the political front and to publicize their case to the world, chiefly through the South West African People's Organization (SWAPO). But peaceful efforts by the African people, both inside South Africa and in Namibia, were met with state violence. Black leaders were harassed, detained, and sometimes killed. On August 26, 1966, the military wing of SWAPO fired its first shots on the South African occupying forces in northern Namibia. The armed struggle began.[2]

This struggle was born of the direct experience of the African people in Namibia, who have suffered systematic genocide for more than a century -- first at the hands of Germany and then at the hands of South Africa.[3] The German Order of Extermination in 1904 left more than 60,000 Namibians dead. More recently, the South African war on Namibia has left at least half the population dislocated and sent another ten percent into exile. These traumas, coupled with South Africa's methodical use of miseducation of Namibians, have crippled nationalist politics among the people and generated a propensity within the leadership to hope that the U.N. or other organizations in the world will solve the Namibian problem for them. As a result, Namibia has not seen resistance as broad or as intense as in South Africa.

Apartheid has been more successful in Namibia than in South Africa; independence for Namibia comes at a time when its people are divided and without clear leadership. South Africa has deliberately fostered a plethora of political parties in Namibia, in order to control and weaken the resistance by the African Namibians. Party divisions generally follow ethnic lines and differences. There is, however, a huge reservoir for consensus among the people on other issues.

Namibia's situation is unique. The process leading to its independence is unlike other decolonization processes in Africa. The first few months of transition in 1989, preceding the scheduled U.N.-supervised elections, point to several problems that will plague an independent Namibia. Namibia's economy remains inextricably linked to South Africa's. This will force any new government to continuously deal with South Africa, which in turn will lead to disillusionment. Popular expectations are too high and unrealistic, like those in other newly-independent African nations in the twentieth century. The party leaders are protective of their own power. The level of tolerance of dissent in these parties, and especially within the leading organization, SWAPO -- taught through years of opposition, oppression, and infiltration, to distrust both agreement and dissent -- is sadly low.[4] An independent Namibia is ripe for trouble. South Africa stands poised to exploit it.

THE U.N. AND SOUTH AFRICA: RELUCTANT PARTNERS

Namibia has not followed the typical pattern of an oppressed people fighting a single colonial power until victory. Rather, its independence movement emerged against a background of struggle and confrontation between the U.N. and South Africa while elements of the Namibian people vied for the support of one against the other. A consequence has been that Namibians themselves have not been able to develop a culture of resistance and self-reliance upon which to build a strong and sovereign nation. Because of the tension between the U.N. and South Africa, the leading liberation movement, SWAPO, was a friend of neither for a long time.[5] However, in 1973, the U.N., succumbing to pressure from the large African bloc in the General Assembly, recognized SWAPO as "the sole and authentic representative of the Namibian people" -- only thirteen years after SWAPO's formation and arguably too early for SWAPO to have built itself into a mass organization. This juridical recognition, apposite as it was, has had negative consequences. It necessarily antagonized South Africa and led it to support or launch a plethora of political parties inside Namibia. SWAPO became the leading liberation movement without experiencing the usual sequence of development crises (identity, legitimacy, participation, penetration, and distribution) inside the country.[6]

Now, as the independence process unfolds, the U.N. has been forced by South Africa to abandon SWAPO, which it had aided for years, to recognize the other parties in Namibia and to accept South Africa's version of the internal situation. In so doing, the U.N. antagonized Namibians, most of whom had come to regard SWAPO as the liberator of Namibia -- not least because the U.N. and other international organizations had previously recognized it as such.

The U.N. commitment to Namibia's independence has been characterized by ambivalence and conflicts of interest. While member states have for years passed resolutions calling for a Namibia free from South Africa's control, the same U.N., through other mechanisms, would in effect defend South Africa's sovereignty over Namibia. The U.N. has been unable to find a legally binding way to get South Africa out of Namibia without breaking the very principles upon which it was founded and which maintain the U.N. as a supra-national organization. Constrained by its own structure and lack of enforcement mechanisms, the U.N. has been largely powerless to deal with a crypto-fascist but sovereign state like South Africa.

In 1978, the U.N. Security Council passed Resolution 435, (UNSCR 435) which spelled out the process that would lead to Namibia's independence. For over ten years, South Africa had refused to implement the U.N. plan, but without officially repudiating it. In order to appear willing to cooperate with the international community, the South African government complained of flaws in 435 to be rectified. Pointing to its stooge political parties inside Namibia, South Africa accused the U.N. of partiality towards SWAPO, for recognizing it and giving it observer status at the U.N. According to South Africa, the U.S. was not fit to supervise the elections as stipulated, unless it no longer supported SWAPO. The five members of the Western Contact Group -- the U.N., Canada, Great Britain, France, and West Germany -- moved the U.N. towards a compromise that reassured South Africa that the U.N. would not favor SWAPO over the forty-five or so other political parties in Namibia. South Africa garnered reassurances that the U.N. would recognize South Africa as the legal administrator of Namibia during the transition to independence, maintaining law and order, carrying out voter registrations and administering the elections. The apartheid government would thus be in a position to dominate, overrule or thwart the U.N. peace-keeping and administrative forces in Namibia. So the U.N. Plan, Resolution 435, resisted by South Africa and embraced by everyone else, is now lauded by South Africa, but judged by other parties to be seriously compromised.

NAMIBIA AND SOUTH AFRICA

South Africa has had many reasons for prolonging Namibia's colonial status. An independent Namibia might bring South Africa's regional wars closer to home, to the Orange River (Namibia border) instead of the Okavango and Kunene Rivers (Angola border). An independent Namibia will also deprive the South African military of continued on-the-job training of men and equipment -- especially training in the counterinsurgency techniques that may one day be necessary to expand against the African National Congress (ANC). Similarly, an independent Namibia will deprive South Africa of continued access to the Caprivi Strip, which has served South Africa as a launching pad for destabilization acts against Botswana, Zambia, and Zimbabwe.[7] As in Angola, Mozambique an Zimbabwe, independence and black majority rule in Namibia pose the threat of emulation from South Africa's own black majority. When Namibia is no longer the object of negotiation and struggle, attention will be focused inside South Africa and the changes that must occur there.

The South African government has tried to keep Namibia as its "fifth province" and to concede only on the basis of a Pretoria-arranged internal settlement. South Africa has attempted two interim governments in Namibia, under the Democratic Turnhalle Alliance (DTA), 1978-83, and the Multi-Party Conference (MPC), 1985-89. In the December 1978 elections, boycotted by SWAPO, the DTA (promoted by South Africa as a "safe opposition" to SWAPO) won eighty percent of the vote and formed a government based on a National Assembly. This government was dissolved and later placed in the hands of a South African appointed Administrator-General.

On March 1, 1984, South Africa released Andimba Toivo JaToivo, (the founder of SWAPO) from seventeen years' incarceration on Robben Island. His release was sudden and unconditional. He was given a passport and freedom to travel -- a deliberate attempt by South Africa to split the leadership of SWAPO. South Africa was also testing the utility of clemency, to see if leaders such as JaToivo could be rendered less potent out of jail than in. JaToivo opted to go into exile and join the SWAPO leadership, in order not to lend credence to South Africa's scheme. Nonetheless, South Africa succeeded in reducing the political pressures in Namibia: no longer would Amnesty International have a recognizable name to publicize, no longer would Namibians have a jailed leader to galvanize them and no longer could his possible death in prison spark immediate disorders.

The MPC government (based on a coalition of six 'internal' parties, with the DTA at its center) was installed by Pretoria as a "transitional government of national unity" on June 17, 1985. Under this government South Africa retained direct control over foreign affairs and defense and indirect control over finance; the Administrator General continued to exercise considerable power. Like its predecessor, the MPC was condemned by SWAPO as another South African-backed anti-SWAPO front meant to distract African and Western demands for an international settlement to the Namibian question. Like its predecessor, the MPC was considered unrepresentative of the Namibian people, in the words of SWAPO leader Sam Nujoma, an "illegal puppet regime."[8]

Finally in 1988, ten years after UNSCR 435 was first passed, South Africa was persuaded by its Western allies to agree to the U.N. plan. SWAPO and other actors seeking independence for Namibia also announced they agreed to the plan, as the only workable compromise meeting the requirements of most, if not all parties to the dispute. The Namibian churches voiced their agreement through the Council of Churches, as did most other socio-political organizations in Namibia, except for the right-wing, white groups who saw the U.N. as an organization promoting communism.

South Africa did not drop its policy of war upon and destabilization of its neighbors and opt to negotiate merely because it wanted independence for Namibia and peace in Angola. South Africa did not suddenly agree to the so-called peace-and-independence process due to a profound change of heart. Rather, it succumbed to economic, political, diplomatic, and military pressure from many quarters, internal as well as external: the cumulative effects of moderate economic sanctions and the threat of more punitive actions by foreign banks, corporations, and governments; the worsening political and business climate inside South Africa that has necessitated years of the state of emergency; the military inconveniences inflicted by both SWAPO in Namibia for over twenty-two years and the African National Congress (ANC) in South Africa for over thirty years; and the humiliating defeat of the once-invincible South African military by Angola *cum* Cuba in the Battle of Cuito Cuanavale in Southeastern Angola. The defenders of apartheid have begun to appreciate that the days of this system -- secure white privilege and white supremacy in Southern Africa -- are numbered.

THE AMBIGUOUS INTERREGNUM

UNSCR 435 of 1978 provides for South Africa to oversee the transition to independence in Namibia. Resolution 435 was a compromise: the Non-Aligned Movement and SWAPO preferred Resolution 385 of 1976, which required South Africa to withdraw from Namibia and the U.N. to take control during the transition. Since 1978 Resolution 435 has been the working doctrine for Namibia's independence, grudgingly accepted by South Africa. After the U.S. and South Africa realized the latter could not win the war in Angola, the U.S. pushed South Africa to implement Resolution 435. South Africa, in turn, set out to use the considerable loopholes of 435 to turn the situation to its own advantage.

South Africa scored its first victory when the U.N. Security Council recommended cost-saving measures to reduce the budget and the personnel of the United Nations Transitional Assistance Group (UNTAG) sent to Namibia. The African countries objected strongly to this decision. They were ignored or ridiculed by the powerful, permanent members of the Security Council.[9]

Furthermore, the U.N. is a bureaucracy, expected to do a political job in Namibia without political weapons: no communications system, no independent lines to the Namibian people, a negative attitude towards SWAPO, and total dependence on the colonial power for intelligence on the domestic situation. The U.N. position is subordinate to that of the South African-appointed Administrator General. This inverted arrangement was one of the concessions to South Africa to get it to sign the agreements.

There are other reasons for the U.N.'s problems. For one thing, the South African culture is a Western culture, and most of the U.N. troops are from Western cultures; they feel more comfortable with their South African counterparts than with the black Namibians. Conversely, it is difficult for most Namibians to tell the difference between a South African soldier and an Australian U.N. officer with an accent so similar to the South African. It would have been and less confusing to send people to the northern war zone who looked distinctly different from the South African soldiers.

South Africa clearly has its own agenda and its own interests. If South Africa was genuinely decolonizing in Namibia, the UNTAG would not have been necessary in the first place. The original U.N. Plan for Namibia's independence, U.N. Resolution 385 of 1976, aborted by the Western Contact Group, essentially stipulated that South Africa and its apartheid structures would withdraw, so that the U.N. would take over the administration of Namibia during the transition period. Clearly, if the

U.N. were to be able to execute its task unhindered, neither SWAPO nor South Africa would be in charge of law and order. Every juridical system underscores that a party to a dispute cannot be a judge ("Nome judex in sua causa"). In effect the U.N. has been forced to submit to South Africa's blackmail.

On April 1, 1989, the day the Peace Plan was to commence, the heaviest battle in years occurred between the South African Defense Forces (SADF) and SWAPO. Three hundred sixty Namibians were killed by South African ground and helicopter gun fire. There was clearly a breach of the cease-fire agreement of March 1989. South Africa justified its attack on SWAPO soldiers by citing an apparent infiltration of SWAPO fighters over the border from Angola. Even if there had been no infiltration, there have been hundreds of SWAPO guerrilla fighters operating inside Namibia for twenty-two years. Their presence alone could have constituted adequate provocation for South Africa to justify attacking them or threatening to scuttle the whole U.N. process. Implicit in the cease fire arrangement was the acknowledgement that there was a conflict inside Namibia between SWAPO and South Africa, yet South Africa was permitted to use the mere presence of SWAPO soldiers as proof that the cease-fire had been violated. South Africa since then has held a handful of captured SWAPO fighters, whom it can display to support its claim that there are still SWAPO soldiers violating the agreements, justifying a need to keep South African soldiers on active duty.

Either the U.N. Security Council did not fully comprehend the duplicitous character of the South African state or it had a bizarrely insensitive understanding of the crisis in Southern Africa. Clearly, the U.N. was not prepared to provide for the immediate confinements to base of the SWAPO soldiers in Namibia at the time of the cease-fire. Less than a quarter of the assigned U.N. troops were in Namibia at the time of the cease-fire. None were in the northern Namibian war zone. Thus the U.N. turned to the South African military to control the ostensible provocation of SWAPO. The SWAPO soldiers were victims of a situation for which the U.N. Secretary General and his Special Representative in Namibia must take some responsibility.

The protocols signed between Angola, Cuba, and South Africa in December 1988 were described as a tripartite agreement between these three countries. SWAPO was not a formal party to these agreements, and could therefore technically not have violated them: one cannot go back on the promise one has not made. Nonetheless, SWAPO did show insensitivity to the governments of Angola and Cuba, which had undertaken to use their good offices to keep SWAPO forces safely above the sixteenth parallel, about ninety miles from the Namibia-Angolan border.

The cease-fire that was to begin in the morning of April 1st was an agreement by SWAPO and South Africa with the U.N. to cease hostilities and abide by the U.N. Peace Plan. SWAPO forces apparently entered Namibia from Angola in the early hours of April 1st, seeking the U.N. forces to claim recognition and demand bases. This attempt by SWAPO at Realpolitik, had it worked, would have given SWAPO a huge psychological boost in the electoral politics leading to independence, by claiming that liberated zones were in existence before the elections. There is convincing evidence from villagers in the field that SWAPO had no intention of fighting. SADF unfortunately intercepted them and responded militarily.[10]

South Africa's responsibility upon seeing the SWAPO incursion was to report it to the U.N., not to fire any shots. Thereupon, the U.N. was to see to it that the issue was investigated quickly. Instead, South Africa fired upon SWAPO soldiers without notifying the U.N.; later the U.N. authorized South Africa to reactivate its military and police "to restore law and order". South Africa's idea of law and order was to shoot to kill -- and that is exactly what happened. But it was not only soldiers who were killed. Many people wearing SWAPO T-shirts and celebrating the commencement of the peaceful transition on April 1st were beaten, injured and killed throughout the country by the South African police and soldiers, ostensibly maintaining law and order. One cannot help but wonder whether the U.N. would have responded in a similar way if SWAPO made the claims and demands that South Africa has made. Namibian civilians tried several times to contact the U.N., whose officials told them that there was nothing they could do about the situation -- that it was for South Africa to restore law and order.

The whole course of events is a serious indictment of the U.N. Security Council, in general, and the Special Representative in Namibia, in particular, SWAPO had never been the chief problem in Namibia. The U.N. should not blame the victim for the offense of the real culprits -- apartheid South Africa. The U.N. can make amends by augmenting its forces and by allowing the Joint Monitoring Commission of Angola, Cuba and South Africa, initially set up to monitor the phased withdrawal of Cuban troops from Angola, to work towards placing the peace process back on track, through the spirit of the Mount Etjo Declaration of April 9, 1989, and subsequent agreements, whereby the Joint Commission in effect took over the responsibility assigned to the U.N. by UNSCR 435.[11]

At present South Africa's primary effort focuses on controlling and sabotaging the electoral process to determine the results of the elections slated for November 1989. The National Security Council for Namibia reportedly met in September 1988 to plot such a strategy.[12] Through the Voters' Registration Laws, South Africa retains considerable control. According to the legislation, any person who was born in or whose parents were born in Namibia or who has resided in Namibia four years prior to the elections, is entitled to vote. Some SWAPO officials could technically be excluded from voting, because they were born in Angola or elsewhere in Southern Africa, before growing up in Namibia, but they had not resided in Namibia for the four years preceding the elections. At the same time, over 40,000 Angolans who have fled Angola since independence and who have been integrated by South Africa into local communities in Namibia will be eligible to vote; these Angolans, by virtue of their refugee status, will invariably vote for the DTA, their host and the party favored by South Africa. The six hundred polling stations to be used during the elections to the Constituent Assembly will be staffed by South African-appointed supervisors who will "assist" illiterate constituent to vote.

The elections to the Constituent Assembly will be conducted according to the system of proportional representation, making it very difficult for any party to obtain a clear majority, especially in Namibia, where South Africa has undertaken a conscious policy of creating political parties along tribal and ethnic lines. Today, besides SWAPO, there are approximately forty-five other political parties. In addition, the names on the ballots will be identified as tribal names, a factor which will promote tribal voting.

South Africa has been carrying out a policy of intimidation and harassment of prospective SWAPO voters. SWAPO supporters are monitored. After meeting they are interrogated on a regular basis by South African police and military. Other psychological and physical forms of intimidation have been reported numerous times to and by United Nations personnel.

The nature of power-sharing arrangements between South Africa and the U.N. makes it difficult for the U.N. to guarantee that people can vote without fear. In general, U.N. officials are hampered by not knowing Afrikaans or the local African languages.

South Africa continues to control the bureaucracy, communications, intelligence, and infrastructure in Namibia. This enhances South Africa's ability to control the outcome of the elections. If SWAPO does not get the two-third majority vote required for one party to have legislative power, the other parties will be so divided that South Africa will probably demand a coalition government with SWAPO as a minority party.

The return of thousands Namibians from exile, some of whom have been kept in SWAPO detention camps, will contribute to an already tense atmosphere. In addition, there is the problem of Koevoet ("crowbar"), the dreaded South African-trained counterinsurgency unit in Namibia, which has long been the cutting edge of South Africa's war against SWAPO. This unit has internalized a culture of violence, duplicity and destruction. Koevoet members have been integrated into the "normal" police force that South Africa will use to maintain law and order during the transition.

Given that South Africa is to provide basic security to the SWAPO leadership upon its return, it is possible that the South African-appointed Administrator General, Louis Pienaar, might assign an ex-Koevoet officer to guard the SWAPO president Sam Nujoma.

The U.N. Plan calls for the release of all political prisoners and the scrapping of all restrictive and discriminatory laws in Namibia as a prerequisite for the return of refugees. South Africa in the past has claimed the right to keep or redetain any prisoner for political reasons, under the notorious AG 9, which allows any police officer to arrest anybody for any reason, and to hold him/her ninety days without trial or access to law.

THE QUESTION OF WALVIS BAY

The status of Walvis Bay, which was never part of German South West Africa, and therefore, according to South Africa, not part of Namibia remains unresolved.[13]   Both SWAPO and South Africa vow to have it when Namibia gains independence. Walvis Bay is the most controversial issue that SWAPO and the U.N. have decided to leave to the government of an independent Namibia to negotiate with South Africa. After South Africa incorporated Walvis Bay in 1977, the U.N. passed Resolution 432, calling for the "reintegration of Walvis Bay into Namibia", although it did not require that step as part of Resolution 435. South Africa, however, is committed to retaining the port, and conceded only that it would be willing to negotiate the future of this vital port with a *moderate* government in Namibia.

Walvis Bay is crucial to the Namibia, and the regional economy. It is important for Namibia's access to the world, for its fishing industry and for military installations to provide security against South Africa's destabilization efforts. The port is an alternative to Lobito, Angola, served by the unreliable Benguela railroad; and it could help Botswana to reduce its dependence on South Africa. Given the main emphasis of SADCC on the self reliance in transport and communication, South Africa's insistence on Walvis Bay denies the port a role as a new avenue for all of Southern Africa.

South Africa uses the Walvis Bay issue in electoral politics. According to the Draft Registration of Voters Proclamation (General Notice No.58, promulgated on April 24, 1989), Namibians born in Walvis Bay are not considered "born in the territory". Thus, technically, they are excluded from participating in the elections. If they are allowed to vote in the upcoming elections, there will be much confusion, affecting the results. South Africa thus has created a basis to deny SWAPO access to Walvis Bay in the campaign.

South Africa keeps both army and navy forces in Walvis Bay, while maintaining an intimate relationship with the well-trained, disbanded-but-still-armed black soldiers in the South West Africa Territorial Force (SWATF) -- a constant threat to Namibia's independence. Furthermore, South Africa's bases in Walvis Bay will provide a center for malcontents among the South African trained soldiers of SWATF who will likely be integrated into the new Namibia National Defence Force. This fits with South Africa's "Total Strategy," to keep a stranglehold over Namibia and Southern Africa as a whole. An independent Namibia will have to negotiate the future of its port with the ex-colonial administration. Litigation in the International Court of Justice might be necessary, a long and costly process.[14]

VIABILITY OF INDEPENDENT NAMIBIA

Namibia faces enormous problems in its quest for genuine independence. In addition to the immediate problems of nation-building in an infant nation like Namibia and South Africa's potential for destabilization, there are numerous long-term worries. The biggest task the new government in Namibia will face is economic survival. Namibia's economy is fragile. For the past decade economic growth has averaged only one percent. Population growth is three to four percent. Unemployment may be as high as thirty-three percent. About eighty percent of Namibia's economy is South African. Ninety percent of its exports go to or through South Africa. Namibia is heavily dependent upon the export of uranium, diamonds, base metals, cattle, karakul sheepskins, fishmeal, and fishoil. The economy is dominated by South African investors; thirty-five percent of total Namibian GDP goes to South Africa through foreign mining firms -- (two-thirds of which are South African) -- in the form of remitted profits.[15] Fifteen percent of Namibia's GNP is from agriculture; the export component is produced primarily on settler-owned farms, on arid land. The new government will have to revamp land utilization in order to provide for the essential needs of the Namibian people. To change land use patterns, without disrupting the agricultural economy and alienating the land-owning white farmers, will be an arduous task. Namibia's large white settler farms will continue to dominate agricultural production.

Unlike many African countries, Namibia has a diversified mineral base that can strengthen the country's economy with time and good management. SWAPO is now promising the white settler farmers a mixed economy, that their properties will not be touched without compensation.[16] SWAPO, like the governments of most African countries, has begun to appreciate the dangers of alienating skilled and knowledgeable whites after independence. When they exit, expertise and a fundamental economic base depart. The consequences are deterioration of the economy, leading to increased political instability.

South Africa has long subsidized the Namibian budget with a "contribution" toward defense, which in the estimated 1988/89 budget totaled R308 million. South Africa also transferred an annual sum in lieu of customs and excise receipts, which in 1988/89 totaled an estimated R392 million. South Africa acts as guarantor of about R750 million of commercial debt held by the government in Namibia (out of a total R1 billion incurred by successive interim governments over the past decade), some of which is used to finance the rapidly increasing Namibian budget deficit. Windhoek has had to pick up administrative costs previously covered by Pretoria for police, transportation, and allocations to ethnic authorities (the extremely cumbersome and expensive mechanisms for separately governing the country's ethnic groups).[17]

Up to seventeen percent of Namibia's state budget comes from South African subsidies. Most civil servants are seconded officials whose first loyalty is to their departments in South Africa. These officials are agitating to reverse South Africa's decision to pay the costs for the 1989 financial year. If South Africa wishes to squeeze Namibia, it can do so by refusing to pay the subsidy for 1989-90, which would leave the transitional authorities with the option of raising taxes or cutting services. Most foreign governments are reluctant to give aid to Namibia until independence.[18]

Ironically, the accumulated debt puts Namibia in a marginally favorable position. With over R1 billion owed mostly to South African banks, an independent Namibia can refuse to foot the bill incurred by colonial South Africa. But Namibia uses South African currency and has no central bank of its own, probably keeping Namibia in the South African Customs union and Common Monetary Area for some time. Considerable restructuring will face an economy that imports more than eighty-five percent of consumption and exports ninety percent of production. For example, more radical nationalists in SWAPO have suggested changes in the mining sector, to include a greater role for local and public capital, an increase in parastatal companies, cooperatives and joint ventures, a greater reinvestment of mining returns, higher tax rates and the creation of mineral-based processing industries. Drastic changes in the agricultural and livestock sector could include possible land redistribution. To protect the over-exploited fishing industry a new government in Namibia might resort to establishing a national fishing company and declaring a two hundred mile exclusive economic zone, and allocating quotas and imposing levies on foreign companies.

INDEPENDENCE ISSUES

The expectations generated during the national struggle in pre-nation communities such as Namibia, are enormous and often too high for any government to fulfill. The process leading to Namibia's independence came about largely as a result of sustained pressure on South Africa to cooperate. SWAPO has become the object of South African vilification in its campaign of political, economic and social strategies to prevent a SWAPO government in Namibia. South Africa's economic strategy, started before the transition process, equates a SWAPO victory with "raising the red flag over Windhoek".[19] South Africa has begun the process of auctioning and privatizing parts of the economy in order to thwart any redistribution of land and property.

Namibians have to adjust to the end of war for twenty-two years, not only with South Africa, but with one another. The majority of the people live in the north; they have lived under martial law since the 1970s. The trained soldiers in SWATF, used to steady and lucrative employment, and the eighty thousand returning refugees, will require reincorporation into the economy and civil society. SWATF became the largest employer in Namibia in the 1980's, particularly in the northern war zone.

SWATF troops are being demobilized but they are allowed to keep their weapons and can be called back at short notice. South Africa counts on the effects of efforts to win the hearts and minds of the Namibian people, through psychological Civic Action Programs, such as *Etango* in Owamboland, *Ezuva* in Kavango and *Namwi* in Caprivi. In their attempts to win support, the South Africans distributed economic benefits in return for anti-SWAPO work.[20]

South Africa has prepared a social problem through the Voters Registration Proclamation, to take advantage of tribal and ethnic tensions. The Namibian leadership is tribally and ethnically based. Barring repression it will be politically weak, and thus unable to embark on programs, to distribute resources more equitably or to promote rapid national development. The government will also face an array of anti-SWAPO groups, supported by South Africa, which could take to guerrilla action, similar to RENAMO in Mozambique.

The question of Namibia's territorial integrity remains uncertain. Contrary to international law, South Africa claims that the southern border between the two countries at the Orange River is at the high-water mark on the Namibian side, instead of at the midpoint of the river. The mouth of the Orange River, in the Atlantic Ocean, covers the Kudu gas fields. The waters of the Orange River, flowing from the Kimberley area in South Africa, carry diamonds washed on to land in the Oranjemund area, explaining why South Africa insists on high-water facilities. Walvis Bay remains another crucial territorial problem, already noted.

Namibians have an impressive capacity to want to work together. They have great resilience. The leadership understands what they are up against. But the political dynamics of Namibia's history, a history with many actors achieving little, and a decolonization process left far too much in the hands of the colonizer, point to a new government likely to be concerned mostly about its own survival, unable to mobilize and politicize the masses of the people for real change, genuine freedom and self reliance. The struggle continues. Until South Africa itself is liberated from minority white control, Namibia's independence, although a step in the right direction, leaves much to be desired.

Notes

1. The League of Nations gave Namibia (South West Africa) to South Africa to administer as a Mandate in category C, which meant that the administering authority treated the colony as if it was an integral part of the authority. South Africa therefore did not conquer Namibia. When the U.N. was formed after World War II, South Africa was requested to hand over the territory to the new U.N. Trusteeship system, and South Africa refused to do so. See United Nations, *A Principle in Torment - The U.N. and Namibia* (New York, 1971); John Dugard, *The South West Africa/Namibia Dispute* (Los Angeles: U.C.B. Press, 1973).
2. The war in Namibia has not left a single family untouched. There will be repercussions to this devastation. See David Soggot, *Namibia, The Violent Heritage* (New York: St. Martin's Press, 1986); Reginald Green, *Namibia: The Last Colony* (London: Longman Group, 1981).
3. For a discussion of South Africa's military experience in Angola and in Namibia's decolonization process, see Horace Campbell, "The Military Defeat of the South Africans in Angola," *Monthly Review* 40(11) (April, 1989), 1-15. A good discussion of Namibia is Gretchen Bauer's "Prospects for the Decolonization of Namibia," unpublished research paper (University of Wisconsin-Madison, April, 1989). See also Allard K. Loewenstein, *Brutal Mandate: A Journey South West Africa* (New York: Macmillan, 1962); Ruth First, *South West Africa* (Harmondsworth: Penguin Books, 1963).
4. After the U.N. recognition of SWAPO as the "sole and authentic" representative of Namibia, its attitude towards other parties has been condemnatory and quite hostile. See Na-iem Dollie, *A Political Review of Namibia; Nationalism in Namibia* (Windhoek, Self-published, 1988). See also Robert I. Rotberg, *Namibia: Political and Economic Prospects* (Lexington, MA: Lexington Books, 1983).
5. In the 1970s SWAPO often referred to the U.N. as imperialist, not good enough, and not trustworthy. See William Minter, *King Solomon's Mines Revisited* (New York: Basic Books, 1986), 241.
6. See Leonard Binder, *et al., Crises and Sequences in Political Development,* (Princeton: Princeton University Press, 1971).
7. See Economist Intelligence Unit, *Country Profile: Namibia 1988-1989* (London: EIU, 1988), 12
8. "Null and Void," *Action on Namibia* (January 10, 1985). Members of the Western Contact Group agreed, declaring the transfer of power to the interim government in Namibia null and void.
9. South Africa consistently complained to the U.N. about the size of the U.N. forces to be sent to Namibia. See Archie W. Singham and Shirley Hune,

Namibian Independence: A Global Responsibility (Westport: Lawrence Hill, 1986).

10. See *South Africa Now*, No. 211, TV program, (New York: WNET, April 18, 1989), for disclosures on South African military action surrounding the April 1 incidents. The U.N. and the Western Press were dependent on South African intelligence and communications for most reports. Also see Dave Clemens, "Weak Link in the Namibian Pact," *International Herald Tribune* (April 5, 1989); David Beresford, "SWAPO 'Did Not Sign Accord,' " *Guardian* (London, April 6, 1989); "They Are SWAPO and Dead," *Sunday Telegraph* (London, April 9, 1989).

11. On April 9th, South Africa , Angola and Cuba, with the U.S. and U.S.S.R. acting as observers, signed a pact that would commit them to assist putting the U.N. Peace Plan on track. Subsequent to this, similar meetings were held by the parties to look at the progress of the Plan and the withdrawal of Cubans from Angola as agreed in the Geneva Protocol of December 13, 1988 and the New York Agreement of December 22, 1988. See Southern Africa Research Centre, "The Namibian Transition to Independence: A Dossier of the Principal Documents" (Harare, May 10, 1989).

12. *The Namibian* (June 7, 1989). Significantly, the Elections Officer, Mr. Visser, appointed by the Administrator General, is himself a member of the National Security Council.

13. South Africa's claim to Walvis Bay and the coastal land area of Namibia grew vigorous in the anticipation of Namibia's independence. The claim is legalistic and technical, going as far back as March 12, 1878, when the British annexed the port and surroundings as part of the Cape Colony, thus not allowing it to be part of German South West Africa. South Africa claims that Walvis Bay is neither part of Namibia nor privy to the independence process. See Richard Moorsom, *Walvis Bay: Namibia's Port* (London: International Aid and Defense Fund for Southern Africa in cooperation with the U.N. Council for Namibia, 1984).

14. When questioned by a reporter on Walvis Bay, the U.N. special representative in Namibia , Martti Ahtisaari, replied that it is an issue that will have to be taken up by the new government. See The Lawyers Committee for Civil Rights under Law, "This Week in Namibia: Week of May 28-June 4" (Windhoek, 1989).

15. *Africa Research Bulletin*, Economic Series, (Jan. 31, 1989), 9388; *The Economist* (June 24, 1989), 42. See also Rotberg, *op. cit.*

16. There were meetings between SWAPO and business and community leaders from Namibia in Sweden and in Kabwe, Zambia, in the second half of 1988. See "A Future Economy," *The Namibian* (April 5, 1989), 4, an address by SWAPO to the Business International in London. The "Principles for a Constitution for an Independent Namibia" also call for protection from expropriation of private property without compensation. See Southern Africa Research and Documentation Centre, "The Namibian Transition to Independence: A Dossier of the Principal Documents" (Harare, May 10, 1989).

17. See Economist Intelligence Unit, *Namibia*, 35-36 for a discussion of the military budget in Namibia as a factor that helped force South Africa to employ other methods of conflict resolution.

18. See *Africa Confidential*, 30(10) (May 12, 1989). Also "Fiscal Crisis," *The Namibian* (June 2, 1989).

19. In August 1988, the South African Foreign Minister, Magnus Malan announced that his government will never allow the red flag to fly over Windhoek, referring to SWAPO. See Joseph Diescho, "Freedom Around the Corner?" *Africa Report* 34(1) (January-February, 1989), 27.

20. See Robert Gordon, "The Praetorianization of Namibia" *Transafrica Forum* 6(2) (Winter, 1989), 15-25.

PART THREE

THE USA AND SOUTHERN AFRICA

9

Reconstructionist Strategies in Mozambique: How Insecurity and De-Development in Mozambique Provide an Opportunity for U.S.-U.S.S.R. Co-Operative Action toward Stability and Peaceful Change in Southern Africa

Harvey Glickman

ARGUMENT

Ironically, the present security and development crisis in Mozambique presents an unusual opportunity for an early follow-up of the Angola-Namibia agreement of 1988 in moving toward stability and justice in the region via parallel action and possible co-operation between the USA and the U.S.S.R. By seizing the opportunity to co-operate in what is now a worst case emergency in Mozambique, the superpowers can lay the groundwork for a security system acceptable to their interests and to those of the Africans as well.

Violence and hunger in Mozambique may be the worst in the world. Their basic linkage to the efforts of the present South African regime to de-stabilize the country is unquestionable. The recovery of Mozambique represents a concern for decency and human dignity separate from ideological or strategic interests. Yet recovery in Mozambique, which depends upon the restoration of internal security and a functioning economic system remains enmeshed in regional strategic designs.

The U.S. and U.S.S.R. share common and complementary interests in:

a) The restoration of minimum security and standard of life for the people of Mozambique;

b) A solution to South Africa's troubles based on a government acceptable to all elements in the South African population;

c) Peace and security in the SADCC states of southern Africa leading toward mutually beneficial trade and development with a non-aggressive South Africa and with the rest of the world;

189

d) A security system in southern Africa acceptable to all its citizens that functions normally independent of superpower intervention.

Although the case for assistance to Mozambique can rest on humanitarian grounds alone and can result in parallel action, rather than active co-operation, an assistance effort can also be supported on regional and global strategic grounds. Even further, a Co-operative Reconstructionist Initiative, as suggested here, can continue a process of gradual reduction of tensions in the Southern Africa area as an example of what could evolve in the rest of the world.

The regional strategic case flows from the desire to strengthen SADCC, especially through the reconstruction of transportation routes and ports in Mozambique. Strengthening SADCC helps stiffen resistance to co-optative de-racialization of politics (as distinguished from citizenship equality) in South Africa and contributes to continuing the pressure toward democratic power-sharing there.

The global strategic case reflects the desire of the Superpowers to reduce the arenas of a possible clash of interests, in this case in southern Africa. The success of parallel efforts in Angola and in Namibia, where opportunities for near-term co-operation have borne fruit, attest to new possibilities on South Africa's other front.

There are two operational requirements to fulfill these arguments. The mechanism for reconstruction efforts in Mozambique has evolved with the non-Superpowers beginning to take the lead. The Superpowers' first and main service now lies in the support of the considerable effort under way in the hands of many European countries and public and private international agencies. Second, each Superpower needs also to continue to foster a convergence of policies toward Mozambique. U.S. policy needs to continue to reflect the dominance of the position of its Department of State -- rather than certain Members of Congress -- regarding the non-recognition of RENAMO, and support for the government of Mozambique in its efforts to restore security in the countryside. There is no longer serious evidence for the "global onslaught" view of anti-communism that has been featured by Pretoria as justification for military intervention in the affairs of its neighbors. For Pretoria,the phased Cuban withdrawal from Angola, the acquiescence in the independence of Namibia and the acceptance of Soviet brokerage, alongside the Americans, in the Angola-Namibia Accords, have undermined the rationale for a hard-line regional security policy. The evidence for a threat of proxy Soviet aggression or internal communist subversion is hard to find today. For its part, on the other hand, the U.S.S.R. needs to continue to encourage a version of "perestroika" in Mozambique, to include respect for non-Marxist groups, decentralization and democratization of political decision-making, as well as to continue the encouragement of parallel legal markets in the economy. This can come about by default, by a gradual distancing of the Soviets from active policy advice in Mozambique, which can be just as effective as vocal direction. While the U.S.S.R. may continue as the largest supplier of military aid to Mozambique, as it was in mid-1989, it is in the interest of the U.S.S.R. for Mozambique to continue its evolution toward diversifying its defense and economic development partners (as evidenced by Mozambique's present strong links to the World Bank and the International Monetary Fund) and its own interpretation of non-alignment in world affairs.

Finally, a Co-operative Reconstructionist Initiative by the two Superpowers supports the present efforts by the Mozambique government to begin a dialogue with elements of RENAMO to bring the war to an end. But rather than supporting the rebels and encouraging reconciliation -- the UNITA strategy employed by the USA in Angola --this is a policy to build the administrative and fighting capability of FRELIMO so that it can support and defend its own beleaguered and ravaged population and "de-criminalize" its countryside.

THE PRESENT CONDITION OF MOZAMBIQUE

Not long ago a grisly compilation of the worst locations of human suffering in the world placed Mozambique near the top with a score of ninety-five out of one hundred.[1] The stark figures of human needs denied are relatively well-known. A few will suffice. About 100,000 Mozambicans have been killed by internal war. 200,000 children are homeless. 1.1 million people are being treated as displaced persons (down from 1.6 million in 1986), but 872,800 Mozambicans are estimated as refugees in 1989, (more than doubled since mid-1987), with 450 thousand to 500,000 in Malawi alone. In spring 1988 20,000 to 30,000 people a month were streaming into Malawi.   At the beginning of 1989, 4.8 million people inside Mozambique faced "severe" or "commercial" food shortages and 5.9 million people or forty percent of the population of Mozambique were dependent in one way or another on food assistance. Mozambique's per capita gross domestic product remains $210, among the world's lowest. It declined an average of 8.2 percent per year between 1982 and 1986, although in 1987 GDP was up by about 3.5 percent.[2]

As a result of internal warfare and natural disasters by 1987 two million people had lost access to health care; in 1982-86 213 health care posts were destroyed and 382 were closed; in 1986 there were seventeen doctors left in rural areas; four years of destruction has wiped out thirty percent of the country's health network. Health centers and schools are a prime target of RENAMO attacks. By mid-1988 2,629 primary schools and twenty-two secondary schools were closed due to war destruction. Half a million pupils lost their classrooms. In one major province alone --Zambezia -- in September 1987, more than 2/3 of the 681,809 children between ages seven and fourteen were unable to attend school. More than half the 958 schools have been destroyed since 1982.[3]

The estimated total damage to the economy in 1986 was $6 billion, or roughly sixty times the value of the 1987 exports and twice the value of the country's external debt. Transiting materials through Maputo port alone were reduced from 14.2 million tons in 1973 to 2.2. million in 1987.[4]

Mozambique's problem may be paraphrased from the famous saying concerning Mexico and the USA: so far from God, so close to South Africa. As the late President Samora Machel stated in 1977, "Mozambique became a political entity upon independence in June 1975 but we are still not an economic entity."[5] A commentator later put it more bluntly. "...there never was a Mozambican economy." While a formal colony of Portugal, Mozambique served as a captive market and a labor reserve for South Africa and a transitway and tourist playground for Rhodesia and South Africa.[6] It is not surprising that an observer would allude to South Africa's "own 'Monroe Doctrine'" in relation to Southern Africa, including Mozambique.[7]

Mozambique's economic integration with South Africa also makes for its vulnerability. South Africa is able to punish Mozambique by withdrawal of port and railroad activity, by withdrawal of employment of migratory labor and by sponsorship of guerrilla warfare. The founding of SADCC upon the independence of Zimbabwe in 1980 was meant to create an economic alternative to dependence on South Africa for the Front Line States. Despite the fact that "the obvious outlet for much of SADCC trade would be the ports of Mozambique," and that the non-South African railroads -- including two key rail lines through Mozambique -- should be "natural" entrepots for SADCC countries, South African non-violent and sponsored violent acts have reduced cargo passage through all Mozambican ports from 14.9 million tons in 1975 to 4.2 million in 1986 and railway traffic from 13.4 million tons to 2.9 million tons in the same years.[8] As early as 1981 a Mozambican railroad official described the Mozambican dilemma with regard to South Africa. "They have it both ways. We pay them for the locomotives in precious foreign exchange while they sabotage the port that earns us that foreign exchange."[9]

South Africa can toy with Mozambique's very existence by applying the carrot and the sjambok, since the South African policy of destabilization is part of a regional strategy to prevent the attenuation of economic ties between the SADCC countries and South Africa. In this unequal struggle, South Africa deploys a defense budget in size totalling about the whole GNP of Mozambique. The cost of destabilization to the SADCC countries between 1980 and 1986 has been estimated at $15 billion, more than all the official foreign aid going to the SADCC states at that time.[10]

By far the major contributor to the destruction of Mozambique's economy is the extraordinarily brutal guerrilla warfare pursued by RENAMO, a group brought to life as an"intelligence" force in Mozambique by Rhodesian Special Services in the unsuccessful war against the Patriotic Front prior to Zimbabwean independence. In 1980 it was inherited by the South African military Special Service.[11] At present RENAMO receives financial support from ex-settler Portuguese businessmen in South Africa and Portugal, right-wing groups in the USA and South Africa and backers in Saudi Arabia. It remains dependent for arms, equipment, communications and transport on the South African military, largely on Special Services.[12]

A report commissioned by the U.S. Department of State ("Gersony Report") concludes that probably 200,000 to 250,000 families have been displaced, and about 100,000 civilians were "murdered... in the absence of resistance or defense.." The report extrapolates thousands of instances of "systematic forced portering, beatings, rape, looting, burning of villages, abductions and mutilations...it appears that the only reciprocity provided by RENAMO for the efforts of the civilians is the possibility of remaining alive."[13] "What has emerged in Mozambique is one of the most brutal holocausts against ordinary human beings since World War II."[14] Somewhat dissimilar from UNITA in Angola, RENAMO makes the feeblest of efforts to win the hearts and minds of segments of the local population, nor do these efforts rise much above warlordism and banditry.

A weak but operating RENAMO serves the South African purpose of maintaining sufficient strength to intimidate a government for which South Africa has use as a dependency -- e.g., to provide electricity for the Transvaal via Cahora Bassa dam, to provide a margin of cheap labor for South Africa's gold mines, to provide a short haul transport link to the Indian Ocean at Maputo and to deny sanctuary to the guerrilla wing of the African National Congress. On a broader horizon, keeping RENAMO going creates what right-wing "liberationists" in Western Europe and the USA can believe is a plausible opposition to the FRELIMO government of Mozambique simply in order to receive covert Western assistance (here there is strong similarity to the former role of UNITA in Angola). In addition a bandit RENAMO operates to sufficiently threaten the Beira and other transportation corridors, not primarily to destabilize Mozambique, but rather to maintain Zimbabwe's dependence on South Africa and indeed to sabotage SADCC. The Nkomati Accords of 1984, "renewed" in 1988, which entailed removal of military sanctuary in Mozambique for the ANC in exchange for removal of support for RENAMO by South Africa, and which some people thought marked a watershed in South Africa-Mozambique relations, instead merely reflect two sides of the same policy coin. For South Africa "talking" is not an alternative to "thumping" Mozambique or other SADCC states; it is the other (parallel) side of the same policy of destabilization to achieve dependence in the region.[15]

The parlous condition of Mozambique and its reliance on the indulgence of foreign donors are exemplified in the fact that the country depends on the outside world for ninety percent of its food requirements. (Ninety percent of the budget of the Ministry of Agriculture is supported by assistance from the Scandinavian countries.) Although the Mozambican economy as a whole may have "bottomed out" and begun to improve in 1987, agriculture and transportation have stagnated. 5.9 million people or forty percent of the Mozambican population still depend on some food aid; 3.9 million of that total are completely dependent. In 1988 food aid from all donors exceeded the $700 million contributed in 1987. The marketed production of maize and rice in 1987/88 (sixty thousand tons) covered only seven to eight percent of the estimated needs (although there was a seventeen percent increase in the volume of all marketed agricultural produce). According to the World Food Program, in the year preceding May 1988 unmet cereal needs -- which means people going without grain to eat -- equalled almost one third of estimated minimum requirements.[16]

The final aspect of the alarming deterioration of the Mozambican economy and the extent to which it has become an international ward concern its external debt. Total foreign debt equals $3.2 billion, 1/3 of which is owed to the U.S.S.R. and its allies. In 1988 debt service came to 119 percent of export receipts ($125-175 million, after rescheduling, on $105 million of receipts).[17]

PRESENT EFFORTS TOWARD REHABILITATION

In the past few years without a great deal of fanfare a multi-nation effort to help Mozambique has emerged.[18] It is focussed on security, transport and food. Like other international relief efforts, it is a jumble of global official agencies, multi-national and bi-lateral arrangements, governmental and semi-private, which the Mozambican government attempts to co-ordinate via CENE, the National Executive Commission for the Emergency and supervise via its Department for the Prevention and Combat of Natural Disasters. In 1987 donations of $230-280 million exceeded the target figure of $210 million. The April 1988 joint conference of international donors in Maputo, under the auspices of the UN and the government of Mozambique, was presented with a projection of total financial requirements for relief and rehabilitation in 1988-89 amounting to $332,645,000. The Mozambique government received the aid of an interagency mission of the United Nations (UN Office for Emergency Operations in Africa, UNICEF, UN Development Program, UN Disaster Relief Co-ordinator, UN High Commission for Refugees, World Food Program, FAO and WHO) in preparing its massive 1988-89 Appeal. In April 1989 at the UN Donors Conference Mozambique sought and secured pledges of $350 million for continuing emergency relief. The USA and Italy have been the largest donors to the relief effort.[19]

Debt relief for Mozambique represents an integral part of Emergency assistance. 1988 debt is estimated at $4 billion. Mozambique is seeking a net reduction in debt service of $1053 million in 1988-90. In 1987 the Paris Club of official lenders and the London Club of commercial lenders agreed to $800 million of debt rescheduling. In addition $700 million of new credit was offered. The World Bank offered an $86 million new loan. Reflecting the global reach of Mozambique's debts, in 1987 forty percent of debt was owed Western countries (Italy cancelled its debt in May 1987), twenty-seven percent was owed socialist countries and twenty-one percent was owed OPEC member countries. A 1987 agreement between the U.S.S.R. and Mozambique, specifically covering housing, fishing and agriculture, indicates the range of rehabilitation efforts that can join debt relief. The U.S.S.R. has apparently rescheduled its debt ($2.5 billion) and postponed interest payments, adding a donation of $60 million, a loan of $45 million for raw materials, a commitment to supply 370,000 tons of crude oil, and a promise to pay 265 Soviet technicians on two year contracts in Mozambique.[20]

Efforts by the USA have been substantial, but cyclical and subject to pressures of internal political jockeying in the Executive and Legislative branches of government. American aid reached $10 million in "Economic Support Funds" in Fiscal Year 1987 encumbered by a U.S. Congress prohibition against all military aid to Mozambique. But $59 million got to Mozambique from the USA via Emergency Food Aid (PL 480) and $7 million from Disaster Relief. In FY1988 the U.S. gave $15 million in economic assistance, mostly tools, seeds and fertilizer going to the private sector in agriculture, from the Development Fund for Africa. $59 million went for food aid (PL 480) and $5.4 million for disaster relief in 1988. Mozambique received no U.S. funds going to SADCC in fiscal year 1987 due to pressure by conservative Senators in the U.S. Congress. In FY 1988 no U.S. aid to SADCC went to Mozambique as there was no Presidential determination to do so, which was required. The U.S. is projecting $15 million in private sector agricultural aid in FY 1989, as well as disaster relief and food aid at about $70 million.[21] Clearly the major U.S. effort has been in the form of food relief, growing from $30 million in 1983 and 1984, when Mozambique was headed toward the top of the list in Africa in food assistance from the U.S. In Maputo in April 1988 an official U.S. representative stated," the U.S. will provide both food and financial resources that will in 1988 make Mozambique our largest assistance recipient in Africa."[22] Some of this food assistance takes the form of triangulation, in which maize flows to Mozambique from Zimbabwe and Malawi in exchange for U.S. wheat.[23]

The Beira Corridor is the major transportation project to restore railroad traffic for Zimbabwe and areas north and west in order to reduce dependence on South African ports and transportation. (Zimbabwean use of South African railroads dropped eighteen percent in 1988.) It is to cost $280 million over four years, is funded largely by Netherlands and Sweden and is protected in part by Zimbabwean troops. The rehabilitation of the railway was supposedly completed in 1987. Railways are a prime target of RENAMO. Reconstruction work is currently under way on the Nacala line from Malawi and the Limpopo line from Zimbabwe to Maputo. The Nacala project is funded mainly by the EC, Canada, France, Italy and Finland. It is guarded by Malawian troops and a British-trained local, private security force. The Limpopo project will cost about $90 million. It principal donors are USA, Canada, West Germany, Botswana and Portugal. Zimbabwe has pledged troops. The U.S.S.R. has promised to finance the rehabilitation of the line from Moatize to the Beira Corridor.[24]

Security arrangements perhaps best reflect Mozambique's multiple attachments between global alignments. Italy, France and Portugal have established such relationships. While the U.S.S.R. remains Mozambique's largest supplier of military assistance, Britain and Zimbabwe are now training Mozambican troops. The British are supplying new arms to join Soviet equipment. Zimbabwean, Tanzanian and Malawian troops have fought alongside Mozambican government forces in the field against RENAMO.[25] (Tanzanian troops withdrew in early 1989.)

A CO-OPERATIVE RECONSTRUCTIONIST INITIATIVE

Even during the period of serious strategic conflict in eastern and southern Africa, incidents in the past two decades have demonstrated possibilities for U.S./U.S.S.R. co-operation. Shared interests in relieving starvation in Ethiopia and Sudan and preventing nuclear proliferation in South Africa provide examples of unacknowledged patterns of communication and complementary action. In 1985-86 Soviet trucks transported American grain to the camps of victims of drought in Ethiopia. In 1977 Soviet intelligence tipped the Americans that South Africa was preparing for a nuclear test in the Kalahari desert. Although one test apparently occurred, U.S. and British pressure persuaded the South Africans to de-activate the test facility.[26] By 1988 the international manifestations of the Gorbachev "new thinking" were plain, as the U.S. and the U.S.S.R. each pressured "its side" to come to an agreement on independence for Namibia and for a South African and Cuban withdrawal from Angola. Clearly, there is already considerable open and tacit co-operation between the U.S. and the U.S.S.R. in southern Africa.

On South Africa, we are entering an era where the Superpowers are converging in their approaches toward a peaceful settlement. Despite the controversy over sanctions, the U.S.S.R. does not boycott the marketing of its diamonds through De Beers in order to influence South African politics. The U.S. has applied certain sanctions and reduced its business contacts with South Africa. There are signs that an understanding is emerging in both the U.S. and in the U.S.S.R. that a democratic outcome that avoids a racial bloodbath and social chaos may require the recognition of the utility of political guarantees for minorities and the need for political representation for all groups in the transition to a non-racial political system.[27]

External pressure to raise the cost to South Africa of destabilization of Mozambique represents a first step toward acknowledging a Superpower effort toward peaceful change. The groundwork has already been laid. Soviet and Eastern European countries have reduced their advisers in 1988 in mining alone to several hundred from a high point of two thousand. There were already more Western country civilian advisers (2100) in Mozambique in early 1988 than Eastern European counterparts (1200). The movement of aid and trade in Mozambique exhibits major efforts on the part of countries East and West. In 1986 (the last available figures), while the U.S.S.R. was Mozambique's largest foreign aid donor in money value of assistance, the next three countries in terms of value of aid were Italy, Sweden and the USA. The U.S.S.R. remains the principal supplier of oil and related materials to Mozambique in 1989. Altogether twenty-seven countries and ten official international agencies are contributing to foreign aid. In the Economic Policy Framework, worked out among the World Bank, the International Monetary Fund and the Government of Mozambique for 1988-1991 total donor financing would go from $672 million to $1 billion. In 1986 the U.S. and the U.S.S.R. were virtually tied as the chief source of imports to Mozambique in volume of goods. In 1987 Italy and South Africa surpassed the U.S. (third) and the U.S.S.R. (fourth). Japan and the U.S. were in the same position in 1986 as the main destination of exports by volume from Mozambique. In 1987 they reversed positions, with East Germany, Spain and the U.S.S.R. following. In terms of value of trade in 1986 and in 1987, Singapore and the U.S. led as importers, while Italy and West Germany led as exporters to Mozambique in 1986; Italy and Thailand and then the U.S. in 1987. [28]

Operationally, co-operation builds beyond old alignments. The U.S.S.R. is constructing trawlers for a joint Soviet-Mozambican fishing company, while the Japanese are building fishing quays. Ireland and Yugoslavia sponsor a joint venture of two companies to exploit mineral sands on the coast of Zambezia province.[29]

For a Co-operative Reconstructionist Initiative to succeed, certain trends in Mozambique must continue. These entail more effective management of a decentralized economy, integrated with re-organized military action, supported by significantly rising foreign assistance. The FRELIMO government in effect has recognized some respectability for local complaints upon which RENAMO capitalizes. The July 1989 party congress is expected to hear plans to elect the President of the country through elected provincial assemblies. President Chissano is supposedly interested in a plan for decentralized poles of development proposed by persons with contacts with RENAMO. The U.S. must also recognize that support for market solutions mean functioning local markets alongside a more efficient state sector -- a partially planned wartime economy.[30] The destruction of RENAMO does not entail acceptance of vanguard authoritarianism in the regime leadership of FRELIMO. The U.S. can support moves toward enlarging participation in political decision-making and toward the popular election of a President in Mozambique that have support within FRELIMO, without departing from views already expressed within the State Department ("FRELIMO has retained a remarkable capacity for self-criticism... the top leadership of FRELIMO has remained constant, apparently popular and well-entrenched."[31]) Despite a Treaty of Co-operation and Friendship, the U.S.S.R. in practice recognized a different strategic equation in Mozambique from Angola (and from Ethiopia). Mozambique was rejected for membership in Comecon; there was rather weak underwriting of socialist solidarity.[32] Development prospects sank after five years of attempted class struggle, rural collectivization and political vanguard centralism.

The major question concerns the consequences for South Africa of a more effective Reconstruction effort in Mozambique. In its desire to seek acceptance as a major player in a revised southern African regional order South Africa will probably act as a participant the Reconstruction effort. South Africa has offered to help restore power lines to Cahora Bassa, to redevelop port facilities at Maputo and even to train Mozambican troops. A Joint (South Africa-Mozambique) Development and Economic Committee held a second meeting in Cape Town in February 1989 and established sub-commissions on transport, trade, agriculture, labor and tourism. South African private companies -- including one joint venture with a state enterprise -- continue to operate inside Mozambique.[33] The controversy on this matter in South Africa is between rebuilding Mozambique as a neighborly gesture and in recognition of business advantages in exploiting Mozambican economic resources, on the one hand, and keeping Mozambique sufficiently weak via destabilization acts, on the other hand, in order to claim that black African governments falter without the involvement of a more advanced white-run state.

Within South Africa, the Reconstruction approach to Mozambique has particular appeal to the foreign office and to the business community, while the destabilization approach appeals to the military. The effectiveness of Reconstruction will probably provoke yet another round of resupply efforts for RENAMO. The South African military provides sanctuary for some elements in RENAMO. The military's analysis in particular appeals to extreme conservative elements in a number of countries, who are dedicated to the overthrow of Marxist governments. Yet the South

African military probably benefit from the Marxist label attached to FRELIMO, since it offers license to continue destabilization efforts.[34]

The first priority for Reconstruction in Mozambique is security, which means rebuilding the Mozambican military capability in order to fight effectively in a hit and run guerrilla war. With meager success Mozambique still spends about forty percent of its budget on national defense. Security also means the defense of transportation links, especially those into SADCC states via the Beira and other Corridors. Finally, security means defense of villages and peasant plots, so that refugees can return home and begin the process of restoring food supply and agricultural markets. Enhanced defense capability on the part of the Mozambican military is good news for SADCC in its efforts to reduce its dependence on South Africa, which, in turn reduces the South African ability to pressure the Front Line States.

A major part of Co-operative Reconstruction must be security. An example of East-West co-operation already exists in the military area, with Britain (the largest Western military donor) training Mozambican troops using Soviet weapons. In 1989 the British plan to provide $25 million in new economic assistance and to begin to train three new companies of troops per year. Soviet trucks are now carrying American-supplied food to the countryside. What is now called for is a joint initiative in which the Superpowers "underwrite" a formula for security and rehabilitation in Mozambique. Such a formula places the Superpowers in the background on military matters, allowing the secondary European powers to take the lead, thus continuing the trend in which foreign security assistance is linked to projects involving these countries, especially in transportation and in food relief. A good example is the Beira Corridor where all the countries participating in reconstruction could follow the lead of Zimbabwe (five thousand troops in early 1988) and Britain and get involved in helping provide security for the project. France (in relation to its role in the Nacala Corridor) and Spain are considering ways to contribute to the defense of their aid projects. Malawi troops are already employed on the Nacala line. In April 1989 the Nacala Corridor was reported open with the French and the Portuguese training Mozambique government soldiers.[35]   The U.S.S.R. has agreed to help re-train the Mozambican army as an anti-guerrilla force and will further reduce its heavy weapons technicians in 1990. East Germany, Czechoslovakia, Poland and Hungary, with whom the Mozambican Ministry of Defense has had discussions about co-operation in 1987, are likely to take over part of weapons supply from the U.S.S.R.[36]

In addition to strengthening Mozambique versus South Africa, and increasing the independence of SADCC states from South Africa, a Co-operative Reconstructionist Initiative on the part of the U.S. and the U.S.S.R. announces to Africans that the Superpowers can find common instrumentalities as well as complementary interests in the struggle toward a democratic South Africa. Even more broadly, such an Initiative can provide another example of concrete steps that can follow the ending of an era of confrontation between the Superpowers.

Notes

The author thanks Robyn Gilman, Prexy Nesbitt, Jerry Herman, Tom Brennan, Martin Lowenkopf, Raymond Hopkins, Harry Wilkinson, Don Melville, Stuart Seldowitz, J. Stephen Morrison and Michael Clough for their assistance and Haverford College and IREX for financial support. An earlier version of this chapter was presented as a background paper at the Fourth Soviet-American Conference on Contemporary Sub-Saharan Africa in Moscow, July 11-14, 1988.

1.   Population Crisis Committee, Washington, D.C., Report of 1987, *Informafrica* 1(7) (Lisbon, March, 1988).
2.   Figures taken from Robert Gersony, *Summary of Mozambican Refugee Accounts of Principally Conflict-Related Experience in Mozambique*, Report Submitted to Ambassador Jonathan Moore, Director, Bureau for Refugee Programs and Dr. Chester A. Crocker, Assistant Secretary of African Affairs (Washington, D.C., U.S. Department of State, April, 1988), typescript; National Executive Commission for the Emergency and the Department for the Prevention and Combat of Natural Disasters, *Rising to the Challenge, Dealing with the Emergency in Mozambique, An Inside View* (Maputo, April, 1988); USAID, *Basic Briefing Document on Mozambique* (Oct. 14, 1988); USAID, *Basic Briefing Notes on Mozambique* (Sept. 29, 1988); USAID, *Briefing Book on Mozambique* (prepared for the April 1989 New York Meeting on Mozambique Relief, April, 1989,), 4. [All USAID materials unclassified.]
3.   See above; in addition, see Dr. Abdul Razak Noormahomed and Dr. Julie Cliff, *The Impact on Health in Mozambique of South African Stabilization* (People's Republic of Mozambique: Ministry of Health, December, 1987); *Final Report, Mozambique Health Assessment Mission September 15, 1988* (Indianapolis, Indiana: Indiana State Board of Health, 1989); Economist Intelligence Unit [EIU], *Country Profile, Mozambique* (1988-89), 7.
4.   EIU, *Country Profile*, 27. See also Government of Mozambique in collaboration with the U.N., *The Emergency Situation in Mozambique, Priority Requirements for the Period 1988-89* (U.N., Office for Emergencies in Africa, 1988), 3, 5, 8. Related figures in Economist Intelligence Unit [EIU], *Country Reports T/M, Tanzania/Mozambique* [n. 4 (1987); n. 1 (1988); n. 2 (1988)]; and in U.S. Committee for Refugees, Issue Brief, "Refugees from Mozambique: Shattered Land, Fragile Asylum," *Update* (Washington, D.C., August, 1988), mss.
5.   Samora Machel quoted in the *Washington Post* (April 20, 1977).
6.   Quote in Horace Campbell, "War, Reconstruction and Dependence in Mozambique," *Third World Quarterly* 6(4) (October, 1984), 857; see also L. Adele Jinadu, "Soviet Influence on Afro-Marxist Regimes: Ethiopia and Mozambique," in Edmond J. Keller and Donald Rothchild, eds., *Afro-Marxist Regimes* (Boulder: Lynne Rienner Publishers, 1987), 225-256.
7.   Thomas Callaghy, "Apartheid and Socialism: South Africa's Relations with Angola and Mozambique," in Callaghy, ed., *South Africa in Southern Africa* (N.Y.: Praeger, 1983), 302.
8.   EIU, *Country Profile*, 27. See also Stephen P. Lewis, "Some Economic Realities in Southern Africa," in Coralie Bryant, ed., *Poverty, Policy, and Food Security in Southern Africa* (Boulder: Lynne Rienner Publishers, 1988), 39-92, esp. 49.
9.   Carlos Veloso, in *The Financial Times* (December 1, 1981), quoted in Callaghy, *op. cit.*, 309.

10. Barry Munslow and Phil O'Keefe, "Rethinking the Revolution in Mozambique," *Race and Class* 26(2) (1984), 16; also Joseph Hanlon, *Apartheid's Second Front* (London: Penguin, 1986), 116.

11. Herbert Howe and Marina Ottaway, "State Power Consolidation in Mozambique," in Keller and Rothchild, eds., *op. cit.*, 43-65. esp. 51. For other material on RENAMO, see Steven Metz, "The Mozambique National Resistance and South African Foreign Policy," *African Affairs* 85(341) (1986), 491-507; Mata Lopes, "The MNR: Opponents or Bandits?" *Africa Report* 31(1), 67-73; Paul Fauvet, "Roots of Counter-Revolution: The Mozambique National Resistance," *Review of African Political Economy*, n. 29 (1984), 108-121; Mozambique Angola Committee, *South Africa's Undeclared War Against Mozambique* (London, 1984); William Minter, "What Kind of War?" *Africa News* (December 21, 1987).

12. In addition to the sources above, see Robert Pear with James Brooke, "Rightists in U.S. Aid Mozambique Rebels," *New York Times* (May 22, 1988); also James Brooke, "Rebels Leave Mozambique a Bloodied and Fallow Land," *New York Times* (May 11, 1988). The human and inhumane consequences of RENAMO actions are detailed in William Finnegan, "The Emergency I, II," *The New Yorker* (May 22, 29, 1989), and in William Minter, "The Mozambican National Resistance (RENAMO) as Described by Ex-Participants," Report submitted to The Ford Foundation and Swedish International Development Authority (reprinted by African-European Institute and Dag Hammarskjold Foundation, 1989).

13. See Gersony Report to U.S. State Department, *op. cit.*, 25.

14. Roy Stacy, U.S. Deputy Assistant Secretary of State, text of speech to Donors Conference (Maputo, Mozambique, April 26, 1988), 2, typescript.

15. Gillian Gunn, "Post-Nkomati Mozambique," in Helen Kitchen, ed., *Angola, Mozambique and the West* (N.Y.: Praeger, 1987), 83-92.

16. EIU, *Country Profile*, 34; EIU , *Country Reports T/M* [n. 1 (1988), 27-28; n. 2 (1988), 22-23]. See also Gunn, *op. cit.*, 97.

17. EIU, *Country Reports T/M*, n. 1 (1988), 35-36. The Economst finds unexplained discrepancies between the OECD data and the Comecon data.

18. Published reports name the following individual countries as contributing to various forms of assistance aside from investment in Mozambique: Italy, Sweden, Norway, Denmark, Iceland, Finland, Portugal, Canada, U.S.A., U.S.S.R., Great Britain, Spain, Switzerland, France, West and East Germany, Czechoslovakia, Poland, Hungary, Japan, Australia, India, Zimbabwe, Tanzania, Malawi, Botswana, South Africa. Official international agencies helping Mozambique include six units of the U.N., the World Bank, the IMF, the African Development Bank, the European Community. Unofficial international organizations (PVO's) include the International Committee of the Red Cross, CARE, Doctors Without Borders, The American Friends Service Committee, the Service Order of Malta, World Vision, Planned Parenthood, Save the Children, Church World Service, Oxfam. It is believed that forty official and non-official international organizations are working in the government-controlled areas of Mozambique.

19. U.N. and Government of Mozambique, *Emergency Situation in Mozambique*, 31; *Africa News* (May 1, 1989), 12.

20. EIU, *Country Reports T/M* [n. 2 (1989), 31; 67, n. 4 (1987), 24-25]; Allan Isaacman, "The Escalating Conflict in Southern Africa: the Case of Mozambique" (July, 1987), 23-24, typescript; USAID, *Basic Briefing Notes* (September 29, 1988), 3.

21. Interview with Gregory Lunden, Mozambique Desk Officer, Bureau of African Affairs, U.S. Department of State, July 6, 1988; Interview with Don Melville, Mozambique Desk Officer, Africa Bureau, USAID, June 7, 1989; Interview with J. Stephen Morrison, Staff Assistant, Africa Sub-Committee, Foreign Relations Committee, U.S. House of Representatives, June 6, 1989; see also Bryant, ed., *op. cit.*, table, 279. Gillian Gunn, "Mozambique after Machel," in Kitchen, ed., *op. cit.*, 127, gives figures for U.S. aid for 1983-1986. Salih Booker discusses Congressional restrictions on U.S. aid to Mozambique in "The Other Engagement," *Africa Report* 31(1) (1986), 50-56.

22. Speech by Stacy, *op. cit.* Figures from interview with Lunden *op. cit.*, and *Washington Post* (November 17, 1987, February 15, 1987).

23. Mudziviri T. Nziramasanga, "Food, Aid, Trade and Economic Development in SADCC," in Bryant, ed., *op. cit.*, 228.

24. *Washington Post* (May 28, 1987); EIU, *Country Profile*, 26.

25. See statement by Chester Crocker, U.S. Assistant Secretary of State for Africa, June 24, 1987, "U.S. Policy toward Mozambique," *Current Policy*, 983 (Washington, D.C.: U.S. Department of State, Bureau of Public Affairs, 1987); U.S. Department of State, Bureau of Public Affairs, *Current Policy* n. 980, "Mozambique: Charting a New Course" (June 1987); Isaacman, *op. cit.*, 26-28; Isaacman, "An African War Ensnarls the U.S. Ultra-Right," *Los Angeles Times* (June 28, 1987); EIU, *Country Reports T/M* [n. 1, n. 2, 1988].

26. Soviet-U.S. Cooperation for Africa, *A Report on the Moscow Workshop* (UCLA, Center for International and Strategic Affairs, December, 1987), 2.

27. Private communications from ANC members returning from Moscow, February 1988, and from participants returning from an ANC conference in Tanzania, October 1987; see also *Africa Confidential* 28(8) (April 15, 1987), 7.

28. EIU, *Country Reports T/M* [n. 1 (1988), 36, appendix; n. 2, 1988, 3; n. 1, 1989, appendix]. Memo of March 17, 1988 in USAID, *Briefing Book on Mozambique*; "Questions and Answers on Mozambique," prepared for USAID for Hearings of the Select Committee on Hunger of the Foreign Affairs Committee of the U.S. House of Representatives (Mar. 10, 1988), mss.

29. EIU, *Country Reports T/M*, n. 1, 1988, 30.

30. See Maureen Mackintosh, "Economic Policy Context and Adjustment Options in Mozambique," *Development and Change*, 17(3) (July, 1986), 557-581, esp. 579.

31. USAID, *Basic Briefing Notes on Mozambique*, 1, 2.

32. Winrich Kuhne, "What Does the Case of Mozambique Tell Us About Soviet Ambivalence Toward Africa?" in Kitchen, ed., *op. cit.*, 105-116; Colin Legum, "The Nkomati Accord and its Implications for the Front Line States and South," in Ibrahim S.R. Msabaha and Timothy M. Shaw, eds., *Confrontation and Liberation in Southern Africa* (Boulder: Westview, 1987), 93-94.

33. James Brooke, "South Africa Apparently Shifting Loyalty to Support Mozambique," *New York Times* (May 3, 1988); EIU, *Country Reports T/M*, n. 2 (1989), 25-26.

34. EIU, *Country Reports T/M* [n. 4 (1988), 22; n. 1 (1989), 20]; Robert M. Price, "South Africa and Afro-Marxism: Pretoria's Relations with Mozambique and Angola in Regional Perspective," in Keller and Rothchild, eds., *op. cit.*, 257-277.

35. EIU, *Country Reports T/M* [n. 1 (1988), 24-25; n.2 (1988); 19-20]. *Facts and Reports*, International Press Cuttings on Southern Africa (Amsterdam, Holland, April 21, 1989), 27. Private Mozambican security forces are being trained by the French on the Nacala line. Enterprises run by the British businessman "Tiny" Rowland are also protected by private security. Interview, Africa

Section, Bureau of Intelligence and Research, U.S. Department of State, June 7, 1989.

36.   EIU, *Country Reports T/M*, 67, n. 4 (1987), 24; *Facts and Reports* (June 30, 1989), 25; also above mentioned interview.

10
Southern Africa and American Politics

Howard Wolpe

This Conference comes at an exciting time in the intersection of southern African and American affairs. Implementation of the Angola-Namibia accords began April 1st. In South Africa there is continuing crisis, a change of leadership, a new sense of fluidity of uncertain meaning. There is ongoing American involvement in the war in Angola. In fact the Administration has publicly announced our covert operations as we do these things in America. The *Washington Post* reported that the Administration is seeking a substantial increase in covert assistance for Savimbi's UNITA forces in Angola. Finally, a new Assistant Secretary for Africa, Herman Cohen, is about to be appointed. In sum, both on the American side and on the African side, many inter-related things are happening.

I wish first to devote my remarks to themes that have run through American political culture over many years, that have not always been very much in public view, but that continue to dominate, unconsciously often, the way we see and speak, about African politics. I would argue that these tendencies in American political culture have created barriers to the development of an effective American policy towards Africa. In the second part, I wish to address several issues that will have immediate policy importance in the next several months in the United States.

The first of the historical tendencies that requires far greater acknowledgement is the racial dimension of American political thought. I once taught African politics and the first day of every semester in my classroom I would always ask my students to take out a sheet of paper and put in writing everything they thought they knew about Africa -- all of their images, all of their understandings about the African continent. We would assemble the results and lay it out on the blackboard. What became instantly apparent was that students' ideas, their images of Africa,

This is a slightly revised version of the Opening Address to the Conference, "Toward Peace and Security in Southern Africa," Haverford College, April 29, 1989. [Editor's Note.]

had been largely framed by the most recent Tarzan movie. And that's not
an exaggeration. Moreover, the ideas my students submitted were hardly
unique. If I were to ask my colleagues in the Congress to undertake the
same exercise, we would have the same results. We need to understand
that, because it is naive to think that somehow policy made by American
decision-makers is not informed by that pattern of prejudice, stereotype
and myth that has so dominated American political thought and culture.

The country where this phenomenon becomes most dramatically evident is the country of South Africa. We in this country continue to see
developments there through our own racial prism. We have developed
over the years -- this is not simply a critique of the Reagan
Administration, but rather a critique of Democratic as well as Republican
administrations -- a racial double standard in our approach to South Africa.
Simply ask yourselves the question, "What if the racial composition of
forces in South Africa had been reversed and you had a black minority imposing this horrendously dehumanizing system of apartheid against a
white majority, would we have been engaged in this decades-long debate
over the wisdom, morality and effectiveness of sanctions?" The answer is
self evident; I think we would not have been engaged in that kind of exercise all these many years. And the rest of the world understands that very
clearly.

The rationalizations that keep surfacing to justify our policy of complicity with apartheid, flow from this double standard, in the corporate
community as well as among just average citizens. When we talk about
South Africa, for instance, we use entirely different language than when
we characterize other situations around the world which also involve the
violation of fundamental human rights. Instead of talking about freedom
fighters struggling for liberation, you have the more frequent use of the
term "terrorists" in talking about the African National Congress. When it
comes to South African policy, suddenly the United States becomes the
apostle of non-violence -- at the same time that we are sending guns off to
Afghanistan, using military means in dealing with Nicaragua, or bombing
Libya. Turn to South Africa and we suddenly hear this extraordinary discussion about how our goals ought to be pursued in a strictly non-violent
means. This is not to say that I think American policy ought not to be
to minimize the violence. In fact, what I would argue, is that our policies
are doing just the opposite; they are exacerbating the violence and the
bloodshed in the region by failing to confront the major source of violence, the South African Government, with stiff retaliatory international
sanction. My only point is to emphasize the different nature, the different
texture of the conversation, as we talk about South Africa, by comparison
with other parts of the world.

Compare this with our response when the Soviet Union invaded
Afghanistan: we not only issued moral condemnations but also immediately imposed sanctions. When the Polish government came down on the

backs of the Polish trade union movement, we issued moral condemnations, imposed sanctions, and our President asked all Americans to light a
candle in our windows at night as a symbol of our solidarity with the
Polish trade union movement. When Libya engaged in state terrorism,
we responded with sanctions and with bombs. Somehow, however, we
turn to South Africa and we enter a long tortured debate about the wisdom, morality and effectiveness of sanctions. My point, again, is that
our foreign policy has been very much affected by the racial preconcep-
tions or misconceptions that we bring to the African continent, and has
resulted in policies viewed by the rest of the world as highly contradictory
and inconsistent.

A second issue that affects how we approach the African continent
time and time again is our tendency to see everything in East-West terms.
We are so fixated on the conflict with the Soviet Union that events in
Africa, as in the rest of the third world, come to be understood simply in
terms of our rivalry with the Soviet Union. The results of that approach
can be absolutely disastrous in terms of American interests. For one, we
create the very distancing that we wish to prevent: the dominant message
that is communicated is that peoples in Africa, Asia, and Latin America
are somehow inherently incapable of making political decisions for themselves, that if the Soviets or other communist bloc countries are involved,
then the United States must be there to rescue these countries from subversion and influence from the other side. This is an extraordinary pater-
nalism that underpins American foreign policy. In addition, we often-
times engage in a foreign policy by labels that results, ironically, in
America becoming the manipulated party rather than exercising its own
active power.

Time and time again we have thrown our support to right wing dicta-
torships, whether in Africa or Latin America and around the world, that
have nothing fundamentally in common with American values or
American interests and where we in fact create the very revolutionary
momentum that we seek to avoid by our identification with these inherently repressive regimes. The classic examples in recent years, have of
course been our response to Somoza in Nicaragua and Marcos in the
Philippines. The Marcos case I was hoping would provide a national
teach-in for the United States since we did manage to secure a reversal of
policy, albeit at the eleventh hour. Here, thanks to the leadership of
Richard Lugar, then the Republican chairman of the Senate Foreign
Relations Committee, and Stephen Solarz, then the Democratic chairman
of the Asia sub-committee of the House, we were able to persuade the
President to understand that Mr. Marcos was, despite his claims to be
anti-communist, indeed doing more that any other actor by virtue of his
corruption and human rights violations to encourage the communist insurgency within the Philippines. American national interests were not
being well served by his close identification; millions of tax dollars going

to Mr. Marcos in the name of anti-communism cost Americans very greatly; many of those dollars towards Imelda's clothes and shoes had just about as much effect in terms of protecting and advancing American interests.

It is my hope that Americans are able to extrapolate from the experience in the Philippines to comparable experiences in Africa. For example, in the U.S. approach towards Angola, probably the classic example of a foreign policy by labelling, one sees policies that have been terribly counterproductive in terms of American national interest and blocked our understanding of what's happening on the ground. In the course of the Angolan national struggle, the nationalist movement broke into three principal factions. One of these factions ended up supported by the Soviet Union while Henry Kissinger, in one of his previous incarnations, made the judgment that we of course had to therefore assist the other two factions. We were not alone in helping them: so were the North Koreans, on the one hand, and the Chinese, on the other, which made for an interesting set of relationships, ideologically. The fact of the matter was the divisions among the three key elements of the nationalist movement had very little to do with ideology, and far more to do with ethnicity. Each of these factions had a different ethnic base within the Angolan nation and they had to do with fights among personalities for power within the nationalist movement. But we did not understand all of that and we ended up therefore throwing our support to these factions.

Today, of course, we support UNITA, led by Jonas Savimbi. That support has fed into perhaps the most extraordinary manipulation of the right wing in American politics that has ever occurred by an individual, who has persuaded the right wing in America that he is the embodiment of the anti-communist freedom fighter. Savimbi must be the first Maoist in history to succeed in accomplishing that kind of recognition on the part of the radical right in America. He first went to the Soviet Union for support and assistance, did not get it, turned to China, was trained in China, was an avowed Maoist, and then subsequently turned to South Africa for support and assistance. The only thing that has been consistent in Jonas Savimbi these many years is that there is always a perfect correlation between his ideology of the moment and his source of financial support. And we have now developed an entire foreign policy based upon a mythology that this man is an anti-communist freedom fighter and that America's interest lies in advancing him militarily.

Likewise the Angolan government, this avowedly Marxist government, has been so radical in its approach to the economy that it hired as its principal economic consultant, Arthur D. Little of Boston, Massachusetts. For many years Angola has signalled its desire for normal diplomatic relationships with the United States and for American private investment. Over fifty American companies currently do business in Angola and some of these companies have testified before the Africa sub-committee that there is no government of the African continent with whom they have enjoyed more profitable business-like relationship that with the Angolan government. And yet because we do not understand what our anti-communist labels mean and because of these ideological fixations we throw our support to Jonas Savimbi, a military ally of South Africa, and spurn Angola's government. How does this expand American influence in black Africa? By introducing U.S. assistance, alongside South Africa assistance to UNITA, the Administration only drives Angola into a deeper dependence upon the Cubans and the Soviets, something which was in fact predicted when U.S. assistance was announced in early 1986.

I cite this as an example of where our own ideological fixations have obstructed the development of an enlightened foreign policy toward the African continent. Perhaps, we are finally getting beyond some of these problems through the recently concluded Angola-Namibia accords. But make no mistake about it, those accords could have been concluded long ago. The South Africans clearly decided at the point in 1980 when they were to begin implementation of U.N. Resolution 435 that they could get a better deal from the Reagan Administration than they could have from the Carter Administration. It is rather clear that the only reason that South Africa has signed on now is because of the growing deterioration of their economy and their recognition that they had to do some retrenchment in order to preserve the home front. It was above all else, the Cubans, after increasing their forces from about twenty thousand to in the neighborhood of fifty thousand and delivering several significant military defeats to the South Africans, who facilitated the negotiations that Crocker wanted to implement and the agreement that Crocker wanted to achieve much earlier.

The third point I would like to make is that we have failed historically to recognize the strengths that the United States potentially can bring to the African continent and to our relationships with Africa. We have our own tradition of an anti-colonial struggle with which the African continent can indeed identify. We have an extraordinarily pluralistic society; we have our own history of the civil rights struggle. These all represent points of contact with the African experience. We have the economic strength, the technological skills that Africa seeks and desires to achieve for itself. And yet instead of playing upon these strengths in terms of our own democratic anti-colonial tradition, in terms of our pluralism and the civil rights history, we have gone instead for this extraordinarily paternalistic approach to Africa that is often times had much more of a military thrust to it than an economic thrust.

Let me switch now to several major issue areas in southern Africa that we are going to be addressing in the next several months. I do not think some of these would even be matters in controversy, if we could somehow develop greater self-awareness about some of the issues that I discussed earlier.

First of all, how to continue to deal with apartheid in South Africa? I would argue that sanctions are the only rational, non-violent means to raise the costs of the continuation of the Afrikaner regime and to force movement toward a negotiated settlement. I do not know of any country in the history of the world that has ever seen a governing regime voluntarily relinquish power. Afrikaners are not unique in that regard. The reality is that this regime will not give way and negotiate a new political system until it concluded that it has more to lose than to gain by trying to hold on to its monopoly of power. If that analysis is correct, what that means very directly is that anything the United States or other countries in the world do to bolster the economy of South Africa has the consequence of encouraging the Afrikaners to hold on indefinitely and to resist the onset of negotiations with the authentic representatives of the black majority.

I recall an advertisement that appeared in American newspapers that was signed by leaders of the South African corporate community a while ago that displayed this photograph of big zebra and a caption that read something to the effect, "Shoot the white and the black dies with it." It has been the theme that somehow sanctions are going to "hurt the people you most want to help," which has been the dominant theme advanced by those who are resisting the imposition of sanctions. Frankly I cannot think of anything more obscene that for those who have been the principal beneficiaries of the apartheid system to now hide behind its victims in an effort at resisting the imposition of sanctions. And make no mistake about it, that is precisely what is happening.

We need somehow to address directly the racial implication that underpins this kind of rationalization. I am reminded of the debates over slavery within the United States. There were some, if you go back and read those debates, who would argue that we could not abolish slavery because that would mean that blacks would somehow become economically vulnerable. That was the "enlightened, liberal" point of view that was sometimes advanced. We would not accept that for a moment in this country today as a rationalization for the maintenance of exploitative relationships; we should not accept it in our discussions of the South African scene either.

Beyond that, the thing that really needs to be understood is that the more equivocal we are, the more ambiguous our policy towards South Africa, the more vacillating we are, the greater the likelihood that the struggle will go on for many more years. The more radicalized and polarized and violent it will become. One of the really supreme ironies is that those who talk about the importance of engagement in a non-violent fashion through corporate business activity inside South Africa are themselves, in my judgment at least, greatly increasing the likelihood of much greater violence and bloodshed within that continent. That is why those

African leaders, black African leaders inside South Africa who have the largest constituencies that stand really to lose the most, have been so consistently supportive of the imposition of sanctions, including disinvestment. It is not that they do not recognize that sanctions will have economic costs for the black population, it is rather because they understand that those costs in terms of potential job losses would be far less than the costs in losses of not only jobs but of lives in a long, protracted, violent struggle. Sanctions are not in-and-of-themselves going to bring down apartheid. But they are a means of reinforcing the pressures that are building inside the country -- a way of adding to the cost the regime must bear for trying to hold on to its monopoly of power.

The last observation I would make in this regard is that the extraordinary comments that you hear about the violence of the African National Congress need to be understood against the larger reality that it is the South African regime that is the origin of South African violence. This is a government that exists entirely by means of coercion, by its monopoly over weaponry. Twenty-six million people do not willingly acquiesce in their own subjugation. If we want to deal with the issue of violence, it is the regime that we must focus upon.

Where are we this year in the Congress? We anticipate again seeking comprehensive sanctions against South Africa. The legislation will probably begin to surface in a more public way at the beginning of 1990 or in the latter part of this year. We are hoping to develop a bi-partisan approach with the new Administration. I would like very much for there to be a much more consistent set of messages that goes out from the Administration and the Congress. I have already had some conversations with Mr. Cohen and I look forward to meeting shortly with Mr. Baker to see if we can identify some areas where we can cooperate, where we can advance a common policy toward South Africa. Thus far it is unclear what the outcome of those discussions will be. I do know there are some things this Administration could do, even without Congressional action, that would make a major difference. I would love to see us seek, for example, a joint U.S.-Soviet condemnation of apartheid at the next summit between Mr. Bush and Mr. Gorbachev. This was an idea suggested to me by a Soviet advisor to the government of the Soviet Union, who was here last year. I thought there was some receptivity on the part of the people within the Reagan Administration at the time, but it obviously did not happen. I hope that we might be able to achieve that this year. I think it would have a very significant impact on South Africa. I would to see established a much more open, visible dialogue with the African National Congress and other liberation groups inside South Africa. Thirdly, I would hope that we can get to the point where the United States will stop exercising its veto in the United Nations when it comes simply to pressing through United Nations for current American sanctions to be multilateralized. Even without going beyond the present set of sanctions, to internationalize those sanctions by United Nations Security Council action could be a very significant step forward. There are several steps that the Administration can take on its own that would be quite helpful in building bridges with the Congress in our approach to South African policy.

The second issue affecting Congress involves the implementation of the Angola-Namibia accord. The accord by mid-1989 will have removed Cubans from any plausible threat to the UNITA forces. As the Cubans continue their withdrawal, I hope that fact will force a reappraisal among some Democrats, as well as Republicans, in the Congress who have been at the center of this debate and that they will come to see the wisdom of stopping the covert assistance that continued to flow to Mr. Savimbi. Democrats need themselves to revisit this issue; we do not have consensus yet within our own party, particularly in the Senate. There is stronger opposition to covert operations in the House that there is in the Senate. Fortunately some of the myths surrounding Mr. Savimbi are beginning to be stripped away. There was the recent spate of reports in the European media and in American media about some of the atrocities that have been perpetrated by the UNITA forces and by Mr. Savimbi personally. These revelations are beginning to have some impact, weakening the commitment of some members of Congress to Mr. Savimbi. In any event, our covert operations there have been, I think, terribly misguided; they have, as I suggested earlier, actually undermined American interests and influence in the region. They have slowed the process of reconciliation inside Angola and widened the conflict in many ways, and they have led to enormous destruction. The largest number of amputees in the world -- we estimate between thirty and forty thousand -- is in Angola as the consequence of land mines laid, by both sides, but primarily by the UNITA forces. The principal victims have been women and children throughout the Angolan countryside.

I remain hopeful, but also somewhat skeptical, on what is happening in Namibia. We should get to the elections; I do not think the recent encounters there, the confrontations that occurred between SWAPO and SADF forces will unhinge the agreement. What is less clear is whether South Africa will accept the outcome of a truly free and fair election inside Namibia. It remains to be seen whether they will attempt to subvert the electoral process, or whether they might opt for an unobstructed electoral transition in Namibia. One thing is clear: the least bit of temporizing on America's part, in the event that South Africa's behavior interferes with the electoral process, will only worsen matters.

I am also very concerned about the strength and capacity of the United Nations in ensuring the freedom and the fairness of those election. The United States, the Soviet Union and other members of the Security Council recently voted to reduce the forces that were initially to be committed to the UNTAG peacekeeping force. That was a terrible mistake, since it is going to heighten the insecurities of the population and potentially could create some serious problems over the longer haul. (I will probably be visiting Namibia sometime in July or October 1989, as part of a monitoring group to observe the electoral process.)

One last comment on Angola. I hope that we can quickly move to recognition of the Angolan government and to the establishment of normal, full diplomatic relationships with the government of Angola. In many respects we have had a practical relationship and open discussion; we were even allowing for long-term export-import loans to go to Angola. The government of Angola signalled its desires long ago to have diplomatic relationships with the United States. I think that would go a long way towards signalling to the South Africans the seriousness of our commitment, as it relates to Angola, and our determination that the South African cease their destabilizing activities detected at Angola and the other Front Line States. So I think that would be very helpful -- a new beginning.

We also need to concentrate on strengthening the position of the Front Line States. It is critical to our relationship with Mozambique and Zimbabwe and with SADCC as a whole. It is critical to reduce their dependence upon South Africa and promote their regional economic development. We must staunch the extraordinary devastation that South Africa has inflicted on the surrounding region and which South Africa continues to threaten to do. We are still finding that tremendous amount of support and assistance flows to RENAMO in Mozambique. Botha proclaims that the South African government is not officially behind that assistance, but there is very little evidence that anyone is trying to stop those who are carrying logistical supplies and support from South Africa into Mozambique. There is wide suspicion that elements of the military are directly involved in some of this activity. It is not at all clear to me that the United States has really indicated, by any means that would be considered forceful, our opposition to that activity.

Regarding SADCC, we have earmarked in the foreign assistance legislation that passed the subcommittee in late April 1989, some fifty million dollars, primarily for the transportation and communication sector in the next fiscal year. I would like to see a much greater expansion for that assistance for southern Africa generally. We are enormously constrained in terms of the whole foreign assistance budget by the deficit crisis and the Gramm-Rudman guidelines. So we can probably not do better that what I have just described. We have, overall, about a 550 million dollar African regional account that is called for in legislation. We need, I think, to at least consider providing, as the Reagan Administration had proposed a few years ago, a non-lethal security system to Mozambique, not in any serious effort to correct the regional military imbalance, but rather as a sign again of the seriousness of our commitment to Mozambique's security. Only then will it become clearly understood by the South Africans, that an attack on their regional neighbors is an attack upon people whom we regard as friends and with whom we want to have positive, constructive relationships. The State Department report that was issued in 1988, the so-called Gersony Report, documented the extraordinary brutality of the RENAMO forces, the slaughter of some one hundred thousand civilians. That report has put the right wing in this country a bit on the defensive.

I conclude by simply observing that our African policy will require a continuous struggle, simply for attention. Africa remains low on the totem pole of foreign policy concerns for the United States. I hope that under the Bush Administration it may acquire increased salience and importance. Mr. Bush seems to be making some effort to reach out to the minority community in the United States. I hope he begins to understand these issues of southern African policy are as much civil rights questions as they are foreign policy questions. If he does, then we may be able to get a somewhat more sensitive, different kind of approach. But in the final analysis it will remain grassroots political mobilization that will determine our degree of success in increasing the salience of these questions and in helping to frame a policy towards southern Africa that is far more consistent with both American values and American national interests than the policy that has been pursued over the last several years.

11
Constructive Engagement at Work in Southern Africa: A View from the Inside

Herman J. Cohen

I begin with a biographic note. If you accept that "constructive engagement" was an eight-year phenomenon coinciding with Chester Crocker's term as Assistant Secretary of State, then my status as an inside player was valid only for the last two years, 1987 to 1988. As the National Security Council's Senior Director for Africa, I worked closely with Dr. Crocker on the tripartite negotiations leading to the agreements of December 22, 1988. Between 1981 and 1987, I had positions in the State Department from which I could observe constructive engagement at work, but I was only peripherally involved.

I would like to state right at the outset my view that "constructive engagement" was not a policy. It was a method selected for the purpose of achieving certain policy objectives. I realize that Chester Crocker utilized the term "a policy of constructive engagement" in his famous 1980 article in *Foreign Affairs* entitled "Change in South Africa." However, I am sure that he would be the first to agree that method is not policy, although in his case it was often interpreted as such, and caused him considerable grief.

The reason I make this point about method versus policy is my contention that the Reagan Administration policy on Southern Africa was squarely in the mainstream of U.S. policy since the early 1960s. It was a policy of continuity and not a policy of innovation.

What were the main lines of U.S. policy in Africa during the twenty year period preceding the Reagan Administration? I would summarize them as follows:

1. *Support the Process of Decolonialization* U.S. policy never failed to be on the right side of the African decolonialization process between 1960 and 1980, although we did a better job in some instances than in others. We were particularly lax, in my view, in failing to pressure Portugal over Angola, Mozambique, Bissau and Sao Tome. In the case of the Portuguese, U.S. NATO commitments and our base in the Azores inhibited us from doing much for the liberation of Lusophone Africa beyond

a scholarship program for FRELIMO students. Nevertheless, we never failed to support freedom for all colonies, at least in our rhetoric if not always in our actions.

2. *Counter Soviet Intervention and Compete with Soviet Influence.* When William Rogers became the first Secretary of State to visit Africa in the early 1970s, he made a speech in Addis Ababa in which he described U.S. policy as seeking to "keep the cold war out of Africa." What he meant by that was mutual restraint between the superpowers in arms deliveries to the African continent and in support for African insurgencies. That element of detente was shattered in 1974 and 1975 with massive Soviet arms deliveries and Cuban troop interventions in both Ethiopia and Angola. In any event, U.S. policy never ceased to focus on the East-West dimensions in Africa.

3. *Work to Diminish Sub-regional Conflict and Encourage Regional Cooperation.* In our military assistance policy as well as our diplomacy in Africa, the U.S. has consistently sought to avoid fanning the flames of conflict. Our policy in the Horn of Africa provided the best example of that view in the 1970s and 80s.

4. *Speak Loudly and Harshly About Apartheid in South Africa, but Carry a Small Stick.* Every President since Eisenhower has expressed abhorrence of apartheid, but none of them attempted to do anything significant about it.

5. *Encourage Regional Economic Cooperation.* In all of our foreign assistance programs, the U.S. has consistently supported regional economic integration as a key motor of development.

If you examine Chester Crocker's policy objectives and implementation priorities, you will see that he was entirely consistent with the five main elements of policy listed above.

The centerpiece of Crocker's southern Africa policy became the quest for a *negotiated* Namibian independence. Why did he choose that option? There are several reasons:

1. The decolonialization issue has always had broad bipartisan support in the U.S. It was a motherhood issue.

2. The U.S. had always been supportive of Namibian independence. We supported the 1971 International Court of Justice decision. We were instrumental in the passage of U.N. Security Council Resolution 435 in 1978.

3. The Namibian question was a discrete diplomatic challenge that had the clear possibility of reaching a successful conclusion. A new Presidential appointee in a new administration looks for challenges that appear susceptible to victory over a four-year time-frame. That may be all the time available, if that much. Namibia fit that requirement exactly. In his *Foreign Affairs* article, Chester Crocker said that a solution to Namibian problem was "tantalizingly close."

4. A negotiation to achieve Namibian independence was necessary because the U.S. was unwilling to get tough with South Africa which, after all, was occupying Namibia illegally. Even the preceding Carter Administration, which displayed greater rhetorical anger toward apartheid, vetoed a mandatory sanctions resolution against South Africa in the U.N. Security Council over the Namibian question. If a sanctions bill had been presented to the Congress in Reagan's first term, it could not have been enacted. The bottom line was that if coercion was not a realistic option, negotiations were the logical alternative.

5. The Carter Administration made Namibian independence the centerpiece of its southern African policy, and succeeded brilliantly in producing U.N. Resolution 435 in 1978. But there was insufficient time to negotiate implementation, giving the Reagan Administration a strong incentive to finish the job.

6. Finally, the Namibian question had real or potential links to regional conflict and tensions, to regional economic issues, and to superpower confrontation in the Third World, all of which were part of the standard menu of U.S. interests in Africa listed earlier. In addition, the then Secretary Alexander Haig had a particular policy interest in reversing Cuban "internationalism." From that perspective, the idea of linking Namibian independence to Cuban troop withdrawal from Angola was clearly very attractive.

Attention to the core apartheid problem had to take a back seat to the Namibian questions because that issue was very far from being ripe, even for a process of pre-negotiations. In Chester Crocker's own words:

The innovative feature of constructive engagement is in its insistence on serious thinking about the sequencing and interrelatedness of change. Priority ought to be given to those arenas of change that logically lead to, and make possible, future steps.

Namibian independence was clearly the next "arena of change" in Chester Crocker's mind, on the long road to the dismantling of apartheid itself.

With this analysis approved by the Secretary of State, Chester Crocker began an active diplomatic effort on Namibia. South Africa had never rejected the idea of Namibian independence, but had never cooperated in the implementation of either the ICJ decision of U.N. Resolution 435. In the absence of any credible coercive leverage over South Africa, Dr. Crocker had to find an incentive. That incentive was the prospect of removing a perceived major threat to South African security in the form of the presence in Angola of a Cuban military expeditionary force and African National Congress training bases. Thus was born "linkage" -- implementation of U.N. Resolution 435 in return for Cuban troop withdrawal from Angola. In the shorthand of the negotiators, the formula was boiled down to 435/CTW.

The South Africans accepted the linkage package easily. Indeed, some sources say it was originally a South African idea. With hindsight, it is clear that the South Africans must have seen linkage initially as giving them breathing space and a possible opportunity to bring about a phony independence to Namibia without reference to 435. In any event, the South Africans were hooked, in the diplomatic sense, into an agreement on a formula for Namibian independence. All it took, therefore, was to persuade the Angolans that linkage was in their interest. This effort effectively consumed all of President Reagan's first term.

The main argument used with the Angolans was their own rhetoric that Cuban troops were in Angola only because of South Africa's continuous military intervention in southern Angola. Once South African troops were withdrawn from Angola and Resolution 435 implemented, there would no longer be any further need for Cuban forces in Angola. If that was the case, U.S. negotiators argued, why not agree to a simultaneous withdrawal of both South African and Cuban forces from Namibia and Angola? Such an arrangement would be designed to allay South African fears of Cuban intervention in Namibia after the departure of South African Troops. It was only a matter of working out appropriate timetables so that neither side would feel their security threatened.

The Angolans resisted this line of reasoning for four years. They said linkage was unjustified on judicial grounds. The Cubans were in Angola at the invitation of a legitimate government. The South Africans were legally obligated by 435 to get out of Namibia without a *quid pro quo*. It would be immoral to link the two. Toward the end of 1984, however, the Angolans were clearly becoming uncomfortable with the thought that their doctrinal hard-line was being increasingly seen as preventing the independence of Namibia, which, to repeat Dr. Crocker's prognosis, was "tantalizingly close." In 1984, the MPLA government made their first concession which was to offer a reduction in Cuban troop strength "as a gesture" in return for the implementation of 435 in Namibia. This was part of their policy document called "PLATIFORMA." It was at this point that the MPLA became partially pregnant on the linkage issue. Dr. Crocker attempted to build on this doctrinal opening by persuading the South Africans to promise a date certain of August 1, 1986, for the implementation of 435 if the Angolans would agree to a formula of a two-year CTW, with eighty percent of the Cubans departing Angola the first year, and the remaining twenty percent the second year. The MPLA let the August 1st deadline go by without a response.

During 1984 as well, Dr. Crocker achieved two diplomatic successes by brokering regional peace agreements between South Africa and both Angola and Mozambique. The Lusaka and Nkomati accords respectively called for an end to cross border attacks and support for insurgencies between Mozambique and South Africa, and a military disengagement between Angola and South Africa. These accords were short-lived for reasons that will not be discussed here, but they were significant in demonstrating that regional security arrangements between South Africa and its neighbors were feasible, Pretoria's pariah status notwithstanding. Even more important, in my view, the Nkomati accord between Mozambique and South Africa gave President Samora Machel the diplomatic standing to put pressure on his brother Lusophones in the MPLA to do their part to advance the cause of Namibian independence. The MPLA's offer of a gesture to reduce Cuban troop strength in return for the implementation of 435 was legitimized by Mozambique's prior agreement to sign a treaty with South Africa.

Although relatively fragile, Chester Crocker's diplomatic achievements through the summer of 1984 and the strong prospects of Ronald Reagan's re-election gave him the hope that a major breakthrough might be possible in the Administration's second term. But events on the ground in Southern Africa between the summer of 1984 and the end of 1986 threatened to destroy the process Chester Crocker had meticulously constructed over four years.

In South Africa itself, the establishment in mid-1984 of a new constitution with a tricameral parliament that excluded the black majority unleashed the longest and most successful black challenge to white minority rule in the country's history. The resulting repression and massive human rights violations by the white security apparatus caused the Reagan Administration to impose selective economic sanctions by executive order in 1985, and the Congress to enact more comprehensive sanctions over the President's veto in 1986. These actions placed U.S.-South African relations in the deep freeze, and jeopardized any further South African cooperation leading to the implementation of 435.

In Angola, the MPLA Government launched a major offensive against UNITA strongholds in the southeast in the 1985 dry season utilizing Soviet arms and close Cuban logistical support. This called into question the MPLA's commitment to peaceful solutions, and gave conservatives in the U.S. Congress the ammunition needed to repeal the Clark Amendment. That legislative action in 1985 was followed by the beginning of U.S. covert assistance to UNITA in early 1986. Within the executive branch during 1985, the State Department opposed the establishment of a U.S. assistance program to UNITA because such an action was expected to cause the MPLA to break off negotiations on 435/CTW. This is exactly what happened. The "tantalizingly close" Namibian independence became depressingly distant as all negotiations on 435/CTW were suspended from late 1985 to the spring of 1987. For most of us observers and players in government, the process of constructive engagement leading to 435/CTW appeared "dead in the water."

During the first quarter of 1987, we started receiving signs that all was not necessarily lost. The President of the Republic of the Congo sent word to Dr. Crocker that the MPLA might be willing to explore the possibility of reopening negotiations. In early April, Dr. Crocker went to Brazzaville where he met with an Angolan delegation. The result was an agreement to meet in Luanda for a series of three-day discussions at six-week intervals that were to carry the process to 1988. The results of the 1987 Lusanda cycle may be summarized as follows:

1. Acceptance by the MPLA of a *de facto* linkage between 435 and CTW, but with the insistence that about fifty percent of the Cuban contingent of forty thousand troops be allowed to remain in the northern part of Angola indefinitely after Namibian independence.

2. Insistence by the MPLA that U.S. aid to UNITA would have to be stopped as part of the package deal.

3. A request by the MPLA that Cuba be allowed to join the talks.

In January 1988, the Secretary of State agreed to our sitting at the same table as the Cubans provided that the Cubans were part of the Angolan delegation and that no U.S.-Cuban bilateral issues could be raised. The first meeting at which the Cubans were present provided a major breakthrough with the acceptance for the first time of the concept of total Cuban troop withdrawal in return for Namibian independence. Although the time-frame proposed for total CTW was unrealistic -- four years after Namibian independence -- the acceptance of total CTW by the Angolans gave Dr. Crocker what he needed to go back to the South Africans.

Dr. Crocker met with South African Foreign Minister Pik Botha in Geneva in March 1988. That meeting took place seventeen months after the passage of the sanctions legislation of 1986. While bilateral relations were still frigid, enough time had gone by to give the South African government a new perspective on their needs as well as on their international relations. At that point, the South African government could not place itself in a position of blocking the prospect of a Cuban troop evacuation from Angola. The South Africans did not want to alienate those members of the U.S. Congress who were reluctant to pursue further sanctions. So the South African government agreed to participate in tripartite negotiations with the Cubans and Angolans.

The first tripartite negotiating roundtable took place in London in May 1988, with Dr. Crocker designated the official mediator. At that session, the head of the South African delegation held up a copy of U.N Resolution 435 and said his government would "implement the resolution to the letter" provided a satisfactory schedule for Cuban troop withdrawal could be negotiated. At that point it became clear that a basic breakthrough had been achieved. There remained to be negotiated only the details of military disengagement, Cuban withdrawal schedules, and verification. The basic linkage concept of 435/CTW was deceptively simple. The details to be negotiated were incredibly complex. We had some very tough negotiating rounds between June and December, but the eventual successful outcome was never really in doubt given the basic mutual commitments advanced in May.

Why was Dr. Crocker able to pull off this tripartite deal in 1988 when he had been unable to do so in the previous seven years? There were a number of primary motivating factors, but to understand them we must first look at two additional developments on the ground between the summer of 1987 and May 1988.

In the 1987 dry season, the MPLA undertook a second major offensive against UNITA strongholds that was even bigger than the one that failed in 1985. Soviet arms deliveries were estimated to have been worth approximately $1 billion. Logistical preparations alone took eighteen months. With the help of superior South African artillery and outstanding UNITA tactics, however, the offensive was a disastrous failure. By the end of 1987, the MPLA had been driven back to its starting point of Cuito Cuanavale with the loss of massive amounts of equipment to UNITA.

The end of the offensive led to the second development which began in December 1987. The Cubans began a major transfer of twelve thousand of their best troops and their equipment from duty in Cuba to Angola. These troops were not rotational. They represented a new infusion of fighting forces that brought total Cuban strength up to fifty-two thousand. By May 1988, the time of the first negotiating round in London, the additional Cuban forces were being deployed to the southwestern border between Angola and Namibia.

These two developments were very important factors in the negotiating matrix. In my view, the fundamental motivating factors leading to the successful conclusion of the negotiations were the following:

1. A Soviet desire to cut down on its Third World security commitments so that resources could be put to higher priority use at home. The defeat of the MPLA forces in the 1987 offensive was an indication that a military victory over UNITA would be impossible. Continued U.S. assistance to UNITA could only serve to reinforce that analysis. Hence, negotiations were necessary to wind down the drain on Soviet resources. In this respect it should be noted that Soviet government representatives were present "in the corridors" at all of the tripartite negotiating sessions in order "to be helpful." They were helpful.

2. A Soviet desire to eliminate irritants in their relationship with the U.S. Angola was one of the irritants in the "regional conflicts" category.

3. Growing domestic opposition within the South African white community to what appeared to be an unbending and increasingly expensive military commitment in southern Angola and northern Namibia.

4. An increasing need for resources on the part of the South African government to finance more black education, black housing and other social welfare projects designed to coopt blacks into a more benevolent system of white domination. This requirement was a direct outgrowth of the

1984 to 1988 wave of massive black opposition and unrest. The very large subsidy to the Namibian colony and the high cost of military occupation of southern Angola and Namibia were obvious sources of funding. In addition, the new Cuban military presence on the Namibian border brought home the reality that the days of South African military domination of southern Angola were over.

5. The Angolan economy had become a basket case, with low world oil prices, and low agricultural production brought on by the war and Marxist disincentives. The Angolans were no longer able to pay their bills or feed their people. Arrears on bills owed to both Cuba and the Soviet Union were in the hundreds of millions of dollars. The Angolans were badly in need of a settlement.

There was an irony in the entire process. The internal upheaval and repression in South Africa leading to subsequent U.S. sanctions, and the program of U.S. covert aid to UNITA virtually caused the negotiations to collapse in 1985 and 1986. But these same factors were important in causing the negotiations to be successful in 1987 and 1988.

In conclusion I offer some comment on the methodology of constructive engagement as it was applied to southern Africa between January 1981 and January 1989.

Without constructive engagement, I do not believe the December 1985 agreements could have been concluded. Certainly Dr. Crocker did not create the convergence of interests that brought the Soviet Union, South Africa, Angola and Cuba to acquiesce in the basic principles of a linked 435/CTW. But constructive engagement positioned Dr. Crocker as the honest broker all the parties felt comfortable with as they got down to hard bargaining in May 1988. In addition, constructive engagement gave Dr. Crocker extensive exposure to all the parties except the Cubans between 1981 and 1988, thereby enabling him to shape the negotiations for maximum chances of success. Most of the negotiating rounds were centered on Dr. Crocker's intensive shuttle diplomacy among the parties. Only someone who knew the parties intimately from years of contact could play that game effectively. Constructive engagement gave Dr. Crocker the diplomatic tools that nobody else had.

The methodology of constructive engagement caused Dr. Crocker considerable grief in U.S. domestic politics. Although the United States Government never failed to condemn reprehensible acts of repression committed by the South African government during Dr. Crocker's tenure, the anti-apartheid forces could not forgive him for maintaining a modicum of normal communications with the white minority regime. What is often overlooked, however, is that "constructive engagement" was applied to all of the government of Southern Africa, and not only to South Africa. For important segments of the U.S. political spectrum, Angola and Mozambique had, and continue to have, pariah Marxist regimes. The application of constructive engagements to those governments outraged many people who did not hesitate to make their feelings known in a number of troublesome ways. When we used to joke that Dr. Crocker was hated by both the left and the right -- so he must have been doing something right -- we were only partially in jest.

If we define constructive engagement as a methodology that seeks to deal with power structures as they exist rather than as we would like them to be, and which seeks incremental results that are achievable within reasonable time-frames, then it was the right methodology to use between 1981 and 1989. I am not saying that the same methodology will be pursued in southern Africa by the Bush Administration. That decision must await the policy review that is currently underway. But I invite you to compare the use of constructive engagement in southern Africa by the Crocker African Bureau with the methods of total isolation, boycotts and total economic sanctions utilized in other parts of the world in recent years, and judge the results for yourselves.

12
What Role for the U.S. in Resolving Conflict in Southern Africa?

Pauline H. Baker

THE REGION AT A CROSSROADS

The success of the Reagan Administration in brokering a settlement in southwest Africa represents an important breakthrough in U.S. diplomacy as well as a major turning point in the region. Even before President George Bush named his Assistant Secretary of State for African Affairs, trial balloons were floated about the possibility of this agreement being used as a model for conflict resolution elsewhere in the area.[1] Attention focused on achieving national reconciliation in Angola, an end to the insurgency in Mozambique, and negotiations for dismantling apartheid in South Africa.

Not since the 1979 British-sponsored Lancaster House negotiations, which ended the war in Rhodesia and brought Zimbabwe to independence, have international expectations been so high. This optimism has emerged in spite of the fact that, compared to other conflict zones, southern Africa remains a relatively low foreign policy priority for Washington. The slow pace of appointments in the Bush Administration, although not unique to Africa, and the lack of an emerging strategy for southern Africa underline the point. By contrast, during Bush's first one hundred days in office, the outlines of U.S. policy toward Central America and the Middle East had taken shape. In Central America, military support for the contras came to an end, the Arias peace plan assumed center stage, and the White House reached a political compromise with Congress. In the Middle East, a three-track policy unfolded that opted for gradual promotion of negotiations through separate approaches to Israel, the PLO and the Soviet Union, with an endorsement of the Israeli plan for West Bank elections.[2]

With the exception of a statement of support for UNITA, the Angolan rebel movement, no comparable indicators of U.S. strategy were revealed with regard to southern Africa. Even the letter of support written by President Bush to Jonas Savimbi just two weeks before his inauguration

to allay conservative criticism of the southwest Africa accord was somewhat ambiguous. It did not promise unlimited aid, but tied assistance to
national reconciliation, though it is not clear how that goal will be pursued or what it means precisely.

The administration's caution, while perplexing, could be seen as a favorable sign. Africa could once again become a backwater foreign policy
issue, but it is equally plausible to hypothesize that a threshold of diplomatic involvement has been reached from which there is no turning back.
Cautious policy responses could indicate reappraisal in light of this commitment. Giving the new administration the benefit of the doubt, therefore, what diplomatic role could the U.S. realistically play at this juncture?

Press speculation and academic assessments have focused predominantly on the opportunities for U.S.-Soviet cooperation. They point to
the constructive role of the Soviet Union throughout the 1988 negotiations on Angola and Namibia, and to Moscow's shift in policy toward
South Africa, which have included contacts with high level officials from
Pretoria and statements in support of political solutions. Southern African
conflicts, it is argued, can now be addressed, not in terms of superpower
confrontation, but as an arena for superpower collaboration.

It is noteworthy that while differences between Moscow and
Washington remain in Nicaragua and Afghanistan, southwestern Africa
remains "the one regional conflict where the superpowers have cooperated
successfully to bring about a resolution."[3] Moreover, there appears to be
a solid convergence of interests between the superpowers on the Angola-
Namibia pact. The Soviet-American partnership was not shaken, for example, by the violence which erupted on the first day of implementation,
when SWAPO guerrillas based in Angola crossed the border into Namibia
on a scale that threatened to collapse the agreement.

But can the meeting of minds reached on Angola-Namibia be applied
to other disputes? Each of three ongoing conflicts in the region is different in origin, nature and level of external influence. Simmering unrest or
insurgencies that were dormant or insignificant in the 1970s have exploded
into violent confrontations in the 1980s. And no one should be sanguine
about the Angola-Namibia accord itself. Many things could still go
wrong during the complex twenty-seven month long process, which involves the withdrawal of some one hundred thousand Cuban and South
African troops from Angola and Namibia, a territory that is roughly comparable in size to the United States east of the Mississippi. Several loopholes and unresolved questions remain in the U.N. plan, including the
critical issue of what happens if the U.N. mandate runs out before
Namibia is free. Preoccupation with keeping this agreement on track
could distract the international community from other regional concerns.

If there is a further role for the U.S., therefore, then it must be carefully targeted. Defining the priorities in the subcontinent is the central

challenge for the United States as a new regional political map is drawn. By 1991, if everything goes according to plan, Cuban forces should be out of Angola; Namibia, Africa's last colony, should be independent; South Africa will lose its last strategic buffer; the African National Congress (ANC) will relocate its military bases outside the subcontinent; and UNITA would become almost wholly dependent for military support on the United States.

These are important new developments which are complemented by equally significant trends independent of the peace agreement. In South Africa, a new generation of National Party leaders is poised to take over the reins of power after President P.W. Botha steps down and a parliamentary election is held in the fall of 1989. The Soviet Union is repositioning itself to play a broader, more political role in the region, including in South Africa. European diplomacy, led by Great Britain, is becoming more active. South Africa's economic involvement in the black-ruled states is expanding, reinforcing the interdependence between Pretoria and its neighbors. And Nelson Mandela is standing in the wings, ready to lead the next phase of black resistance to apartheid if he is free.

From this perspective, the accord in southwest Africa should not be seen as a event confined to Angola and Namibia alone. It draws to a close two major chapters of African history: colonial rule and, hopefully, the Cold War. In the process, new dynamics have been unleashed. The pact thus marks the beginning, not the end, of a wider political process in which an entirely new regional order is taking shape. It is in this context that the United States' diplomatic role in Southern Africa must be re-evaluated.

ANGOLA

Angola represents part of the unfinished agenda of the past. During the Reagan years, the United States resumed its military involvement in the Angolan civil war, after a lapse of nine years, providing covert assistance to Jonas Savimbi, head of the antigovernment UNITA guerrilla force. The debate over aid to UNITA remains a troubling and controversial legacy. Unless internal peace can be achieved, UNITA could threaten the Angola-Namibia accord and undermine the ability of the administration to create a broad consensus for its southern Africa policy.

Yet President Bush began his term, in what the *Washington Post* described as his first foreign policy commitment, by promising "all appropriate and effective assistance" in order "to provide maximum support to a process of negotiation leading to national reconciliation."[4] UNITA guerrillas are regarded by supporters of the Reagan Doctrine as "freedom fighters" and Savimbi is often portrayed as a charismatic exponent of democracy and free enterprise. Nevertheless, today the guerrilla movement is walking what may be the most delicate tightrope in its existence. While Bush's statement of support was welcome news to Savimbi, it was poor consolation for the cut-off of direct South African military and financial assistance which was necessary to obtain the agreement on Angola and Namibia. Pretoria's agreement to end aid to UNITA was the *quid pro quo* for Angola's agreement to close down military bases of the ANC, South Africa's oldest and most popular liberation movement.

Deprived of South African air cover and ground support, as well as a lifeline of South African-supplied material, UNITA is now dependent on the United States. Since 1986, Washington has helped Savimbi by funnelling aid through Zaire in a covert military program, reported to be started at an annual level of $15 million and raised to $30 million.[5] UNITA wants that level to be increased further, to a minimum of $45 million in fiscal 1990, to include nonlethal goods formerly obtained from South Africa and a new generation of high-tech anti-aircraft missiles, artillery and anti-tank weapons.

Substantial support exists for UNITA on Capitol Hill, including among some Democrats. But the rationale for supporting UNITA seems to be shifting to a tactical one, justified on the grounds of keeping the Angola-Namibia accord on course and exercising leverage on the Angolan government. Nevertheless, pro-UNITA ideological fervor among conservatives remains high. Unless negotiations take place to achieve an internal settlement in Angola, the debate over the U.S. military program could threaten the Bush administration's relations with Congress, just as contra aid plagued the Reagan administration.

Problems could also arise because of dwindling interest in funding insurgencies in other regions. Support for these operations is winding down as aid to UNITA is increasing. This means that the issue could become more of a litmus test of conservative loyalty to the anti-Marxist strategy identified with Ronald Reagan than a political strategy for achieving long-term peace and stability in Angola.

Critics see Savimbi, not as a pro-western freedom fighter, but as one observer put it, "a political chameleon of passing persuasion but steady ambition."[6] They argue that American military aid erodes Washington's ability to act as an honest broker, inflames rather than resolves the civil war in Angola, and undercuts American credibility and influence in Africa as a whole. South African blacks, for example, have cited U.S. aid to UNITA as evidence of their perception that the United States silently supports South Africa.

For its part, the Soviet Union seems similarly entangled with its Angolan ally. Although Moscow collaborated with the United States in persuading the Cubans to go home, it is still the major military supplier of the MPLA government and seems unprepared to disengage in a precipitous way. Conceivably, both superpowers may see it in their interest to exercise influence on their respective clients to negotiate. At the moment, however, the MPLA and UNITA seem inclined to test each other's military strength on the battlefield without foreign backers before they enter talks. Should that be the case, then the United States and the Soviet Union will have to decide whether to stand by their clients and supply additional weapons for another confrontation. Sustaining aid, especially in light of allegations of atrocities, could lead to a backlash in American public opinion and risk a downturn in superpower relations.[7]

MOZAMBIQUE

A second conflict in the region is the RENAMO insurgency in Mozambique. After years of deadly warfare and economic mismanagement, this former Portuguese colony has, in effect, become a ward of the international community. Malawi, Tanzania and, most of all, Zimbabwe have deployed troops in Mozambique to defend vital outlets to the sea; the British supply military training to the Mozambican army; and the Western world is shoring up the economy with economic aid, including more than $450 million pledged for the rehabilitation of the Beira Corridor, the central railway, road, pipeline, port and town that serves as a transportation artery to the sea for the region as a whole.[8]

Yet, for all this assistance, Mozambique continues to reel from the brutal activities of RENAMO, a force consisting of bands of marauding guerrilla fighters originally created as a fifth column by the white minority regime in Rhodesia. Since 1980, when Zimbabwe gained its independence and South Africa took over responsibility for training and equipping the rebels, RENAMO has intensified its attacks, including on civilians and other non-military targets, such as schools and health centers. Several sources, including the State Department in a 1988 report, describe RENAMO as a force that regularly commits atrocities. The State Department concluded that the right-wing rebels killed at least one hundred thousand Mozambicans and had turned one million others into refugees.[9] Besides having a deplorable human rights record, RENAMO also lacks a coherent program, clear leadership and historical roots as an anti-colonial liberation movement.

Having had a hand in creating this undisciplined force -- which, among other things, has attacked pylons from the Cahora Bassa hydroelectric project that supplies power to Pretoria -- South Africa decided to distance itself from RENAMO as part of a wider campaign launched in mid-1988 to improve its international image. Radically reversing its position on Mozambique, Pretoria formally declared that it was no longer aiding RENAMO, though it never officially admitted to having done so as a matter of policy. Pretoria also revived the 1984 non-aggression pact with Mozambique, known as the Nkomati Accord; concluded an agreement to upgrade the Cahora Bassa hydroelectric project in Mozambique; supplied non-lethal military equipment to help defend the project's installations; and lifted restrictions on Mozambican migrant workers imposed in 1986.

But there have been charges, emphatically denied by Pretoria, that the South African military is still secretly supplying RENAMO and elements of the United States Government, including the Pentagon and right-wing conservatives, remain sympathetic. In this context, Pretoria's suggestion, offered in February, that the U.S. and the USSR broker a settlement in Mozambique, similar to the one negotiated in Angola, raises puzzling questions.[10] Is there a genuine role for outside powers or is this an attempt to entice the international community into a process that would legitimize discredited rebels that still retain ties to their benefactor?

One notable feature of the conflict is the way in which the government of Mozambique has lined up international support. Indeed, Mozambique seems to have generated more of a consensus than any other conflict in the region. RENAMO has not succeeded in winning the official backing of any country, with the possible exception of South Africa; and even Pretoria, whose role in supplying the rebels remains unclear, has been forced to keep its distance.

But this international consensus does not lead to easy solutions. Pressing the South Africa government to shut down all aid to RENAMO, if that is the obvious point of departure, is not a simple task. Pretoria denies official involvement, may be unwilling to crack down on RENAMO supporters for political reasons, or might be unable to shut down the operation which has developed a life of its own.

The Soviet Union's assessment seems to be equally at a loss for solutions that could bring peace to Mozambique in short order. Moscow appears to have concluded that, outside of an international plan for economic assistance, not much can be done. Alexei Makarov, a Mozambique expert from the Soviet Ministry of Foreign Affairs, has described Mozambique as a nation suffering from general social disintegration because, among other things, of failed socialist policies. Mass violence in the rural areas cannot be solely laid at the doorstep of the anti-government forces, Makarov argued, and the poorly clothed and fed Mozambican army and police also commit "acts of robbery" that "are particularly brutal."[11] "Forcing the liquidation of RENAMO with military or other means is not going to change anything fundamental in this country," he concluded. "Mozambique has only one exit out of this tormenting, endless crisis - to create the economic mechanism, to develop the money-based market in the country, to transform their feudal peasantry into goods producers,...and to create an effective and relatively non-bureaucratic government and army." The author dismisses the possibility of Soviet military involvement and calls instead for "international cooperation in helping the development of Mozambique" as the way to eliminate the country's crisis.[12]

SOUTH AFRICA

The third and, for the United States, most salient conflict concerns South Africa. This issue stands out as one in which there is a strong domestic interest that must be taken into account. Congress, in particular, has a key role to play. Indeed, an important threshold was crossed in relations between Pretoria and Washington when sanctions were enacted by a bipartisan vote of Congress in October 1986, over the veto of President Reagan. Even with that momentary unity of purpose, built on outrage over the continuing violence and repression in South Africa, sanctions remain a matter of considerable debate.

There will be no going back on these measures unless and until there is significant progress toward granting blacks full political rights, as detailed in provisions of the Comprehensive Anti-Apartheid Act of 1986. But it is an open question whether new sanctions will be adopted and, if so, whether they will be as extensive as those proposed in the so-called Dellums Bill, a measure which calls for comprehensive sanctions. It is also unclear whether, in recognition of the fixed congressional position, the administration will try to use sanctions creatively, as a lever to exert influence on South Africa along with diplomatic pressure and aid to anti-apartheid groups. If so, it would stand in stark contrast to the Reagan administration, which adopted a stance of blanket opposition to economic sanctions of any kind.

It is possible that the Bush administration will move further than Reagan did on seeking to harmonize American policy on South Africa with its allies, some of which are taking advantage of American sanctions to advance their own trading relationships with Pretoria. Collaboration with the Soviet Union may also be in the cards. Moscow has revised fundamental tenets of its approach toward South Africa by downplaying revolution, pushing for a political settlement, encouraging preservation of the economy and calling for recognition of the importance of ethnicity and group rights. Moscow has also expanded ties with liberal whites, academics and journalists in South Africa, and has developed direct contacts with Pretoria. South African officials have even hinted of establishing diplomatic relations with the Soviet Union, an idea that would have been unthinkable a short time ago.

However, a broad accommodation between the U.S. and the USSR seems to be a long way off and it probably will not be possible until there is some attempt to build a consensus at home. In the meantime, the search for an effective policy on South Africa consistent with American values and strategic interests has put the U.S. in the curious position of both opposing and working with Pretoria. Washington and Pretoria are now estranged partners, deeply divided over apartheid while linked to a regional peace process in which both have vested interests.

THE DOMESTIC SCENE

The complex of issues that arise in southern Africa could present formidable problems as well as opportunities for the United States in the years ahead. In addition to the considerations mentioned above, a domestic political agenda will also enter into play. Republicans have declared their intention of seeking to capture the black vote; yet Democrats, who elected a black American as national party chairman, are dedicated to holding onto their most loyal voting bloc. In the contest over black votes, both parties must demonstrate sensitivity to African issues, particularly South Africa. Blacks had an unprecedented impact on shaping U.S. policy toward South Africa during the Reagan years and Bush, who raised expectations early by meeting with prominent black political leaders, will be obligated to listen to rising black voices. Jesse Jackson's call for twelve percent of the American population to identify as African-Americans is a signal of growing pressure on this front.

Bush's concern with a bipartisan foreign policy and the quest for black support are two imperatives that could set a new direction for the U.S. in the region. But Bush also is keen to avoid alienating the right, which has targeted Southern Africa as an area of concern and drives policy toward an opposite course. A central dilemma for the Bush administration at this juncture, therefore, is whether a genuine political consensus can be achieved, taking these domestic and international factors into account, or whether paralysis will set in as a result of political polarization.

It is significant to note how much the U.S. has changed in this regard. Public opinion will be an important factor shaping future policy, in contrast to previous administrations. Active American diplomacy in southern Africa started in 1976, when former Secretary of State Henry Kissinger embarked upon last- minute shuttle diplomacy during the Ford administration to achieve a settlement of the conflicts in Rhodesia and Namibia. It continued through the Carter administration, which succeeded in forging a multilateral initiative, known as the Contact Group (consisting of the U.S., U.K., France, West Germany and Canada) which negotiated the U.N. plan for Namibia that is the basis for the current accord. Public opinion did not play a strong role in either of these efforts.

Even the first term of the Reagan administration conformed to the pattern. Crocker worked in relatively obscurity, without much public scrutiny, and with virtually a free hand from the start. Not until 1984, when an uprising in South Africa propelled apartheid into the mainstream of public attention, did "constructive engagement," Reagan's southern Africa policy, come under fire.

It was in the second term of the Reagan administration that the situation changed dramatically, bringing new perspectives to U.S. policy in southern Africa in more ways than one. The public outcry over repression in South Africa and the failure of the United States to respond appropriately resulted in an overwhelming vote for sanctions that had two central messages: one registered opposition to apartheid; the other signaled no confidence in the administration's policy. It took some time for this to sink in fully and the trappings of the administration's policy remained in place, but the congressional vote did have an effect.

Gradually, there appeared some adjustments to U.S. policy toward South Africa. This was seen in the meeting of Secretary of State George Shultz with ANC president Oliver Tambo and in the appointment of a new black American ambassador to South Africa who reached out to South African blacks. There was also a new flexibility in regional diplomacy. By stealth rather than by grand design, Crocker moved away from his own policy, not by bowing to public opinion, but by responding to changing regional realities. Geostrategic shifts, a change in the military balance of power as a result of Cuban escalation, and mounting economic pressures on Pretoria changed the regional political calculus and moved U.S. policy as well.

Public opinion, congressional input and intensive diplomacy are all now part of the U.S. policy process. There are also new tools and tactics available. A substantial aid program to anti-apartheid groups was introduced during the Reagan years, and military assistance to UNITA was resumed. Depending upon how the administration acts, in particular if it can reach an understanding with Congress, these developments could either present new manholes into which the U.S. can fall, or windows of opportunities for applying pressures and incentives that had once been considered unacceptable.

CONCLUSION

Clearly, in the last decade of this century, a new fluidity is emerging in southern Africa that offers opportunities for international influence. While there remain differences between them, the superpowers are now working as partners, not rivals, in resolving conflicts in the area. Foreign military forces are withdrawing to their own borders. South Africa is coming under new economic and political pressures at the same time it is undergoing a change of political leadership at the center. And the U.S. has created a record of involvement that makes it a central player.

Thus, the U.S. diplomatic role appears to be a certainty. It is already a guarantor of the Angola-Namibia accord, a supporter of the Mozambique government and a military backer of UNITA. But the scope and nature of its future involvement is open to question.

Can the U.S. be effective without a domestic political consensus on Angola and South Africa, two issues around which hard-core constituencies have emerged? Is the Bush administration prepared to face up to the challenge of apartheid, which for the last fifteen years has been pushed to the bottom of the hierarchy of southern Africa priorities in order to deal with other regional issues, such as Rhodesia, Namibia and Angola? Is the administration prepared to maximize its leverage by using sanctions more creatively and joining in a multilateral initiative? Is there a solid basis for working further with the Soviet Union and, if so, can it be done in a way that does not alienate African opinion? These are the more fundamental questions that will determine whether the American role will be effective or whether it will be paralyzed by domestic politics, rival foreign policy concerns or lingering contradictions and suspicions from previous involvements.

For its part, the Bush Administration could make a promising start by putting aside Reagan's discredited policy of "constructive engagement" and building a bipartisan approach together with Congress. First, President Bush should state his own position on U.S. policy toward South Africa, emphasizing the goal of negotiations with genuine black leaders, not race-based reforms. Secondly, he should strive for the short-term goal of getting Pretoria to permit legitimate political dissent by releasing political prisoners, ending the state of emergency and legalizing the opposition, including the ANC.

Third, Bush should forge a compromise with Congress on sanctions. To give the administration time to coordinate with the allies and perhaps, the Soviet Union, to press for these objectives, Congress could agree to a one-year sanctions moratorium and grant Bush a qualified presidential waiver that would allow him, with the approval of appropriate congressional committees, to lift sanctions selectively in response to positive steps by South Africa. Alternatively, if Pretoria remains intransigent or tries to adopt half-measures, the U.S. could adopt more sanctions.

Thus, for example, if Nelson Mandela, the ANC leader, was released, the ban on Kruggerands could be suspended. However, if Mandela was released but immediately placed under restrictions, as many other detainees have been, the U.S. could block U.S. banks from rolling over loans or extending trade credits, withdraw military attaches from the U.S. embassy in South Africa, or support tougher U.N. resolutions.

Close consultations with anti-apartheid figures, trade unionists and community leaders regarding the nature, scope and timing of U.S. actions will strengthen the hand of blacks by allowing them to coordinate international responses with internal developments. Conversely, the prospects of having sanctions lifted would undermine the argument of white hard-liners that there is nothing to be gained by responding to international pressures.

Creative, flexible but firm measures, such as these, could end the stand-off with Congress on South Africa, convert sanctions into an instrument of political leverage and enable Americans to speak with one voice on apartheid instead of dissipating their energies by fighting each other.

Notes

1. John Felton, "Angola Pact Poses Policy Challenges for Bush," *Congressional Quarterly* 47(6) (February 11, 1989).
2. Howard J. Wiarda and Ieda Siqueria Wiarda, "The United States and South America: The Challenge of Fragile Democracy," *Current History* 88(536) (March, 1989); "Baker's Mideast: Three Legs of a Triangle," *New York Times* (March 6, 1989); and "Baker's Pace for Mideast," *New York Times* (March 16, 1989).
3. David Ottaway, "Diplomatic Confrontation Looms on Regional Issues," *Washington Post* (April 16, 1989).
4. *The Washington Post* (January 12, 1989), 1. The Bush statement was contained in a letter dated January 6, 1989.
5. David Ottaway, "Angola Rebels Ask Risks in US Aid," *Washington Post* (April 25, 1989).
6. John A. Marcum, "Africa: A Continent Adrift," *Foreign Affairs* 68 (1988/89), 162.
7. See, for example, *Angola: Violations of the Laws of War by Both Sides, An Africa Watch Report* (April, 1989).
8. *The New York Times* (February 21, 1989), 4.
9. See also the research report by William Minter, "The Mozambican National Resistance (RENAMO) as Described by Ex-Participants," submitted to the Ford Foundation and the Swedish International Development Agency (Washington, D.C., March, 1989).
10. *The Washington Post* (February 11, 1989); and *The New York Times* (February 12, 1989).
11. Alexei Makarov, "On the Problem of Internal Conflict in Mozambique" (unpublished paper, April, 1989).
12. *Ibid.*

Steps Toward A More Effective U.S. Foreign Policy in Southern Africa: A Comment

Gail M. Gerhart

Pauline Baker's chapter puts forward a judicious and realistic assessment of the current American position, and I have found little in it with which I can seriously take issue. I would like to have seen some more specific prescriptions for future American action. However I would like to mention a few points that to me stand out as priority considerations for the Bush administration.

Although I believe that South Africa is the most important item pending on the Bush agenda, I will mention Mozambique's situation first, because it seems to me the administration has a major opportunity to demonstrate its commitment to peace and security in the region through increasing aid to Mozambique, and bringing diplomatic pressure for an end to the war there. Although we have been told that the United States has committed major financial resources to strengthen the SADCC countries, the sums are really quite paltry. Mozambique is a country on which I think a domestic consensus can be reached, because rightwing support for RENAMO has been undermined by the exposure given to its methods in a major State Department report last year. Assistant Secretary Cohen has said that all parties to the Mozambican conflict may be ready to look seriously for a way out, and surely this is an area where there is room for creative American diplomacy, in conjunction with an increased commitment to the reconstruction of Mozambique's shattered economy and society.

Another priority target for the Bush administration must be to establish much stronger rapport between the U.S. government and the organizations working for fundamental change in South Africa. During the Reagan years, the White House transmitted many discouraging signals to South Africans working for genuine change, particularly organizations representing the black majority. The Bush administration now has an opportunity to reestablish America's firm identification with the values of democracy and racial equality by encouraging closer communication with anti-apartheid groups inside South Africa and with the externally based liberation movements.

It was suggested in reference to Robert Price's model of the negotiation process, that it would be unrealistic for the U.S. to expect all movement towards the "zone of agreement" to take place from the right, by whites moving towards acceptance of majority demands, without also expecting some movement towards that zone by the ANC, UDF, and other opposition forces. Yet in the last few years there has in fact been significant movement from South Africa's opposition towards a potential accommodation of minority fears. We have seen the leaders of the ANC maintain their principles on the restrained use of violence and strongly resist pressures from within their own ranks to adopt terrorist tactics. We have seen significant moves by the ANC to open a dialogue with whites and to develop new thinking and new vocabulary to deal with their fears. About a year ago, the ANC issued an impressive set of guidelines for a future South African constitution, in which there is little that most Americans would dispute and a great deal that they can applaud. It seems to me that the guidelines represent a very significant movement on the part of the ANC towards a "zone of agreement."

Not all South African opposition groups endorse these guidelines, and there are shades of black opinion that lie both to the left and to the right of the ANC's position. Nevertheless our policy-makers ought to appreciate that in the case of the ANC, which is South Africa's most significant organization standing for fundamental change, there is definitely movement in search of common ground, and this is an ongoing process. As testament to that, in early February 1989 there was a major meeting between the ANC's Department of Legal and Constitutional Affairs and about thirty Afrikaner lawyers, law professors, and even a few deans of South African law faculties, who travelled to Harare to engage in discussions of the ANC's guidelines document. At the end of the five day meeting, a joint statement was issued indicating that there were very substantial areas of agreement between the ANC and these Afrikaner intellectuals and opinion leaders. There were hardly any major areas within the purview of the guidelines on which there was significant disagreement, and both sides endorsed the goal of creating conditions in which all South Africans would enjoy full and equal political, economic, social and cultural rights. This demonstrates a serious ongoing effort to seek out the parameters of a consensus.

If the United States during the Bush administration is to play a more positive role in finding a solution to the South African conflict, it must urgently seek ways to demonstrate its support for those who have committed themselves to the struggle against apartheid. Rhetorical support can never suffice, nor can primarily symbolic gestures like invitations for anti-apartheid leaders to visit the White House, though these do have a role to play in American diplomacy. On a more substantive level, there is one particular gesture that I would like to see the Bush administration make in order to move this country away from its tilt toward the white regime during the Reagan years, and that is to reconsider its position on intelligence sharing. This is an issue normally almost totally out of public view. *The New York Times* ran a front page story on this issue in July 1986, at the height of the sanctions pressure in Congress, and the story was picked up by newspapers around the world, including a number in South Africa. The story was by Seymour Hersh, and it revealed in considerable detail the extent of intelligence sharing between the United States, Britain, and the Pretoria government. Hersh's sources described a session, for example, at the Cheltenham intelligence headquarters in Britain, at which arrangements were discussed for *weekly* sharing of information between British, American, and South African intelligence sources, where the South Africans gave to the British and Americans information on Soviet shipping and submarine traffic. In return Britain and the United States offered to South African intelligence information on the activities of the ANC in the Front Line States, picked up through communications eavesdropping and other sources in the region. I should mention that Secretary Shultz denied before a Congressional committee that such intelligence sharing took place, or to be more precise he said that William Casey had denied to him that it took place. However, on February 9, 1989 in a televised question-and-answer session between Chester Crocker and Professor Thomas Karis, Crocker confirmed that the arrangements for intelligence sharing were still in place. Since, according to Hersh, this sharing of information on the liberation movements was halted during the Carter administration, it can hardly be vital to American interests. It seems to me that it will be very hard for the United States in future to aspire to the role of an honest broker in the South African conflict if it continues under Bush to show its true colors in this way. I also think it will be hard for the Bush administration, with its ambition to attract black support domestically, to succeed politically if it is known to be clearly aligning itself with the Pretoria government and against South Africa's black majority in this way.

13
In Conclusion: Charting a Path toward Peace and Security in Southern Africa

Harvey Glickman

FOCUS ON SOUTH AFRICA

Southern Africa as a region derives its coherence largely from the predatory role of South Africa. It is not surprising that the policy implications of the contributions to this volume are governed by developments in South Africa. Yet one overall message of the contributions taken as a whole is that international pressures, more than ever (writing in July 1989) are shaping events in South Africa. For example, putting aside opinions on whether justice has triumphed in Angola, in fact the killing has stopped; the South Africans have withdrawn, the Cubans have completed phase one of their reciprocal withdrawal, and the MPLA government is negotiating with the UNITA rebels. None of this would have come about without the active involvement of the U.S.A., the U.S.S.R. and several African states, as noted in the chapter by Herman Cohen. In Mozambique, somewhat contrary to what Harvey Glickman's contribution would have defined as justice, and after his chapter was written, the FRELIMO government announced its willingness to negotiate with the RENAMO "bandits." A multiform international effort could be said to have negatively shaped events, as it proved unable to mount a fully effective counter-insurgency effort in association with the Mozambique military. Decolonization in Namibia for years remained hostage to South African and Cuban disengagement in Angola. While the United Nations served as an arena for debate about Namibia and as a conduit of international legality, its effectiveness in administering the long-sought election of a constituent assembly and an independence government depend upon the willingness of the major powers to provide financial resources. As implied by Joseph Diescho in his chapter, of all of Africa's liberation movements, SWAPO's success may be the most dependent on international action.

Larger international forces are conspiring to reinforce a climate for negotiations in southern Africa. The watershed event here is the virtual dis-

241

appearance of the Cold War. A parallel dwindling in the defense budgets
of the Superpowers is occurring; the position of Southern Africa in a
global strategic design is waning. Although never a priority, southern
Africa in the role of a major strategic asset to either side grows increasingly implausible. At the same time, the dream of a partnership of
Marxist-Leninist states in southern Africa, via socialist development
strategies, with a mentor in the Soviet Union, has died. The Marxoid
model of development dictatorship in the Third World has failed. That nationalism in Africa automatically means a flirtation with socialism and
that re-distributionist rhetoric automatically means a hand-out from the
U.S.S.R. are dismissable notions today. When Oliver Tambo of the
African National Congress turns up at Business Seminars in Britain, it is
increasingly difficult to sustain the view that the ANC in a future South
African government means the beginning of a Stalinist Five Year Plan.
Finally, the advent of "modernization" in China and "perestroika" in the
U.S.S.R. and their consequences have permanently undermined socialist
revolutionary authority. Even a Communist Party member within the
ANC in South Africa must pause before assuming the redemptive charac-
ter of a revolutionary takeover.[1] In the year of the anniversary of the
French Revolution it is clearer than ever that the stupidity of *ancien
regimes* makes for revolutions; once made they are poor instruments for
institutionalizing the reforms the denial of which brought them about.
What seems increasingly apparent today is that white intransigence rather
than black mobilization will make for revolution in South Africa.

THE INTERNATIONAL CONDITIONER

A major theme that emerges from this volume is that the struggle inside southern Africa is played to an audience outside and is meant to influence attitudes and steps taken by actors external to southern Africa. What
external actors do inclines tropistically toward events in South Africa.
While the struggle inside South Africa will in the last analysis be determined by the South African people themselves, the resources in that
struggle are increasingly conditioned by outsiders, and importantly by the
actions of the U.S.A.

All the authors in Part One of this volume agree on a number of de-
scriptive elements in the situational analysis of "The South African
Cockpit." They agree, sometimes only by implication, that apartheid is
dying, but not yet dead; that the South African government's response has
been technocratic and co-optative but oscillating between repression and
defensive, ad hoc schemes at the local level for increasing African well-being; that a grass roots, mass opposition has been growing, in the form of
trade unions and community activist groups; that amidst the extra-parliamentary opposition to the government the ANC has assumed a leading

position; and that cosmopolitan elements in the business community find themselves pushing for the liquidation of racialist socio-economic restrictions and the elimination of the obstacles to mass, non-racial political participation.

While no one denies that the South Africans themselves make their own history, to paraphrase Marx, the conditions of history are not of their own choosing. We are approaching the endgame in the battle of the South African government to defend racial oligarchy with reforms that invite selective involvement but deny mass political participation by blacks. South Africa's internal situation is vulnerable to outside pressures. As Robert Price makes clear in his chapter, the extroverted nature of the South African economy makes it sensitive to "market sanctions." Aside from the continuing black uprising, which has caused the government to maintain the state of emergency for five years, the greatest single force for change is the erosion of confidence on the part of international business. Disinvestment by the giant Mobil Oil Company in April 1989 and the decline of the rand to record lows in June 1989, represent just two leading signs of an economy increasingly starved of foreign capital. Inflation adjusted growth in Gross Domestic Product is expected to shrink to zero in 1990.[2]

The self-styled, pro-Western alignment of the South African government has lost its strategic vitality in an era of detente between previous Cold War rivals. The utility of a South African military commitment to the strategic defense of southern Africa declines drastically, although this has not stopped the South African military from increasing its strike capability to include submarines and intermediate range missiles. The focus of attention, however, shifts more intensively to the internal security role of the military and its relation to domestic political coalitions. The problem of foreign suppliers, such as Israel and West Germany, maintaining a connection to a military increasingly centered on internal repression continues to draw international criticism. Finally, the feeble and tattered liberal tradition in South Africa has undergone a certain transfusion from the democratic uprisings in authoritarian countries around the world. As well, the debate over a revised constitution for South Africa draws on the experience of liberal regimes modified elsewhere by confederalism and consociationalism.[3]

On the whole, the authors in this volume accept the view that the balance of forces inside South Africa has shifted toward the non-parliamentary opposition. Nevertheless, as Henry Isaacs notes, what are major concessions for whites are still seen as minor by blacks. The authors differ perhaps on how much coherent initiative can be exercised by the government. The chapter by Isaacs and the commentaries by Joe Thloloe and Moeletsi Mbeki do not dwell on the differences among mobilized blacks or on potential ethnic, regional or class divergences in the black population. They accept the fact of the present leadership of the African

National Congress. As Isaacs puts it, the ANC has been "de-demonized." And in fact government-sponsored reform has created the legal space for the formation of new groups whose interests are complementary to the ANC. Price expects the opposition as a whole to negotiate for nothing less than majority rule. The discussion of internal forces in South Africa in this volume centers on two major vectors in the struggle for majority rule: the ability of the black opposition to raise the costs of a non-democratic order and the will and ability of the government to resist in order to maintain white privilege.

THE REVISED MILITARY CHALLENGE

The key factor, as noted in the chapter by Kenneth Grundy, is the relative autonomy of the military vis a vis the National Party government. The militarization of the policy process has been exhaustive. The implication in the discussions of Grundy and Isaacs is that the post-apartheid Africanization of the military may pose the greatest challenge to democratic power sharing.

Until the Angola-Namibia Accords in 1988, the driving force of foreign policy in the region for almost fifteen years has been "de-stabilization" of neighboring states, despite treaties of friendship, such as the Nkomati agreement with Mozambique and the Lusaka agreement with Angola in 1984. Central to the domestic reform process is the National Security Management scheme in which military officers supervise community development and welfare in the townships, simultaneous with police and military pacification. The military have been active in anti-SWAPO activity in Namibia in the run-up to the November 1989 election; the military permit or cannot prevent "rogue" elements from supplying RENAMO guerrillas in Mozambique despite the official withdrawal of support by the South African government.[4] Yet, as Mbeki notes, the reduction in destabilization actions against neighboring states also reduces divisive issues within the military, such as rising casualties in Angola or maintaining a long-term presence outside the borders of South Africa. Indeed the willingness of the military to cut back on deployment in Angola and Namibia, and, perhaps in Mozambique, may also contribute to increasing its political influence, as South Africa tries a new ploy in its campaign to appear a trustworthy partner to the West. (This is also an interesting implication of the commentary by Walter Barrows.)

THE NEGOTIATIONS ATTRACTION

To summarize, analysts of the transition to a South Africa after apartheid must therefore track the interaction of three major variables: the

military and its ability to maintain its coherence as a political force; the
non-parliamentary, mass opposition and its ability to prevent disintegration of the anti-apartheid coalition; and international pressures, especially on the troubled South African economy. (Compare Samuel P.
Huntington, "At some point in the next decade or two, some combination
of black mobilization, economic trouble, and external threat are likely to
create a crisis within the South African political system that will only be
resolved by fundamental change of that system."[5]) But, as Price points
out, the types of domestic changes designed by the South African government to satisfy the desires of the international community are not designed to meet the demands of the black opposition. Given the trends in
authoritarian countries of the Left and the Right toward inclusive, popular
elections with competition among electoral groups --albeit not necessarily
equal competition-- and representation of individual citizenship as well as
other forms of group representation, it seems probable that a future constitutional settlement will consist of provisions for individual and group
representation in South Africa.[6] The extant example provided for South
Africa in neighboring Zimbabwe of temporary, constitutional guarantees
of minority rights and minority representation remain problematic for
both privileged whites (and Asians too) as well as claimant blacks.
Whites want political guarantees, blacks want compensatory, affirmative
action in the economic and social spheres.[7] The implication of our analysis of "The South African Cockpit" is that the interested international actors will be satisfied with a negotiating formula that provides for minority
guarantees in a system of formal majority rule. Neither side at present
will settle for that. But the pressures from the outside are toward that
type of negotiated settlement.

REGIONAL SUPPORT FOR NEGOTIATION

Turning to international pressures manifest in the region, contrary to
the object toward which the major regional instruments of co-operation
were conceived, the Southern Africa Development Co-Ordinating
Conference (SADCC) and the Front Line States have not been able to put
significant pressure on South Africa in the anti-apartheid struggle.
Structurally related to the South African economy and open to destabilization interference by South African military and para-military forces, the
states in the region have in fact exercised limited leverage. Their primary
role as sanctuary for ANC and SWAPO guerrillas has been eliminated in
Lesotho, Swaziland and Mozambique and reduced in Botswana, Zimbabwe
and Angola by relentless pressure from South Africa. In Zambia the
ANC maintains an administrative center, despite several South African air
raids, and in Tanzania -- out of normal range of the South African air force
-- the ANC has a training and education facility.

At present Zimbabwe, Zambia and Malawi share a strong interest in an end to the fighting and in political reconciliation in Angola and Mozambique, in order to rehabilitate railway lines and ports that restore lower costs for international trade. As described in Gilbert Khadiagala's chapter, SADCC's influence would grow if the Superpowers reduced their entanglements in southern Africa , what he calls a "condominium." But a Superpower "partnership" would dictate events and SADCC's influence would diminish, as illustrated by the reduction of financing for UN troops in Namibia by the Security Council, over the protests of the African countries and SWAPO. (Harvey Glickman labels this phenomenon "parallel action" on the part of the Superpowers, in discussing Mozambique and the background to the Angola-Namibia Accords.) On the other hand, spurring the "peace process" in Namibia, Angola and Mozambique is in the long term interest of the economic health of several of the SADCC states, especially Zimbabwe and Zambia. In acquiescing to a tension reduction environment, SADCC interests and the newly-emergent Superpower partnership threaten to diverge from the bargaining interests of the ANC. Both Isaacs and W. Ofuatey-Kodjoe express concern on this score. The implication is to expect more differences to emerge among the states of southern Africa.

A routine, low-level flow of aid continues to SADCC from the West. But a number of European governments appear to have abandoned a regional strategy of building SADCC as a major lever of international pressure on South Africa in favor of more selective rehabilitation targets, such as the Beira Corridor project in Mozambique, directly linked to Zimbabwean interests, and the Nacala Corridor plans, linked to Malawi. Whereas some ANC supporters feared that aid to SADCC would siphon off assistance to the ANC, Western policy today simply favors certain countries over others in the region for tactical reasons. In both the cases of aid to SADCC and aid to targeted states in southern Africa the reduction of dependence on and the hostility of the South African government do not add up to direct help for the ANC cause.

AMERICA AND SOUTH AFRICA

The final Part of this volume treats American foreign policy. Despite a number of attempts on the part of groups concerned with moral priorities in foreign policy over nearly three decades to treat the anti-apartheid struggle in South Africa as an anti-racism crusade comparable to anti-fascism in the Spanish Civil War of the late 1930's, policy toward South Africa in the U.S.A. is governed by global strategy toward the U.S.S.R., yet it remains tied internally to civil rights politics. Domestic coalitions on civil rights issues tend to gravitate toward policy toward Africa as part of their purview.[8]

In 1989 the basic difference in activity toward resolving the South African conflict is between pacifying the parties (letting the South Africans work out their own destiny) and support for insisting on popular rule (democratic majority rule), with the civil rights supporters in the U.S.A. calling for renewed pressure on South Africa. In this case the active interventionists favor stronger and more comprehensive sanctions (see the chapter by Howard Wolpe), while the pragmatists favor negotiations to reduce violence and find a route toward a political settlement. The official U.S government position on South Africa in 1989 resembles the position taken with regard to opposition groups that are competing with the Communist Parties in the U.S.S.R. and in Eastern Europe. As stated by Herman Cohen in the Senate hearings on his nomination to the post of Assistant Secretary of State for Africa, "...we must work every day to promote a negotiated, non-violent transition to a new constitutional system which will guarantee equal political rights and equal economic and social opportunity for all South Africans regardless of race or ethnic affiliation."[9]

President Bush has received anti-apartheid leaders from South Africa in the White House, but policy toward South Africa receives scant attention compared to Europe or the Middle East or, in days gone by, Central America. The flurry of attention paid to achieving agreements in Angola and Namibia serves to generate an aura of respectability about the government of South Africa, so the U.S. awaits the next election to the restricted parliament, the new moves expected by F.W. de Klerk, who replaces P.W. Botha as head of the National Party, a possible new constitutional dispensation, and the next wave of government-proffered reforms. One can compare that stance to a U.S. Ambassador holding regular talks with representatives of the Palestine Liberation Organization in Tunis or President Bush meeting directly with Lech Walesa and other leaders of Solidarity in Poland. In a parallel vein, one might also compare the position of U.S. Administrations (not Congress) on sanctions versus South Africa with the position on sanctions in recent years in the the cases of Panama, Nicaragua, or the U.S.S.R.

Without major military-related goals in southern Africa and in the presence of concerns for the infrastructure (including access to minerals) of the southern African regional economy, the U.S. may express the goal of equal rights for all, but even a policy of communication with all parties is bound to await the initiatives of the South African government.[10] An impartial observer has to conclude that the involvement of the South African Communist Party in the activities of the ANC and the socialist rhetoric of the militant elements in the ANC continue to make the U.S. Administration uncomfortable in supporting the ANC in the effort to establish a democratic system in South Africa. Similarly, one has to conclude that the attitude and positions taken by the U.S.S.R. in regard to change in South Africa will influence the U.S. position enormously. It was the Soviets who began the process of persuading the U.S. that the ANC is not the vanguard of Soviet strategy when they began calling for support for all the democratic elements in the South African opposition.[11] As Cohen observes in his chapter, the Soviets made a significant contribution to bringing the Angola-Namibia agreement to fruition.

WINDOW OF OPPPORTUNITY

A unique opportunity looms; in effect, both the Americans and the Soviets are already acting in concert in the region. For the U.S. to maintain its leadership in contributing to a settlement in South Africa, it needs to recognize the realities already described in the chapter by Pauline Baker and the commentary by Gail Gerhart. But U.S. policy needs to align itself even more actively with the "pro-democracy" elements in South Africa. The object is to expand the resources of the extra-parliamentary opposition. Those resources grow positively through expanding aid to build the black infrastructure of associational life. They grow also by reducing the repressive resources of the government. Major steps in that direction would be, for example, the vigorous enforcement of sanctions on technology relating to weapons, especially with regard to military allies of the U.S.A., and abandoning information sharing arrangements with the South African military. Adding Oliver Tambo to the series of anti-apartheid leaders meeting President Bush in the White House would underscore the seriousness of our resolve.

A multi-racial democratic South Africa will remain central to peace and security in the region. Geo-politics cannot be repealed. Yet the legacy of the struggle to end apartheid informs the politics of southern Africa in ways that offer hope for an era of co-operation deeper and more comprehensive than elsewhere on the continent.

Notes

1. The Seventh Party Congress of the South African Communist Party in June 1989 adopted a new program, "The Path to Power." The program acknowledges that guerrilla warfare will not overturn the apartheid system and that nationwide unity would be weakened if resistance groups emphasized socialism. *Weekly Mail* (Johannesburg, June 23, 1989).
2. *The Times* (London, June 16, 1989). Cf. Robin Cohen, *Endgame in South Africa?* (Trenton, Africa World Press, 1988).
3. See, for example, F. van Zyl Slabbert and David Welsh, *South Africa's Options: Strategies for Sharing Power* (Cape Town: David Philip, 1979); Frances Kendall and Leon Louw, *After Apartheid, The Solution for South Africa* (San Francisco: ICS Press, 1987); see also Arend Lijphart, *Power Sharing in South Africa* (Berkeley: University of California, Institute of International Studies, 1985).
4. (Namibia) *Southscan* (June 28, 1989); (Mozambique) *Africa Confidential* (July 7, 1989).

5. "Reform and Stability in a Modernizing, Multi-Ethnic Society," *Politikon* 8(2) (December, 1981), 11.

6. Compare I. William Zartman, "Negotiations in South Africa," *The Washington Quarterly* (Autumn, 1988), 145: "...it is within this federalist area that the negotiated solution to the greatest satisfaction of the values and interests of both sides can be found."

7. *Ibid.*, 13; Murray Forsyth, "Constitutional Proposals: The Middle Ground," in Jesmond Blumenfeld, ed., *South Africa in Crisis* (London: Methuen, 1987), 126-147; Herman Giliomee, "The Elusive Search for Peace," *Optima* 36(3) (September, 1988), 126-135.

8. The annual TransAfrica Forum in Washington, D.C. (June 9, 1989), began with a panel on the recruitment of blacks to the U.S. Foreign Service and ended with a panel on the future of Namibia.

9. *Washington Post* (May 4, 1989), A21.

10. For a shrewd review of the premises of U.S. policy toward Africa, see Helen Kitchen, *Some Guidelines on Africa for the Next President* (Washington, D.C.: Center for Strategic and International Studies, 1988).

11. See Harvey Glickman, "Perspectives on Africa from the Fourth American-Soviet Symposium on Contemporary Sub-Saharan Africa," *Issue - A Journal of Opinion* 17(1) (Winter, 1988), 4-6.

INDEX